AMERICAN RACING

Tom Burnside

AMERICAN RACING

Road Racing in the 50s and 60s

Text by Denise McCluggage

KÖNEMANN
Verlagsgesellschaft mbH

CONTENTS

INHALT · SOMMAIRE

FROM THE OTHER SIDE OF THE LENS

JOHN WEITZ

Polo, sailing, flying, tennis all had their golden years. It had nothing to do with how fast they sailed, how high they flew, how hard they served or how much money was earned. The best part of any sport has to do with the people who love it and are willing to do battle for the sheer joy of it.

For sports car racing on this side of the Atlantic, the nineteen fifties and sixties were its golden years. From Mosport to Maine and from Sebring to Venezuela, Tom Burnside was there to record it with his camera. In those years race drivers were a wondrous mix of visiting foreign professionals and American amateurs, all competing on the same course. The champions from Britain, France, Italy, Germany and Argentina were heroes to their countrymen but known to us only from pictures in racing magazines. In person they seemed at first a bit cynical and jaded, probably because they viewed us with suspicion, but once the starter's flag fell they were keen to compete. And they taught us sportsmanship. A *maestro* from Torino would forgive an amateur from Connecticut for blocking his way into a hairpin turn. A great British champion would wave his thanks for giving him room to pass. What's more, the visitors quickly found out that not all American racers were novices or weekend warriors. Several of our drivers could match their skills, and one became champion of the world.

One of the best American amateur race drivers of the golden time was Denise McCluggage, who learned the sport on a small road course in Connecticut and soon was given the supreme compliment, an invitation to race on a team, or even better, the loan of a great, expensive, dazzling, superfast exotic car for the next race. Fortunately for the sport, Denise was and is an incisive, precise and instinctual writer, a skilled professional journalist with the ability to sum up happenings and feelings and the very *sense* of what is going on.

In those days, when we raced, we were quite alone. Not lonely, just alone. Our races were not like the Mille Miglia in Italy or the Carrera Panamericana in Mexico where you could shout at your co-driver to find out what lay behind the next blind turn or who was chasing you. Today's drivers have earphones and pit-to-car communications for relaying information, but then, all we had was a sign held up by our crew onto which someone had chalked drivel like "D + 25" which meant either that Dodd was twenty-five seconds ahead

Polo, Segeln, Fliegen, Tennis – jede dieser Sportarten hatte ihre goldene Ära. Das Tempo, die Höhe, die Aufschlaghärte, sogar der Verdienst spielten nur eine untergeordnete Rolle. Ausschlaggebend sind in jeder Sportart die Menschen, die ihren Sport lieben und aus reiner Freude am Wettkampf ihr Bestes geben.

Der Autorennsport hatte seine Glanzzeit in den USA während der 50er und 60er Jahre. Von Mosport bis Maine, Sebring bis Venezuela – Tom Burnside war dort und hat die Rennen mit seiner Kamera festgehalten. In jenen Jahren präsentierte sich die Fahrergilde als skurrile Mischung aus ausländischen Profis und amerikanischen Amateuren. Die Champions aus England, Frankreich, Italien, Deutschland und Argentinien waren Helden in ihrem eigenen Land, aber wir kannten nur ihre Fotos aus den Motorsportzeitschriften. In Persona wirkten sie zuerst etwas zynisch und emotionslos – vielleicht auch, weil sie uns zunächst mit Mißtrauen begegneten – aber sobald die Startflagge gefallen war, zählte auch für sie nur noch das Rennen. Und sie lehrten uns Fairneß. Großzügig verzieh da ein Turiner *Maestro* einem Amateur aus Connecticut, der ihn vor einer Haarnadelkurve behindert hatte. Und ein berühmter britischer Champion bedankte sich mit einem Winken, wenn man ihm Platz zum Überholen machte. Außerdem stellten die ausländischen Gäste bald fest, daß längst nicht alle amerikanischen Rennfahrer reine Anfänger oder Wochenendfahrer waren. Viele unserer Piloten erwiesen sich als ebenbürtige Konkurrenten, und einer erkämpfte sich sogar den Weltmeistertitel.

Denise McCluggage gehörte in dieser goldenen Zeit des Rennsports zu Amerikas besten Amateurfahrerinnen. Ihre ersten Sporen verdiente sie sich auf einer kleinen Rennstrecke in Connecticut, aber schon bald darauf erhielt sie das Angebot, als Teamfahrerin an einem Rennen teilzunehmen – ein immenses Kompliment für einen Amateur. Besser noch: Für das nächste Rennen stellte man ihr einen großen, teuren, superschnellen, exotischen Rennwagen zur Verfügung. Es ist ein Glücksfall für den Rennsport, daß Denise darüber hinaus auch eine scharfsinnige, präzise und instinktsichere Autorin war und ist – eine begabte Profijournalistin mit dem Talent, Ereignisse und Emotionen auf den Punkt zu bringen, und das Gefühl des Geschehens zu vermitteln.

In jenen Tagen waren wir auf der Rennstrecke völlig allein. Nicht einsam, aber allein. Unsere

Le polo, la voile, les sports aériens, le tennis ont tous eu leur Age d'Or. Une période faste qui ne fut pas dictée par la vitesse des voiliers, l'altitude des planeurs, la force des services ou les sommes d'argent gagnées. La meilleure part de n'importe quel sport raconte une histoire d'amour vécue par des gens prêts à combattre pour le plaisir.

Les années cinquante et soixante ont vu l'Age d'Or du sport automobile de ce côté de l'Atlantique. De Mosport à l'Etat du Maine et de Sebring au Venezuela, Tom Burnside était présent partout, pour l'immortaliser avec son appareil photographique. A cette époque, les pilotes constituaient un mélange insolite de professionnels venus de l'étranger et d'amateurs américains qui s'alignaient dans les mêmes courses. Les champions britanniques, français, italiens, allemands ou argentins, héros dans leurs pays, ne nous étaient connus qu'à travers les images des revues de sport automobiles. Quand nous les rencontrions en chair et en os, ils nous semblaient un peu cyniques et blasés au premier abord sans doute parce que nous leur étions suspects. Mais ils étaient là, prêts à foncer, dès que le drapeau du départ s'abaissait. Et ils nous ont appris le fair-play. Un *champion* de Torino savait pardonner à un amateur du Connecticut qui le bloquait dans un virage en épingle. Un as britannique remerciait d'un signe de main quand on s'écartait pour lui laisser le chemin libre. Par ailleurs, nos visiteurs célèbres réalisèrent bien vite que les coureurs américains n'étaient pas tous des novices ou des gladiateurs du dimanche. Certains étaient de taille à lutter contre eux et l'un devint même champion du monde.

Denise McCluggage fait partie des meilleurs pilotes amateurs américains de l'Age d'Or. Après avoir effectué son apprentissage sur un petit circuit du Connecticut, elle eut l'honneur ultime d'être invitée à rejoindre une écurie de courses et plus encore, de courir dans un bolide coûteux, aussi éblouissant que performant. Une grande chance pour le sport : Denise est une chroniqueuse innée, à l'écriture incisive et concise ; une journaliste professionnelle sachant relater l'événement, décrire l'émotion et l'ambiance avec brio.

A cette époque, nous étions seuls durant la course. Seuls, mais non pas esseulés. Nos courses ne ressemblaient en rien aux Mille Miglia d'Italie ou à la Carrera Panamericana du Mexique. Nous n'avions pas de coéquipier pour nous indiquer qui étaient nos poursuivants ou ce qui nous attendait

John Weitz, Arnolt-Bristol, Sebring, 1957.

of you or that you were twenty-five seconds ahead of Dodd. Sometimes in the excitement you forgot the code.

Often, our only real contact with the outside world was a man with a camera. At first we did not notice the lens pointed at us, but after a half hour of racing we even knew who the photographer was, and sometimes we mugged for him. Tom Burnside was one of the most exciting pointers of cameras around a race track. When used with his skill, the camera amplified the joy and pain of sports car racing more than words or movie film or draftsmanship. There is that precise act of opening a shutter for a mini-second when aimed at a car traveling at high speed and capturing, encapsulating, presenting the car, the driver, the course, the moment suspended in time. Tom's eye and shutter finger matched the hand and foot of the best of the race drivers. He could also catch a driver out of his car, on foot, unaware, vulnerable.

The photographs on these pages bring back the golden years' magic moments with an immediacy and a poignancy you will not forget. I promise that after you have finished your first reading you will return to these pages over and over again. There are so many things to discover. What an adventure!

Rennen waren nicht wie die Mille Miglia in Italien oder die mexikanische Carrera Panamericana, wo man sich durch Zurufe mit seinem Beifahrer darüber verständigen konnte, was hinter der nächsten Spitzkehre lag, oder wer einem im Nacken saß. Heute erhalten die Rennfahrer über Kopfhörer Informationen von ihren Boxen, aber uns hielt damals bestenfalls ein Crewmitglied ein Schild entgegen, auf das jemand mit Kreide Absurditäten wie »D + 25« gekritzelt hatte – was bedeutete, daß Dodd entweder 25 Sekunden vor oder hinter dir lag. In der Aufregung vergaß man eben manchmal den Code.

Der Mann mit der Kamera war nicht selten unser einziger Kontakt zur Außenwelt. Anfangs bemerkten wir die auf uns gerichtete Linse gar nicht, aber nach einer halben Stunde auf der Piste kannten wir den Fotografen und legten uns manchmal sogar extra für ihn ins Zeug. Tom Burnside gehörte zu den wohl besten Fotografen auf den Rennkursen. In seinen geschickten Händen offenbarte die Kamera Freud und Leid des Rennsports eindringlicher als alle Worte, Filme oder Zeichnungen. Es gehört unglaublich viel Präzision dazu, den Verschluß des auf den vorbeirasenden Wagen gerichteten Objektivs in genau jenem Bruchteil einer Sekunde zu öffnen, in dem man Wagen, Fahrer und Strecke in diesem einen Augenblick, in dem die Zeit stehenbleibt, erfassen, einfangen und zeigen kann. Toms Auge am Sucher und sein Finger am Auslöser standen der Hand- und Fußarbeit der weltbesten Rennfahrer in nichts nach. Und er fing die Fahrer auch außerhalb ihrer Wagen ein – zu Fuß, nichtsahnend, verletzlich.

Die Fotos auf diesen Seiten bringen die magischen Augenblicke dieser goldenen Jahre mit unvergeßlicher Eindringlichkeit und Präzision zurück. Glauben Sie mir, Sie werden dieses Buch auch nach dem ersten Lesen immer und immer wieder zur Hand nehmen und immer wieder Neues entdecken. Welch ein Erlebnis!

derrière le prochain virage sans visibilité. Aujourd'hui, les pilotes portent des écouteurs et sont directement branchés avec le stand. Pour toute aide, nous n'avions qu'un tableau que nous regardions en passant et sur lequel quelqu'un de l'équipe avait gribouillé des signes tels que « D + 25 », ce qui signifiait que Dodd avait 25 secondes d'avance ou que vous aviez 25 secondes d'avance sur Dodd. Mais quelquefois, dans l'excitation, on oubliait le code.

Souvent, les photographes étaient notre unique contact réel avec le monde extérieur. D'abord, on ne remarquait pas l'objectif braqué sur nous, mais après une demi-heure de course, on avait reconnu l'homme derrière l'appareil-photo et parfois, on « posait » pour lui. Tom Burnside était un des plus brillants opérateurs des circuits. Entre ses mains, l'appareil-photo captait les joies et les souffrances du sport automobile avec une intensité que ne rendaient ni les mots, ni les films, ni les illustrations. Il s'agit d'ouvrir l'obturateur pour une mini-seconde, à l'instant décisif, afin de capturer la voiture qui file à toute vitesse, le pilote, le circuit, le moment suspendu dans le temps. Le regard et les doigts experts de Tom égalaient les pieds et les mains des meilleurs pilotes. Il savait aussi saisir à l'improviste un pilote sans sa voiture, à pied comme le commun des mortels, vulnérable.

Les photographies de ces pages évoquent les moments magiques de l'Age d'Or de la course automobile avec une intensité dramatique inoubliable. Je suis certain que vous rouvrirez cet ouvrage maintes et maintes fois après en avoir fait une première lecture. Ses pages recèlent tant de choses à découvrir. Quelle aventure !

Lime Rock, 1989

AN ERA IN TRANSITION

DENISE McCLUGGAGE

"I don't know who discovered water, but I'm sure it wasn't a fish."
– MARSHALL McLUHAN

An era gets a name in retrospect. Those living it cannot discern its significance until they glance backwards over their shoulders from far down the road and behold the totality of its shape. Then they can say with a gasp of surprise and pride: "I was there; I lived history."

Such a time in motorsports occurred in the United States from the early 1950s to the late 1960s. It was an age of transitions. Some changes came tumbling quickly one after another; some advanced in a more sedate progression.

European influence was strong as more Americans rediscovered the car as an implement of sport. American car makers were of little help, turning as they did in the post-war years to putting wheels on upholstered parlors featuring marshmallow-soft suspensions and vast expanses of sheet metal. Those who cared about the car as something more than mere transportation, or a status symbol to adorn a suburban driveway, had to look abroad for their machines or turn to their own backyards and garages and build inventive specials. Two basic paths of American car-sport led from there.

Those intrigued by "foreign cars" bought imported spoke-wheeled MGs and swoop-fendered Jaguars and drove them on weekends to back country sites where they adorned them with numbers and raced each other over blocked-off roads. Not that racing on roads was new to the US. A rich history of such racing was attached to the early years of the century and the period between the World Wars, but in its revival after World War II road racing wore a distinct "Made in Europe" tag.

America's native racing was largely oval in shape, from the quarter-mile dirt tracks on the outskirts of many small towns to the half-mile or mile circuits common to state and county fairgrounds. These were often used for horse racing as well as for auto "thrill" shows (cars leaping from ramps, through burning hoops and slamming into huge walls of ice.)

"Auto racing" was the home-grown product; "motor racing" was the import. Auto racing was done on tracks, motor racing on road courses. Some auto racing tracks had steeply banked turns made of wood. Some were asphalt. Indianapolis, the dream of most of those who drove these ovals, was originally paved with bricks.

»Ich weiß nicht, wer das Wasser entdeckt hat, aber ich bin sicher, daß es kein Fisch war.«
– MARSHALL McLUHAN

Eine Ära erhält ihren Namen immer erst im Rückblick. Diejenigen, die sie erleben, begreifen ihre Bedeutung nicht, bis sie, am Ende des Wegs angelangt, über ihre Schulter zurückblicken und die Zeit in ihrer Gesamtheit sehen. Erst dann können sie erstaunt und stolz sagen: »Ich war da, ich habe Geschichte gelebt.«

Für den US-Motorsport war die Spanne zwischen Anfang 1950 und dem Ende der 50er Jahre eine solche Epoche. Es war eine Übergangszeit. Manche Veränderungen stürzten in rascher Folge auf uns ein, andere entwickelten sich gemächlicher.

Als immer mehr Amerikaner das Auto als Sportgerät wiederentdeckten, war die europäische Führungsrolle enorm. Die amerikanische Automobilindustrie war keine große Hilfe. Sie hatte sich in den Nachkriegsjahren darauf verlegt, Räder unter bequeme Wohnzimmer mit butterweicher Federung und reichlich Blechverkleidung zu montieren. Wer im Auto mehr als ein bloßes Transportmittel oder Statussymbol für die vorstädtische Hauseinfahrt sah, mußte sich im Ausland nach geeigneten Fahrzeugen umsehen oder in den eigenen Hinterhöfen und Garagen mit viel Phantasie renngeeignete Umbauten konstruieren. Hieraus entwickelten sich zwei Grundtrends des amerikanischen Motorsports.

Diejenigen, die ihr Herz an ausländische Marken gehängt hatten, fuhren an den Wochenenden importierte MGs mit Speichenrädern oder Jaguars mit verbreiterten Kotflügeln zu den Rennplätzen im Hinterland, wo sie die Wagen mit Startnummern versahen und auf abgesperrten Straßen gegeneinander antraten. Nicht, daß solche Straßenrennen eine Novität in Amerika gewesen wären. Sie hatten zu Beginn des Jahrhunderts und zwischen den beiden Weltkriegen eine bewegte Vergangenheit, aber nach dem Zweiten Weltkrieg trug das Comeback des Road Racing eindeutig den Stempel »Made in Europe«.

Die ursprünglichen US-Rennstrecken waren meist oval. Man fuhr auf den eine Viertelmeile langen Sandbahnstrecken außerhalb der Kleinstädte oder auf Halbmeilen- und Meilenkursen, die sich in allen Staaten und Counties auf Festplätzen fanden, und die häufig auch als Veranstaltungsort für Pferderennen und Stunt-Shows (bei denen die Fahrzeuge über Rampen, durch

« J'ignore qui a découvert l'eau, mais je suis certain que ce n'était pas un poisson. »
– MARSHALL McLUHAN

Une époque reçoit rétrospectivement une appellation. Ceux qui l'ont vécue ne se rendent compte de son importance qu'au bout du chemin parcouru, lorsqu'ils regardent en arrière et se disent avec étonnement ou fierté: « J'y étais, j'ai vécu une page d'histoire. »

Pour le sport automobile aux Etats-Unis, une telle époque s'inscrit du début des années cinquante à la fin des années soixante. Ce fut une période de transition. Certains changements furent précipités, d'autres prirent plus de temps pour s'imposer.

L'influence européenne joua un rôle déterminant lorsque de plus en plus d'Américains redécouvrirent la voiture dans un contexte sportif. Dans les années d'après-guerre, l'industrie automobile américaine construisit des intérieurs feutrés montés sur roues, dotés de suspensions molles comme de la guimauve et enrobés de vastes carrosseries. Ce n'était pas ce qu'ils recherchaient. Les Américains pour qui la voiture représentait davantage qu'un simple moyen de transport ou qu'un symbole de réussite sociale à exhiber devant une villa de banlieue, devaient soit acquérir des voitures européennes ou s'ingénier à construire leurs propres modèles dans leurs patios ou garages. Ces deux alternatives allaient constituer les bases du sport automobile américain.

Les passionnés de « marques étrangères » achetaient des MG avec des roues à rayons ou des Jaguar aux ailes aérodynamiques. Les week-ends, ils se retrouvaient dans des coins de campagne isolés, collaient des numéros sur leurs véhicules et se poursuivaient sur des routes fermées à la circulation pour la course. En fait, utiliser les routes comme circuits n'avait rien de nouveau aux Etats-Unis. Ce genre de rencontre sportive était déjà très populaire au début du siècle et entre les deux guerres. Cependant, le renouveau de la course sur route, après la Deuxième Guerre mondiale, portait indéniablement le label « made in Europe ».

Les tracés traditionnels américains avaient une forme ovale, depuis les circuits d'un quart de mile que l'on trouvait aux abords de nombreuses petites villes à ceux d'un demi-mile ou d'un mile aménagés sur les champs de foire locaux ou régionaux. Ces derniers servaient également d'hippodromes et de scènes pour des spectacles de cascades (les voitures s'élançaient sur des rampes,

Oval-track drivers were pros or semi-pros see-king from the start the monetary support of local garages and body shops. The sponsors' names and logos grew increasingly large, corporate and numerous as this form of racing evolved, particularly in the south, into the most popular spectator event of any kind.

Road racers looked down their noses at such commercialism. They were haughtily amateur as they drew on their knit-back gloves and imported crash helmets. Beyond their weekends of motor sport they aspired, if at all, to compete in the Twenty-four Hours of Le Mans or at American venues such as Sebring in Florida where displaced Europeans, or those inspired by the continental scene, evoked the great sports car races of Europe.

As the mid-century decades ripened, the transitions in "motor racing" accelerated. Here are some of those changes:

• Races, once staged on existing roads which were closed for the event, moved to courses laid out on airports and then, increasingly, to the purpose-built road courses common today. Hybrid circuits still exist – modified ovals, pieces of airports. And, with portable barriers and fencing, temporary racing circuits spring up in the hearts of cities for special occasions.

• Engines moved from front to rear and grew increasingly more powerful. Tires progressively fattened and so did steering wheels as they shrank in diameter.

• Race cars, once driven to and from the racing circuit, were first towed, then transported by simple trailers which became increasingly complex, grew covers and were themselves supplanted by huge 18-wheelers which altered the appearance of the paddock the way skyscrapers alter the sky line of a city.

• Safety measures transformed the appearance of cars and drivers. Roll bars appeared on the cars. Crash helmets evolved from what were essentially modified polo wear to full-faced helmets made of space-age composites. Driving garb went from ordinary casual wear – short-sleeved polo shirts were popular – through a period when driving clothes were dunked in a boric acid solution for fire retardation and then to made-to-order fire-proof suits.

• Drivers changed in this time from weekend road warriors – ardent amateurs seeking respite from law offices, dental chairs, stock exchanges and factory floors – to professionals, or would-be professionals, making a career of racing. With

brennende Reifen oder in riesige Eiswände rasten) dienten.

Die einheimische Version des Rennsports nannte man »Autorennen«, den Import »Motorrennen«. Autorennen fuhr man auf Pisten, Motorrennen auf Straßenkursen. Auf manchen Rennpisten waren die Steilwandkurven aus Holz, auf anderen aus Asphalt. Indianapolis – Traum der meisten Piloten – war ursprünglich mit Ziegelsteinen gepflastert.

Auf dem Oval der Rennbahnen fuhren Profis oder Halbprofis, die sich von Anfang an bei örtlichen Werkstätten und Karosseriebauern um finanzielle Unterstützung bemühten. Mit der Beliebtheit des Motorsports, der vor allem im Süden zum zuschauerträchtigsten Sportereignis wurde, wuchsen auch die Namen und Logos der Sponsoren, sowohl vom Firmenprestige als auch von der Anzahl her.

Die Fahrer von Straßenrennen hatten für diese Kommerzialisierung nur Verachtung übrig. Sie waren stolz auf ihren Amateurstatus, wenn sie ihre mit Strickrücken versehenen Autohandschuhe anzogen und die importierten Sturzhelme aufsetzten. Über die Wochenendrennen hinaus träumten sie höchstens von der Teilnahme am 24-Stunden-Rennen von Le Mans oder von US-Rennsportereignissen wie in Sebring (Florida), wo Exil-Europäer und Anhänger der europäischen Rennszene die großen europäischen Sportwagenrennen heraufbeschworen.

Gegen Ende der 50er und 60er Jahre veränderte sich das »Motorrennen« immer schneller. Hier einige der wichtigsten Entwicklungen:

• Rennen, die vorher auf normalen, während des Rennens für den übrigen Verkehr gesperrten Straßen ausgetragen wurden, verlagerten sich zunächst auf Flugplatzstrecken und dann zunehmend auf die heute üblichen, eigens hierfür angelegten Straßenkurse. Aber es gibt immer noch Mischkurse, wie etwa modifizierte Ovalstrecken oder Flugplatzkurse. Und manchmal entstehen mit Hilfe beweglicher Barrieren und Abgrenzungen auch mitten im Herzen der Städte zu besonderen Anlässen noch vorübergehend Rennkurse.

• Die Motoren wanderten zwischen Fahrer und Hinterachse, während ihre Leistung beständig zunahm. Die Reifen wurden breiter, die Lenkräder griffiger und kleiner.

• Die Rennwagen, die die Fahrer einst selbst zum und vom Rennplatz fuhren, wurden zunächst zur Strecke geschleppt, dann auf einfachen Anhängern transportiert. Die Anhänger wurden

traversaient des cercles de feu et se précipitaient dans des parois de blocs de glace).

« Auto racing » (courses de voitures) définissait la version typiquement américaine tandis que « Motor racing » (course automobile) était la version importée. Les courses de voitures se déroulaient sur des circuits, les courses automobiles sur des routes. Quelques circuits avaient des virages serrés recouverts de bois ou d'asphalte. A l'origine, Indianapolis – le rêve de tous les pilotes – était pavé de briques.

Les pilotes qui tournaient sur les pistes ovales étaient des professionnels ou semi-professionnels qui, dès le départ, recherchaient le support financier de garages et carrossiers locaux. Les noms et logos de sponsors ne cessèrent d'augmenter en nombre et en prestige avec la popularité de ce genre de course qui commença à attirer de larges foules, notamment dans le Sud.

Les pilotes de « motor racing » (courses sur routes) méprisaient cette commercialisation. Ils enfilaient leurs gants tricotés sur le dessus et arboraient leurs casques importés d'Europe avec toute la fierté de leur statut d'amateur. S'ils aspiraient à davantage que leurs courses du week-end, c'était de participer aux 24 heures du Mans ou à un meeting américain, comme celui de Sebring en Floride, où les Européens exilés et les passionnés du sport automobile européen s'extasiaient devant les bolides du Vieux Continent.

Les changements dans le « motor racing » s'accélérèrent lorsqu'on approcha des années soixante. En voici quelques-uns :

• Les courses qui s'étaient déroulées sur des routes provisoirement fermées à la circulation, furent d'abord déplacées sur des pistes d'aérodromes, puis eurent de plus en plus souvent lieu sur des circuits spécialement construits pour le sport, comme c'est le cas de nos jours. On trouve encore des circuits hybrides composés d'ovales modifiés et de segments de pistes d'aérodromes. Parfois, en certaines occasions, les centres des villes sont aussi transformés en circuits temporaires à l'aide de murs et barrières amovibles.

• Les moteurs changèrent de place, de l'avant à l'arrière, et devinrent plus puissants. Les pneus s'élargirent progressivement de même que les volants dont le diamètre se réduisit.

• Les pilotes n'arrivèrent plus sur les circuits au volant de leurs véhicules. Les voitures de courses furent d'abord tirées par des câbles avant d'être transportées sur des remorques ouvertes, puis fermées par des bâches. Les re-

professionalism came another change:

• Amateur drivers, even the professionals in the early days, were accessible to the public, to the press and to each other. They sat on pit walls or stacks of tires and chatted informally. That was before there were motor homes to disappear into, before post-race press conferences, before helicopters came to whisk the stars away. In short, before racing became big business and lost some of its soul to commerce.

Tom Burnside's pictures on these pages chronicle these transitions. To one who was there – sometimes in a race car, sometimes in the press box – the pictures sting with nostalgia. They provide the over-the-shoulder glance back, the recognition that this was, indeed, a time worthy of note. Let us note it. Live it, or re-live it, now.

immer komplexer, dann mit einer Verkleidung versehen und schließlich durch riesige 18rädrige Trucks ersetzt, die das Erscheinungsbild der Fahrerlager in etwa so sehr veränderten, wie Wolkenkratzer eine Stadt-Silhouette.

• Durch die Sicherheitsvorkehrungen veränderte sich das Aussehen von Wagen und Fahrern. Die Autos bekamen Überrollbügel. Die Sturzhelme, ursprünglich modifizierte Polohelme, mutierten zu Integralhelmen aus Raumfahrtmaterialien. An die Stelle der normalen Freizeitkleidung, die die Fahrer während der Rennen trugen (sehr beliebt waren kurzärmelige Polohemden), trat übergangsweise eine zum Brandschutz in Borsäurelösung getauchte Rennbekleidung, die inzwischen längst durch maßgeschneiderte feuersichere Monturen ersetzt ist.

• Während dieser Zeit wurden aus den Fahrern – einst begeisterte Amateure, die in den Straßenrennen am Wochenende einen Ausgleich für ihren Alltag als Anwalt, Zahnarzt, Börsenmakler oder Fabrikarbeiter suchten – Profis oder Möchtegern-Profis, die Rennfahren als Beruf betrieben.

• Die Amateurfahrer, und anfänglich auch die Profis, waren immer für Publikum, Presse und auch füreinander da. Sie saßen auf Boxenmauern oder Reifenstapeln und plauderten ungezwungen miteinander. Das war die Zeit vor den Motorhomes, in die man verschwinden konnte, vor den Pressekonferenzen nach einem Rennen, vor den Helikoptern, die die Stars abholten. Kurz gesagt, es war die Zeit, bevor der Rennsport zum Big Business wurde und einen Teil seiner Seele an den Kommerz verkaufte.

Tom Burnsides Fotos in diesem Buch dokumentieren diese Veränderungen. Für jemanden, der diese Zeit miterlebt hat – manchmal auf der Pressetribüne, manchmal am Steuer eines Rennwagens – bergen seine Bilder geradezu melancholische Nostalgie. Sie erlauben den Blick zurück über die Schulter, sie lassen erkennen, daß dies wirklich eine Zeit war, die unsere Aufmerksamkeit verdient. Schenken wir ihr diese Aufmerksamkeit, um sie heute neu- oder wiederzuerleben.

morques de plus en plus perfectionnées furent ensuite remplacées par les gigantesques camions de transport à 18 roues qui ont autant modifié l'aspect des paddocks que les gratte-ciel la physionomie des villes.

• Les mesures de sécurité transformèrent l'apparence des voitures et des pilotes. Les voitures étaient désormais dotées d'arceaux de sécurité. Les pilotes qui avaient porté une version modifiée des casques de polo, cachèrent leurs visages sous des casques intégraux en matériau « aérospatial ». Leur habillement évolua également. La tenue de sport désinvolte – le polo à manches courtes était très prisé – fut abandonnée pour des vêtements trempés dans l'acide borique aux fins de retarder l'inflammation, puis plus tard, pour une combinaison ignifugée confectionnée sur mesure.

• C'est à cette époque que les coureurs, gladiateurs du dimanche – amateurs enflammés cherchant à oublier le cabinet d'avocat, le cabinet dentaire, la bourse ou l'usine le temps d'un week-end – mutèrent en professionnels ou désireux de le devenir, transformant le sport automobile en carrière.

Le professionnalisme entraîna d'autres changements :

• Les pilotes amateurs et même les professionnels entretenaient des relations entre eux. Ils étaient accessibles au public et à la presse. Ils venaient s'asseoir sur les murets des stands ou sur les piles de pneus et on pouvait discuter avec eux. Cela changea avec l'apparition des motorhomes où les pilotes s'enfermaient, avec les conférences de presse officielles après la course, avec les hélicoptères qui déposaient et emportaient les vedettes. En bref, tout changea lorsque le sport automobile devint synonyme de business et vendit une partie de son âme au commerce.

Les clichés de Tom Burnside illustrent cette période de transition. Ils emplissent de nostalgie ceux qui l'ont vécue, que ce soit au volant d'une voiture ou dans le box de la presse. Ils nous permettent de regarder en arrière, de reconnaître que cette époque mérite sa place dans la mémoire. Immortalisons-la, vivons-la ou revivons-la, maintenant.

PHOTOGRAPHER'S STATEMENT

EINFÜHRUNG DES FOTOGRAFEN · L'ENONCÉ DU PHOTOGRAPHE

This book is drawn from photographs I made for various American periodicals ranging from the motoring monthlies to LIFE magazine between the years 1954 and 1968. We look back on those years as golden but anyone suggesting such a thing at the time would have been labeled a lunatic. *Golden?* This hodgepodge of amateurs and professionals dodging each other on closed-off roads and airport runways in everything from big-engined American specials to sleek European imports. *Golden?*

It was easy to overlook the warm camaraderie, the casual effect of open paddocks and shared pits, of borrowed tools and tape, the thrill of brilliant spur-of-the-moment innovations; to discount the all-embracing class-rating system that allowed tiny engines in there with the behemoths; to ignore the absence of crowd control and safety precautions, the knowing disregard of mortal peril. Yet these seemingly unremarkable but defining characteristics, as much as the cars themselves, drew me to motor racing and directed my picture-making.

By the late '60s the sport had undergone many profound changes. Safety and security measures now distanced drivers from spectators both physically and emotionally. Casual interaction and openness succumbed to tight security and secrecy when commercial sponsors, attracted by the sport's increased popularity, stepped in to protect their interests. I stopped photographing motor racing when I realized that the *feel* of the sport had changed for me irrevocably.

This book is not meant to document a period in motor racing history but to celebrate some of the qualities that made it special. These include the fabulous cars with but a single-season lifespan and the great champions and amateurs alike for whom competing was everything. I salute them all.

Tom Burnside, June 1996.

Die Fotos in diesem Buch entstanden zwischen 1954 und 1968, ursprünglich für verschiedene amerikanische Zeitschriften, von Motorsport-Illustrierten bis hin zum LIFE Magazin. Rückblickend nennen wir diese Zeit eine goldene Ära, aber damals hätten wir diese Bezeichnung für verrückt gehalten. *Golden?* Dieser Kuddelmuddel von Amateuren und Profis, die sich auf abgesperrten Straßenkursen und Flugplatzpisten gegenseitig auszutricksen versuchten – mit Fahrzeugen, bei denen von großmotorigen US-Spezialanfertigungen bis zu geschmeidigen Europa-Importen alles vertreten war? *Golden?*

Nur allzu leicht übersah man die Kameradschaft, die Ungezwungenheit offener Fahrerlager und geteilter Boxen, geliehener Werkzeuge und Klebestreifen oder die Faszination spontaner und oft brillanter Innovationen. Wir unterschätzten das tolerante Klassifizierungssystem, das leistungsschwache Fahrzeuge zusammen mit Rennboliden auf eine Strecke schickte, ignorierten die fehlenden Sicherheitsmaßnahmen, übersahen bewußt die tödliche Gefahr. Aber neben den Wagen selbst waren es gerade diese scheinbar irrelevanten aber charakteristischen Qualitäten, die mich am Motorsport faszinierten und meine Fotoarbeit dirigierten.

Gegen Mitte der 60er hatte sich der Sport grundlegend verändert. Unfallschutz- und Sicherheitsvorkehrungen trennten Fahrer und Zuschauer sowohl räumlich als auch emotional voneinander. Unbeschwertes Miteinander wich strengster Sicherheit und Geheimhaltung, als die Sponsoren, die auf die gestiegene Popularität des Sports aufmerksam geworden waren, zur Wahrung ihrer Interessen in das Geschehen eingriffen. Ich stellte fest, daß sich die gesamte Atmosphäre für mich unwiderruflich verändert hatte und beendete meine Karriere als Motorsport-Fotograf.

Dieses Buch soll weniger eine Periode der Rennsportgeschichte dokumentieren, sondern vielmehr jene Qualitäten feiern, die diese Zeit besonders machten. Hierzu gehören die phantastischen Rennwagen, die oft nur eine einzige Rennsaison lang gefahren wurden und die großen Sieger ebenso wie die Amateure, denen die Teilnahme am Rennen alles bedeutete. Ich grüße sie alle.

Tom Burnside, Juni 1996.

Cet ouvrage contient une compilation de photographies que j'ai prises entre les années 1954 et 1968 pour divers périodiques américains, depuis des revues mensuelles de sport automobile au magazine LIFE. Aujourd'hui, nous appelons ces années l'Age d'Or du sport automobile, mais quiconque les aurait qualifiées de telles à l'époque, aurait été traité d'aliéné. *L'âge d'or?* Cette époque où un salmigondis d'amateurs et de professionnels se pourchassaient sur des routes fermées à la circulation ou sur des pistes d'aérodromes, au volant d'une gamme de véhicules qui englobait aussi bien de grosses américaines que des voitures européennes racées. *L'âge d'or?*

On prenait pour argent comptant la chaude camaraderie et l'atmosphère relaxe qui régnaient dans les paddocks ouverts à tous. Les équipes se partageaient les stands, se prêtaient les outils et se réjouissaient ensemble des innovations aussi astucieuses que spontanées. On ne questionnait pas le système de classification qui permettait d'aligner côte à côte petits moteurs et bolides ou l'absence de mesures de sécurité. On connaissait le danger mortel, mais on ne voulait pas en entendre parler. Autant que ma passion pour les voitures, ce sont ces aspects, banals en soi, mais si évocateurs, qui m'ont attiré vers la course automobile et ont inspiré mon oeuvre photographique.

Le sport avait déjà subi de profonds changements au milieu des années soixante. Des mesures de sécurité et de prévention séparaient désormais les pilotes des spectateurs. Cette distance était autant physique qu'émotionnelle. Les échanges spontanés et ouverts succombèrent aux mesures de sécurité rigoureuses et à l'atmosphère de secret établie par les sponsors attirés par la popularité croissante du sport et qui tenaient à défendre leurs intérêts commerciaux. J'ai cessé de photographier les courses automobiles à partir du moment où j'ai réalisé que ce que j'avais aimé dans ce sport était, pour moi, perdu à jamais.

Cet ouvrage recherche moins à décrire une page de l'histoire du sport automobile qu'à célébrer les qualités qui ont caractérisé cette époque. Il évoque les voitures fabuleuses qui souvent ne couraient que le temps d'une saison et les grands champions et les amateurs liés par la passion de la course. Je les salue tous.

Tom Burnside, Juin 1996.

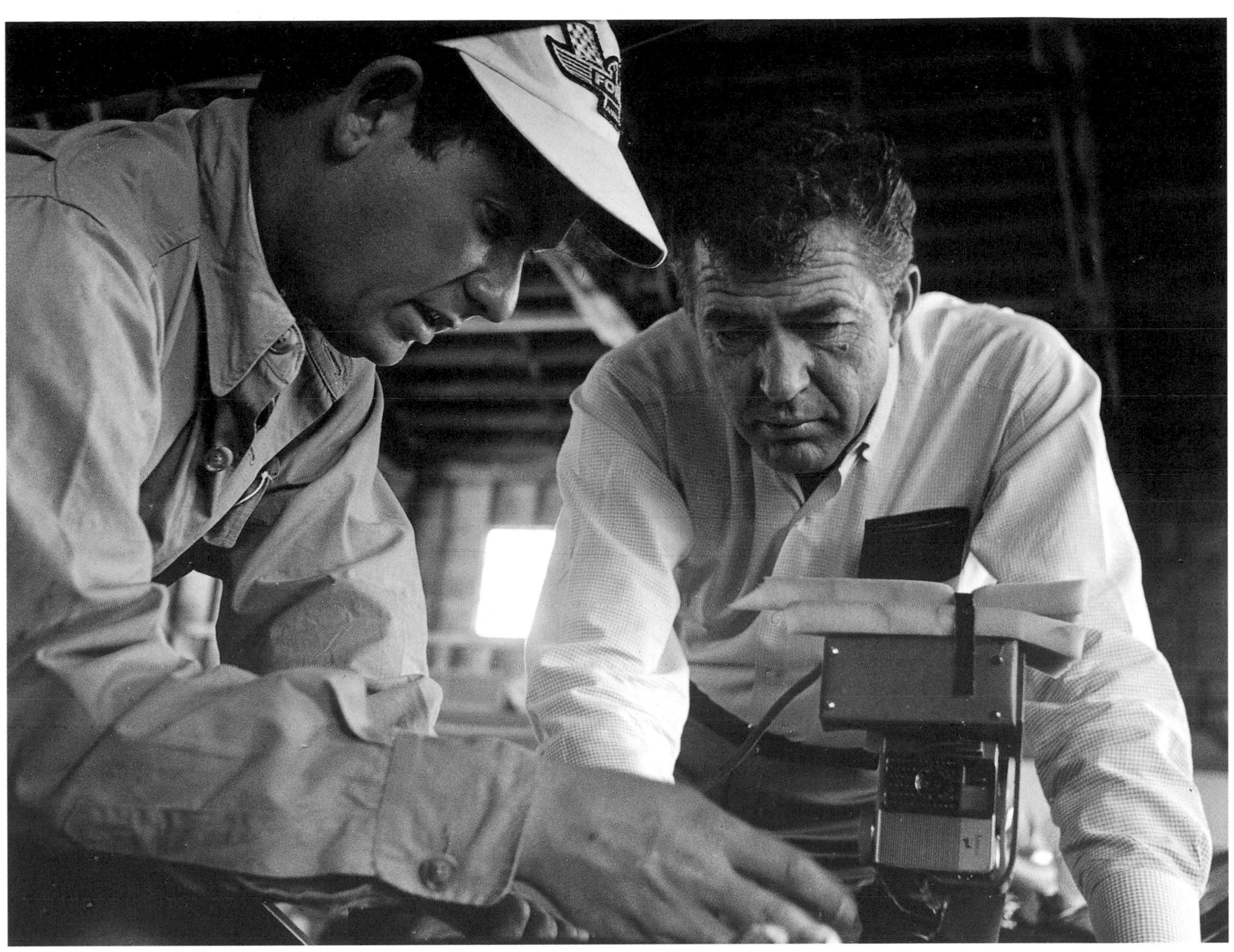

Tom Burnside with Carroll Shelby, installing a radio-operated, remote control camera in a Cobra. Sebring 1965. (Photo: Elinor Burnside)

Tom Burnside mit Carroll Shelby. Sie bauen eine ferngesteuerte Kamera in einen Cobra ein. Sebring 1965. (Foto: Elinor Burnside)

Tom Burnside avec Carroll Shelby en train d'installer un appareil photographique téléguidé dans la Cobra. Sebring 1965. (Photo: Elinor Burnside)

NATURAL ROADS

STRASSENRENNEN · SUR LES ROUTES

Racing over real roads offered a unique challenge. The roads were narrow and often tree-lined. They were sometimes hump-backed. The surfaces were rough from their real-world experience, with changes in surface texture common. That's what made them fun and challenging. Two such courses over natural roads were Brynfan Tyddyn and Watkins Glen.

The former was the Welsh-named private estate of a Pennsylvania senator who for much of the 1950s granted the use of its narrow, black-top roads to the Sports Car Club of America. The course, near Wilkes Barre, Pennsylvania, was a favorite of drivers who appreciated both its challenge and beautiful setting. Carroll Shelby termed it "a little Nurburgring." Brynfan Tyddyn's tight turns and hilly terrain were best suited to smaller cars and the races were limited to those two liters and under.

The races at Brynfan Tyddyn were usually held in conjunction with a nearby hillclimb called "Giants' Despair" which claimed a history dating back to 1906. On a July Friday and Saturday of racing in 1956 Shelby was the main winner in both events, winning the hillclimb in a Formula I Ferrari which had been brought to the US as a possible Indianapolis contender.

Watkins Glen, in New York's Finger Lakes district, had been the site of a through-the-town race which was discontinued after a spectator's death. But the townspeople liked the sports car racing crowd so they scouted out a series of natural road courses over the years (one of which is photographed here) and finally constructed a purpose-built road course in 1956.

Rennen auf »echten« Straßen boten eine unvergleichliche Herausforderung. Die Straßen waren eng und oft von Bäumen gesäumt. Die Fahrbahnen waren uneben, durch die alltägliche Nutzung rauh, Unregelmäßigkeiten der Oberflächenstruktur üblich – und genau das machte den Spaß und die Herausforderung dieser Strecken aus. Zwei dieser »natürlichen« Kurse waren Brynfan Tyddyn und Watkins Glen.

Erstere Strecke, deren Name aus dem Walisischen stammt, war Privatbesitz eines Senators aus Pennsylvania, der dem Sports Car Club of America während der 50er Jahre die Nutzung dieser engen, schwarzgedeckten Straßen seines Besitzes zugesichert hatte. Der in der Nähe von Wilkes Barre, Pennsylvania, gelegene Kurs gehörte dank seines Schwierigkeitsgrades und der großartigen Landschaft zu den Lieblingsstrecken der Fahrer. Carroll Shelby bezeichnete ihn als »kleinen Nürburgring«. Mit seinen engen Kurven und hügeligem Gelände war Brynfan Tyddyn am ehesten für kleinere Sportwagen geeignet, weshalb zu den Rennen nur Wagen bis zu zwei Litern Hubraum zugelassen waren.

Die Rennen auf Brynfan Tyddyn fanden normalerweise gleichzeitig mit dem Bergrennen »Giants' Despair« statt, das bereits seit 1906 in unmittelbarer Nähe ausgetragen wurde. An einem Freitag und Samstag im Juli 1956 gewann Carroll Shelby beide Rennen hintereinander. Den Sieg im Bergrennen holte er mit einem Formel-1-Ferrari, den man als potentiellen Indianapolis-Anwärter nach Amerika gebracht hatte.

Watkins Glen war ein ehemaliger Stadtkurs im Bereich der New Yorker Finger Lakes, auf dem seit dem Tod eines Zuschauers keine Rennen mehr ausgetragen wurden. Aber den New Yorkern gefielen die Publikumsmengen, die zu den Rennen anreisten, so daß sie im Laufe der Jahre eine Reihe natürlicher Straßenstrecken auskundschafteten (von denen eine hier abgebildet ist) und schließlich 1956 einen ausschließlich für Rennzwecke genutzten Straßenkurs bauten.

Les courses sur les « vraies » routes offraient un challenge unique. Les routes étaient étroites, souvent bordées d'arbres. Elle avaient parfois des dos d'ânes. La plupart des chaussées étaient déformées, la circulation quotidienne ayant usé les revêtements. Mais c'est ce qui faisait le plaisir et la gageure de conduire sur ces routes. Deux des parcours qui empruntaient de « vraies » routes s'appelaient Brynfan Tyddyn et Watkins Glen.

Situé près de Wilkes Barre en Pennsylvanie, Brynfan Tyddyn était le nom gallois du domaine d'un sénateur qui avait permis au Sport Car Club of America d'utiliser les routes étroites et bitumées de sa propriété durant les années cinquante. Les pilotes appréciaient beaucoup ce parcours difficile, situé dans un site admirable. Carroll Shelby l'avait baptisé le « petit Nurburgring ». Brynfan Tyddyn convenait surtout aux petites cylindrées en raison de ses virages serrés et de son relief fragmenté. Les voitures ne devaient pas dépasser les deux litres pour être admises aux courses.

Les courses de Brynfan Tyddyn se déroulaient en même temps que l'épreuve de montagne appelée « Giants' Despair » (Désespoir des Géants), qui existait depuis 1906. Shelby remporta les deux compétitions un vendredi et un samedi de juillet 1956. Il gagna le « Giants' Despair » au volant d'une Formule I Ferrari, amenée aux Etats-Unis pour participer à Indianapolis.

La course de Watkins Glen, dans la région new-yorkaise des Finger Lakes, se déroulait à l'origine à travers la ville. On abandonna ce parcours à la suite de la mort d'un spectateur. Mais les habitants de la ville appréciaient tant l'atmosphère du sport automobile qu'ils dénichèrent différents parcours sur routes « normales » au fil des années (l'un d'eux est photographié ici) et finirent par construire un circuit permanent en 1956.

Bob Goldich, Ferrari 500 Mondial (#30); Carroll Shelby, Ferrari 500 TR (#128); Porsches; MGs, Brynfan Tyddyn, 1956.

BRYNFAN TYDDYN 1956

Sitting on the fence watching all the cars race by, led by a Morgan.

»Zaungäste« bei einem Straßenrennen. An der Spitze ein Morgan.

Assis sur la barrière pour regarder défiler les voitures menées par une Morgan.

A Lotus peeks over the hill.
Ein Lotus vor der Talfahrt.
Une Lotus apparaît en haut de la colline.

MGs all. Bob Holbert (#6) makes a pass with Alan Day (#54) following.

Alleingang der MGs. Bob Holbert (Nr. 6) überholt, gefolgt von Alan Day (Nr. 54).

Toutes des MG. Bob Holbert (n° 6) double ; Alan Day suit (n° 54).

Otto Linton, OSCA MT4.

Bob Grossman, Porsche 550 Spyder (#43), Charlie Kolb, Triumph TR2 (partly hidden/teilweise verdeckt/en partie caché), Anthony Koveleski, MG (#44).

2

3

4

(1) Emil Pupulidy, Porsche 356 coupe (#58) passes Henry Wessells III, Alfa Romeo Giulietta Spyder. They were first and second in G Production.
(2) The crowd hunkers down to watch Bill Lilley, Porsche 356, on his way to a Class F Production victory.
(3) Bud Kinne, Porsche 356 Speedster, leads an MG A and a Triumph TR3.
(4) Tom Fleming (Lotus) whips past the railbirds. Jack McAfee, who was to chase Shelby's Ferrari in the main event with his Porsche 550 Spyder, perches on the fence, center, wearing a white paper hat.

(1) Emil Pupulidy, Porsche 356 Coupé (Nr. 58) überholt Henry Wessells III. Alfa Romeo Giulietta Spyder. Sie erreichten den ersten und zweiten Platz in der G-Klasse.
(2) In Hockstellung verfolgen die Zuschauer, wie Bill Lilley im Porsche 356 die letzten Meter zum Sieg in der F-Klasse zurücklegt.
(3) Bud Kinne im Porsche 356 Speedster vor einem MG A und einem Triumph TR3.
(4) Tom Fleming (Lotus) fegt an den Zaungästen vorbei. Jack McAfee, mit dem weißen Papierhut in der Mitte, machte später im Hauptrennen mit seinem Porsche 550 Spyder Jagd auf Shelbys Ferrari.

(1) Emil Pupulidy, Porsche 356 coupé (n° 58) double Henry Wessells III. Alfa Romeo Giulietta Spyder. Ils seront premier et second en groupe G.
(2) Les spectateurs se baissent pour regarder Bill Lilley au volant d'une Porsche 356. Il remportera la victoire en groupe F.
(3) Bud Kinne, Porsche 356 Speedstar, mène devant une MG A et une Triumph TR3.
(4) La Lotus de Tom Fleming fonce devant Jack McAfee, perché sur la barrière, (au centre) coiffé d'un chapeau de papier blanc. Jack poursuivra la Ferrari de Shelby sur une Porsche 550 Spyder durant la course principale

(1, 2 & 5) Carroll Shelby checks his engine, smiles in victory and acknowledges the crowd in a 500 TR Ferrari. Shelby was raking in victories in 1956 like autumn leaves.

(3) Roland Keith urges his Cooper Formula III to victory. These quick little machines were well suited to the Brynfan Tyddyn course and held the lap record for a time. They were looked upon by drivers of "real" cars as an amusing aberration (who knew that their rear engines anticipated the future). Temperamental, their attrition rate was high, which seemed just fine with Formula III drivers, most of whom ranked tinkering with dead engines on a par with actual racing.

(4) Duncan Black, a familiar figure in many races, took a 2nd in class here in his Lotus IX.

(1, 2 & 5) Carroll Shelby beim Motorcheck, mit einem Siegerlächeln und während der Ehrenrunde in seinem 500 TR Ferrari. Shelby heimste 1956 einen Sieg nach dem anderen ein.

(3) Roland Keith jagt in seinem Formel-3-Cooper dem Sieg entgegen. Diese rasanten kleine Monoposti waren für den Brynfan-Tyddyn-Kurs wie geschaffen und hielten für eine Weile sogar den Rundenrekord. Die Fahrer der »richtigen« Autos sahen in ihnen eher eine amüsante Verirrung (wer wußte damals schon, daß solchen Mittelmotorkonstruktionen die Zukunft gehörte). Die Ausfallquote der temperamentvollen Kleinen war hoch, aber den Formel-3-Fahrern, die mit dem Herumbasteln an defekten Motoren größtenteils ebensoviel Zeit verbrachten wie mit dem eigentlichen Rennen, war das nicht unrecht.

(4) Duncan Black, Star vieler Rennen, hier als Zweiter in seiner Klasse im Lotus IX.

(1, 2 & 5) Carrol Shelby vérifie son moteur, sourit à la victoire et plus tard au public au volant d'une Ferrari 500 TR. Shelby ramassera les victoires comme des feuilles d'automne durant la saison 1956.

(3) Roland Keith conduit sa Cooper Formule III vers la victoire. Ces petites mécaniques rapides étaient idéales sur le circuit de Brynfan Tyddyn et conservèrent le record de tour pendant quelque temps. Les pilotes de « vraies » voitures s'en amusaient (ils savaient que leurs moteurs arrière présageaient l'avenir). Nerveuses, les formules III s'usaient rapidement, mais cela ne semblait pas gêner leurs pilotes pour qui le bricolage de moteurs épuisés faisait partie de la course.

(4) Duncan Black, un habitué des courses, va prendre une deuxième place au volant de sa Lotus IX.

1

2

3

4

5

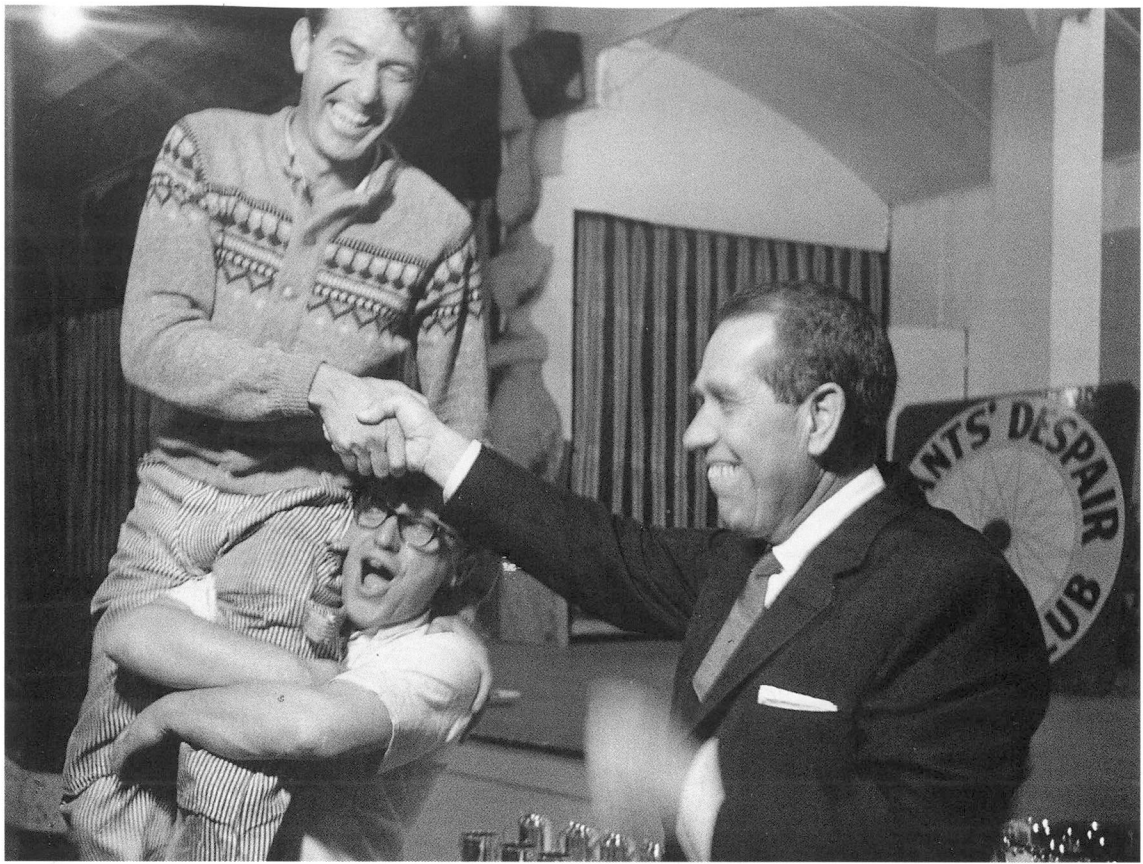

1

(1) Carroll Shelby accepts congratulations from a shoulder perch.
(2) Shelby in close conversation with Luigi Chinetti, U.S. Ferrari distributor. Driver Paul O'Shea is on the far right.

(1) Auf den Schultern eines Fans nimmt Carroll Shelby Glückwünsche entgegen.
(2) Shelby im Zwiegespräch mit Luigi Chinetti, Ferraris U.S.-Importeur. Ganz rechts der Fahrer Paul O'Shea.

(1) Félicitations pour Carroll Shelby, perché sur les épaules d'un admirateur.
(2) Shelby en grande conversation avec Luigi Chinetti, concessionnaire Ferrari aux USA. Le pilote Paul O'Shea est à l'extrême droite.

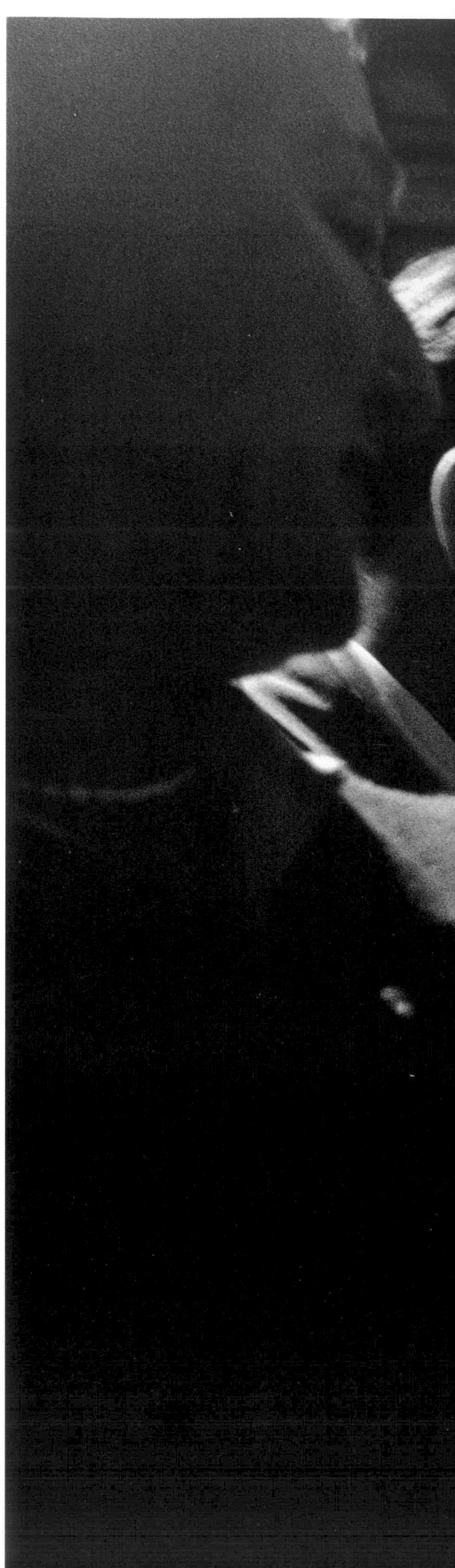

2

WATKINS GLEN 1955

A paddock line-up for the Watkins Glen Grand Prix, September, 1955. Bill Lloyd (Maserati 300S), Sherwood Johnston (D-type Jaguar) and Bill Spear (Maserati 300S) finished the 22-lap feature race Johnston, Lloyd, Spear.

Vorstartaufstellung für den Watkins Glen Grand Prix im September 1955. Bill Lloyd (Maserati 300S), Sherwood Johnston (D-Type Jaguar) und Bill Spear (Maserati 300S) gewannen das 22-Runden-Rennen. Zieleinlauf: Johnston vor Lloyd und Spear.

Queue au paddock lors du Grand Prix de Watkins Glen en septembre 1955. Bill Lloyd (Maserati 300S), Sherwood Johnston (Jaguar Type D) et Bill Spear (Maserati 300S) ont terminé la course de 22 tours. Classement : Johnston, Lloyd et Spear.

(1) The Briggs Cunningham team was one of the first to use large transport trucks, this one housing a D-type Jaguar and spare wheels.

Das Briggs-Cunningham-Team setzte als erstes große Transport-Lkws ein, hier mit einem Jaguar D-Type und Ersatzreifen.

L'écurie Briggs Cunningham sera l'une des premières à utiliser les grands transporteurs. Celui-ci abrite une Jaguar Type D et des pneus de rechange.

1

(2) The Queen Catherine Cup Race, 11 laps for F Production Porsches and Modified cars under 1500 cc, led here by Warren Steele, Porsche 356. Among the Porsches are an Alfa Romeo Giulietta and 2 MG TDs.

Das Rennen um den Queen Catherine Cup, 11 Runden für F-Klasse-Porsche und modifizierte Fahrzeuge unter 1500 cm3, hier angeführt von Warren Steele, Porsche 356. Zwischen den Porsche ein Alfa Romeo Giulietta und zwei MG TDs.

La Queen Catherine Cup Race ; 11 tours pour les Porsche de groupe F et les voitures modifiées de moins de 1,5 litres. En tête ici : la Porsche 356 de Warren Steele. Une Alfa Romeo Giulietta et deux MG TD sont parmi les Porsche.

2

Flying through Valents' farm at the old Glen, a Cadillac engine in the leading Cheetah being driven to a class victory by John Plaisted, with George Rabe's Ford Riley (the ex-Miles Collier "Ardent Alligator") in pursuit.

Im »Tiefflug« durch Valents' Farm auf dem alten Glen rast John Plaisted in einem Cheetah mit Cadillac-Motor zum Klassensieg, dicht gefolgt von George Rabes Ford Riley – dem »Ardent Alligator«, der vorher Miles Collier gehörte.

La Cheetah équipée d'un moteur Cadillac fonce dans le Valent's Farm sur l'ancien tracé de Watkins Glen. John Plaisted la propulse vers une victoire de groupe, poursuivi par la Ford Riley de George Rabe (l'ex « Ardent Alligator » de Miles Collier).

Preston Gray, Ferrari 340 Mexico Spyder.

Fred Wacker, Cunningham C4RK.

AIRPORTS

FLUGPLATZKURSE · AERODROMES

Airports and their support roads offered a safer, more easily controlled venue than public roads for racing. As the dangers to the drivers of deep ditches, solid trees and narrow roads and to the spectators of problematical crowd control became increasingly evident, race organizers sought small-town airports or abandoned military facilities on which to hold their events. Just as races through town streets had yielded to races through the countryside now the countryside was increasingly replaced by airports as the most common site.

Hay bales, cones and stacks of old tires marked the course and cut chicanes out of the featureless expanses. Though drivers could now spin off the course with impunity and spectators could be kept at a safe distance, the lack of variation in terrain or other distinguishing aspects stole much of the flavor of road racing from these venues. Since it was often airports or nothing the choice was obvious.

Many airport courses were used once or twice and never again. But the granddaddy of them all, Sebring, is still in use today, although much modified and using little of the original circuit.

Airports were often highly abrasive (the various courses put together for Nassau Speed Weeks leap to mind). Tires were chewed up at a most expensive rate. But damage from mowing down fences, side-swiping trees or up-ending in a ditch was greatly reduced on the wide open spaces. And racing, after all, wherever it might be, is racing.

Flugplatzgelände und ihre Anlieferstraßen boten den Rennen ein sichereres und leichter kontrollierbares Umfeld als öffentliche Straßen. Die Rennorganisatoren verlegten die Veranstaltungen auf Kleinstadtflugplätze und ehemalige Militärflughäfen, als die Gefährdung der Fahrer durch tiefe Gräben, massive Bäume und enge Straßen und der Zuschauer durch fehlende Ordnungsmaßnahmen immer offensichtlicher wurde. So wie Rennen zuvor bereits von der Stadt aufs Land verlagert worden waren, wich man nun zunehmend von diesem auf Flugplatzstrecken aus.

Strohballen, Pylone und aufgestapelte alte Reifen markierten die Strecke und dienten zugleich als Schikanen in der eintönigen Weite. Obwohl die Fahrer jetzt gefahrlos von der Fahrbahn kreiseln und die Zuschauer auf Sicherheitsabstand gehalten werden konnten, nahm die Monotonie des Geländes und das Fehlen jeglicher Unterscheidungsmerkmale diesen Strecken die für die Straßenrennen charakteristische Atmosphäre. Wenn es aber hieß, Flugplatz oder gar kein Rennen, fiel die Entscheidung nicht schwer.

Die meisten Flugplatzkurse wurden nur ein- oder zweimal benutzt. Aber die Ur-Flugplatzstrecke Sebring wird heute noch gefahren – allerdings mit zahlreichen Modifikationen und nur noch auf einem kleinen Abschnitt des ursprünglichen Rundkurses.

Der Reifenabrieb war auf Flugplatzkursen oft besonders hoch (wie etwa auf den verschiedenen Kursen der Nassau Speed Weeks). Diese Strecken waren teure Reifenfresser. Dafür waren auf den großen Arealen Unfallschäden durch umgerissene Zäune, gestreifte Bäume oder Grabenlandungen weitgehend reduziert. Und ein Rennen bleibt schließlich ein Rennen – egal, wo es ausgetragen wird.

Les aérodromes et les routes adjacentes étaient des endroits plus sûrs et plus facilement contrôlables que les voies publiques. Les organisateurs de courses recherchèrent des aérodromes de petites villes et des aéroports militaires désaffectés lorsqu'on réalisa enfin que les fossés profonds, les arbres et les routes étroites représentaient des dangers pour les pilotes et qu'il fallait faire quelque chose pour assurer la sécurité des spectateurs. Les courses qui s'étaient d'abord déroulées dans les rues des villes, puis sur les routes de campagne, auraient dorénavant de plus en plus souvent lieu sur des aérodromes.

Les aérodromes étant des étendues planes, on dessinait le tracé du parcours à l'aide de bottes de paille, de pylônes et de piles de pneus. Les pilotes pouvaient désormais foncer sans crainte et le public, éloigné à une distance respectueuse, était à l'abri. Mais le manque de relief du terrain et de ce qui avait fait le charme des courses sur routes enlevaient beaucoup à l'atmosphère des compétitions. Néanmoins, on n'avait pas le choix. La plupart du temps, c'était les aérodromes ou pas de courses.

La plupart des parcours d'aérodromes ne furent utilisés qu'une ou deux fois. Cependant, on court encore à Sebring, un des plus anciens. Le tracé en a cependant été très modifié et n'inclut plus qu'un petit segment du circuit d'origine.

Les courses sur les pistes d'aérodromes maltraitaient les roues des voitures (on se remémora les divers parcours des Nassau Speed Weeks). L'usure des pneus revenait très cher. Par contre, les accidents de barrières défoncées, d'arbres effleurés et de chutes dans le fossé étaient bien moins fréquents sur les vastes espaces ouverts. Et puis, une course de voitures, où qu'elle ait lieu, reste une course de voitures.

An AC Bristol and braces of Arnolt-Bristols, Austin-Healeys and Triumph TRs negotiate the runways and access roads of Cumberland airport, 1956.

Ein AC Bristol und je zwei Arnolt-Bristols, Austin-Healeys und Triumph TRs meistern die Rollbahnen und Anlieferstraßen des Flugplatzkurses von Cumberland, 1956.

Une Bristol AC suivie d'une armada d'Arnolt-Bristol, Austin-Healey et Triumph TR négocient les pistes et routes d'accès de l'aérodrome de Cumberland, 1956.

CUMBERLAND 1956

1

2

(1) Alfred Momo (with cap) oversees preparation of the Briggs Cunningham D-type Jaguars.
(2) Airports rarely lacked space.
(3) Bill Lloyd, center, points out something in his Maserati 300S engine to photographer Richard Thierry (left) and mechanic Joe Growalski. Lloyd was 3rd in the Vandegrift Memorial Trophy race.

(1) Alfred Momo (mit Kappe) beobachtet die Arbeiten an den Jaguar D-Types von Briggs Cunningham.
(2) Auf den Flugplätzen wurde es nur selten zu eng.
(3) Bill Lloyd (Mitte) zeigt dem Fotografen Richard Thierry (links) und dem Mechaniker Joe Growalski etwas am Motor seines Maserati 300S. Lloyd wurde Dritter im Rennen um die Vandegrift Memorial Trophy.

(1) Alfred Momo (avec casquette) observe les préparations effectuées sur des Briggs Cunningham Jaguar Type D.
(2) Les aérodromes avaient de la place à revendre.
(3) Bill Lloyd (au milieu) discute du moteur de sa Maserati 300S avec le photographe Richard Thierry (à gauche) et le mécanicien Joe Growalski. Lloyd se placera 3ème dans l'épreuve Vandegrift Memorial Trophy.

3

1

2

(1) Austin-Healeys set for the Cumberland Cup race.
(2) J.L. King, Allard J2X, leads Dick Perrin, Corvette, and Gene Greenspun, Ferrari 250 MM, through a turn.
(3) 1-2-3, everybody lean! An MG TF (#38) and two MG As.
(4) Paul O'Shea, Mercedes-Benz 300SL, winner of the Lion's Club Trophy, leads Bark Henry, Corvette, who was 5th.

(1) Austin-Healeys vor dem Start zum Rennen um den Cumberland Cup.
(2) J.L. King, Allard J2X, führt in einer Kurve vor Dick Perrin, Corvette, und Gene Greenspun, Ferrari 250 MM.
(3) 1-2-3, alle Augen nach links! Ein MG TF (Nr. 38) und zwei MG As.
(4) Paul O'Shea, Mercedes-Benz 300SL, Gewinner der Lion's Club Trophy, führt vor Bark Henry, Corvette, der als Fünfter ins Ziel kam.

(1) Des Austin-Healey au départ de la Cumberland Cup.
(2) J.L. King sur une Allard J2X entraîne la Corvette de Dick Perrin et la Ferrari 250 MM de Gene Greenspun dans un virage.
(3) Un, deux, trois, tout le monde se penche à gauche! Une MG TF (n° 38) et deux MG A.
(4) Vainqueur du Lion's Club Trophy, Paul O'Shea sur une Mercedes-Benz 300 SL, en pole position devant la Corvette de Bark Henry qui se classera 5ème.

3

4

The Cunningham Jaguars were vanquished by
Walt Hansgen in another D-type, Jack McAfee in a
Porsche 550 Spyder and Bill Lloyd in his 3-liter
Maserati.

Die Cunningham Jaguars wurden von Walt Hansgen, ebenfalls Jaguar D-Type, Jack McAfee, Porsche 550 Spyder, und Bill Lloyd, 3-Liter-Maserati
besiegt.

Les Cunningham Jaguar seront vaincues par Walt
Hansgen sur une autre Type D, Jack McAfee sur
une Porsche 550 Spyder et Bill Lloyd sur une
Maserati 3 litres.

Walt Hansgen, D-type Jaguar, winner of the hour-
long feature race for the Vandegrift Memorial Trophy.

Walt Hansgen, Jaguar D-Type, Gewinner des ein-
stündigen Hauptrennens um die Vandegrift
Memorial Trophy.

Walt Hansgen, Jaguar Type D, vainqueur de
l'épreuve d'une heure pour le Vandegrift Memorial Trophy.

Frank Baptista, Lotus IX was 3rd in Class G-Modified/Er wurde Dritter in der modifizierten G-Klasse/Il se classera 3ème dans le groupe G-modifié.

S.H. "Wacky" Arnolt in his Arnolt-Bristol (#9); R.B. Wilson, Triumph TR3 (#41); K.H. Wilson, Austin-Healey (#55).

MONTGOMERY 1956

1

2

3

(1) Carroll Shelby in John Edgar's Ferrari 857 S on his way to one of two victories at the August 1956 meet (his 18th and 19th of the season).
(2) A smiling Bill Lloyd in his reliable Maserati 300S was twice 2nd to Shelby.
(3) Hay bale chicanes were a staple of airport courses and Montgomery, an old Air Force field, had several. George Constantine, D-type Jaguar, followed by David Darrin, C-type Jaguar, a brace of Austin-Healey 100Ms and an Austin-Healey Special.

(1) Carroll Shelby in John Edgars Ferrari 857 S, auf dem Weg zu einem von zwei bei dieser Veranstaltung im August errungenen Siegen (Saisonsiege Nr. 18 und 19).
(2) Bill Lloyd hat gut lachen. Mit seinem zuverlässigen Maserati 300S wurde er beide Male Zweiter hinter Shelby.
(3) Montgomery, ein ehemaliger Luftwaffen-Flugplatz, wartete mit mehreren der auf Flugplatzkursen üblichen Heuballen-Schikanen auf. George Constantine, Jaguar D-Type, vor David Darrin auf Jaguar C-Type, umrahmt von mehreren Austin-Healey 100M und einem Austin-Healey Special.

(1) Carroll Shelby au volant de la Ferrari 857 S de John Edgar, fonce vers une des deux victoires qu'il s'adjugera à la rencontre d'août 1956 (ses 18ème et 19ème de la saison).
(2) Un Bill Lloyd radieux au volant de sa fidèle Maserati 300S. A deux reprises, il s'est placé 2ème derrière Shelby.
(3) Les bottes de foin dessinaient des chicanes sur les tracés d'aérodromes. Il y en avait plusieurs à Montgomery, un ancien aéroport de l'aviation militaire. George Constantine, Jaguar Type D, suivi de David Darrin sur une Jaguar Type C, deux Austin-Healey 100M et une Austin-Healey Special.

1

2

3

(1) Bill Lloyd, Maserati 300S, amid the shredded bales.
(2) Carroll Shelby, Ferrari 857 S, winner.
(3) Paul O'Shea, George Tilp's Ferrari 750 Monza was 3rd behind Shelby and Lloyd in two races.
(4) John Alderborgh, Abarth.
(5) Chet Flynn, Mercedes Benz 300SL, 2nd to O'Shea's MB 300SL.
(6) Mike Marshall, Porsche 550 Spyder.

(1) Bill Lloyd, Maserati 300S, landet im Heu.
(2) Carroll Shelby, Ferrari 857 S, Sieger.
(3) Paul O'Shea belegte mit George Tilps Ferrari 750 Monza in zwei Rennen den dritten Platz hinter Shelby und Lloyd.
(4) John Alderborgh, Abarth.
(5) Chet Flynn, Mercedes Benz 300SL, hinter O'Shea im MB 300SL.
(6) Mike Marshall, Porsche 550 Spyder.

(1) Bill Lloyd, Maserati 300S, entre des bottes de paille déchiquetées.
(2) Carroll Shelby, Ferrari 857 S, le vainqueur.
(3) Paul O'Shea sur la Ferrari 750 Monza de George Tilp qui arrivera 3ème derrière Shelby et Lloyd dans deux courses.
(4) John Alderborgh, Abarth.
(5) Chet Flynn, Mercedes-Benz 300SL, 2ème derrière la MB 300 SL de O'Shea.
(6) Mike Marshall, Porsche 550 Spyder.

4

5

6

BEVERLY 1955, 1956

Howard Hanna, Deutsch-Bonnet. 1956.

Chuck Wallace, Mercedes-Benz 300 SL, and Dick Thompson, Corvette – a hairdresser and a dentist/ein Friseur und ein Zahnarzt/un coiffeur et un dentiste au volant. 1956.

The Cad Allard J-R of Bob Bucher (#29), Masten Gregory, Ferrari 750 Monza (#147). 1956.

Jim Johnston, Ferrari 500 TR (#15); David Darrin, C-type Jaguar; Charles Moran, Cunningham C4R; and poor drainage typical of airport courses/und die schlechte Dränage der Flugplatzkurse/et le mauvais drainage des pistes d'aérodromes.

1

2

(1) Airport courses rarely boasted stands or pits – just cars and people.
(2) Sherwood Johnston, Briggs Cunningham D-type Jaguar finished behind the Ferraris of Carroll Shelby and Masten Gregory in the 1956 feature race.

(1) Boxen und Tribünen sah man auf Flugplatzkursen eher selten – aber um so mehr Autos und Menschen.
(2) Der Cunningham Jaguar D-Type von Sherwood Johnston fuhr im Hauptrennen von 1956 hinter den Ferraris von Carroll Shelby und Masten Gregory ins Ziel.

(1) Les aménagements étaient rudimentaires. Il n'y avait pratiquement ni stands, ni tribunes – rien que des voitures et des gens.
(2) Sherwood Johnston au volant d'une Briggs Cunningham Jaguar Type D, terminera la course derrière les Ferrari de Carroll Shelby et Masten Gregory, 1956.

Briggs Cunningham and two mounts in July 1956:
supercharged Jaguar XK140MC and OSCA MT4
(see bottom right).

Briggs Cunningham und zwei Fahrzeuge im Juli
1956: Jaguar XK 140MC mit Kompressormotor
und OSCA MT4 (siehe unten rechts).

Briggs Cunningham a deux bolides en juillet 1956 :
Jaguar XK 140MC gonflée et OSCA MT4 (voir ci-
dessous, à droite).

Peggy Darrin times her husband, David, in the rain. 1956.

Bei strömendem Regen nimmt Peggy Darrin die Zeit für ihren Mann David. 1956.

Peggy Darrin chronomètre son mari David sous une pluie battante. 1956.

Gaston Andrey drove a Morgan Plus 4 to 2nd in Class E Production in July, 1956.

Im Juli 1956 belegte Gaston Andrey mit einem Morgan Plus 4 den zweiten Platz in der E-Klasse.

Gaston Andrey se classera 2e dans le groupe E sur une Morgan Plus 4, juillet 1956.

1

2

3

(1) Charles Moran, Cunningham C4R. 1956.
Moran was one of the founders of the Sports Car
Club of America and a veteran of pre-war road
racing.
(2, 3) Jack McAfee in the Porsche 550 Spyder in
which Hans Herrmann and Wolfgang von Trips
had won the Index of Performance at Sebring,
waged a terrific battle in the Witch City Trophy
race in 1956 only to lose out to Eddie Crawford
in a similar car (#69).
(4) Gene Greenspun's Ferrari 250 MM serves as
a beauty's rest. In the background is the MG A of
Dave Ash and a travel trailer, the beginning of
many to follow.

(1) Charles Moran im Cunningham C4R. 1956.
Moran war einer der Gründer des Sports Car Club
of America und ein Veteran der Vorkriegs-
Straßenrennen.
(2, 3) In einem Porsche 550 Spyder, mit dem
bereits Hans Herrmann und Wolfgang von Trips in
Sebring an die Tabellenspitze gefahren waren,
kämpfte Jack McAfee beim Witch City Trophy
Rennen von 1956 erbittert um den Sieg, den ihm
allerdings Eddie Crawford mit einem ähnlichen
Wagen (Nr. 69) stahl.
(4) Der reine Luxus: ein Mittagsschläfchen auf
Gene Greenspuns Ferrari 250 MM. Im Hintergrund sieht man den MG A von Dave Ash und
einen der ersten Wohnanhänger, die später zum
gewohnten Bild wurden.

(1) Charles Moran, Cunningham C4R. 1956.
Moran était un des fondateurs du Sports Car Club
of America et un vétéran des courses sur routes
d'avant-guerre.
(2, 3) Jack McAfee au volant de la Porsche 550
Spyder sur laquelle Hans Herrmann et Wolfgang
von Trips remportèrent l'Indice de Performance à
Sebring. Après un dur combat pour le Witch City
Trophy de 1956, il devra s'incliner devant Eddie
Crawford qui pilote une voiture jumelle (n° 69).
(4) La Ferrari 250 MM de Gene Greenspun sert de
lieu de repos. A l'arrière-plan : la MG A de Dave
Ash et un des premiers motorhomes.

Len Bastrup was an East Coast fixture in shining Lotus race cars. At Beverly in 1955 he inaugurated his 1100 cc Lotus by winning one race and finishing 3rd overall and 1st in class in another.

Len Bastrup und seine blitzenden Lotus-Rennwagen waren fester Bestandteil der Ostküsten-Rennen. In Beverly weihte er 1955 seinen 1100-cm³-Lotus ein, indem er ein Rennen gewann, Dritter im Gesamtklassement und Klassensieger in einem weiteren Rennen wurde.

Len Bastrup est un habitué des courses de la Côte Est au volant de Lotus impeccables. En 1955, à Beverly, il inaugure sa Lotus 1,1 litre en remportant une course, une 3ème place au classement général et une 1ère place de groupe.

1

2

(1) Phil Hill in George Tilp's Ferrari 750 Monza
(#3) bested the Ferrari 375 MM of Jim Kimberly
to win the 104-mile Beverly Trophy Race. Here he
takes the outside to pass Paul Ceresole, Kieft-
Bristol (#23). Phil was 28 years old and six years
away from his world championship in 1961.
(2) Jim Pauley, Ferrari 500 Mondial (#53) on the
outside of Jack Crusoe, C-type Jaguar (#37) in the
July, 1955 race. Pauley went on to a 1st in class,
Crusoe a 2nd.

(1) In George Tilps Ferrari 750 Monza (Nr. 3)
schlug Phil Hill den Ferrari 375 MM von Jim Kimberly und gewann so das über 166 Kilometer
führende Beverly Trophy Race. Hier überholt er
auf der Außenbahn Paul Ceresole im Kieft-Bristol
(Nr. 23). Phil war 28 Jahre alt und noch sechs
Jahre von seinem Weltmeistertitel 1961 entfernt.
(2) Jim Pauleys Ferrari 500 Mondial (Nr. 53) zieht
im Rennen vom Juli 1955 außen an Jack Crusoe im
Jaguar C-Type (Nr. 37) vorbei. Pauley wurde Klassensieger, Crusoe Zweiter.

(1) Phil Hill sur la Ferrari 750 Monza de George
Tilp (n° 3) devancera la Ferrari 375 MM de Jim
Kimberly pour s'adjuger le Beverly Trophy de 104
miles. Ici, il double Paul Ceresole, Kieft-Bristol,
(n° 23) sur le flanc gauche. Phil qui avait alors 28
ans, sera couronné champion du monde 1961 six
ans plus tard.
(2) Jim Pauley sur une Ferrari 500 Mondial (n° 53)
contourne Jack Crusoe, Jaguar Type C (n° 37),
dans la course de juillet 1955. Pauley s'octroiera
une 1ère place et Crusoe une 2ème dans une épreuve de groupe.

EAGLE MOUNTAIN 1956

PURPOSE-BUILT COURSES

PERMANENTE RENNSTRECKEN · CIRCUITS PERMANENTS

In the progression from the use of everyday roads blocked to traffic for race day to the construction of roads leading nowhere for the specific purpose of racing, it was not that one year all races were on country roads, the next year on airports and then on road courses. They over-lapped. In any racing season drivers might see examples of all, including no few hybrids such as Marlboro Raceway near Washington DC and the old Thompson in northeast Connecticut (and the present day Phoenix for that matter) which began as oval tracks and became road courses by bursting a seam and meandering about outside the perimeter before rejoining the track. Some advantages in converting oval tracks to road course use were found in the pre-existence of grandstands and sometimes in garages and pits.

Perhaps the grandest such hybrid track/road course was at Daytona Beach, Florida. Bill France, the man behind NASCAR, added a road course inside his 2 1/2 mile oval in 1959 and it continues to be the site of international 24-hour races.

Among the purpose-built courses that began snaking about over hill and dale were Lime Rock, in Connecticut (1957), spurred by John Fitch, one of the country's finest drivers; Elkhart Lake in Wisconsin (1955); a new Thompson (1957); Virginia International Raceway, and Bridgehampton amidst the sand dunes of eastern Long Island in New York (both 1957).

Auf dem Weg von normalen Straßen, die am Renntag für den übrigen Verkehr gesperrt wurden, zum Bau spezieller, isolierter Rennstrecken war es keineswegs so, daß die Rennen in einem Jahr nur auf Landstraßen, im nächsten auf Flugplätzen und schließlich auf permanenten Kursen ausgetragen wurden. Die einzelnen Phasen überschnitten sich. Es war möglich, daß die Fahrer in einer Rennsaison alle Varianten sahen, darunter nicht wenige Mischkurse, wie den Marlboro Raceway nahe Washington DC oder den alten Thompson-Kurs im Nordosten Connecticuts (und übrigens auch die heutige Rennstrecke von Phoenix), die sich von Ovalkursen zu echten Rennstrecken entwickelten, indem man an den Rundkurs eine Strecke außerhalb dessen Grenzen anhängte, die später wieder an die Ursprungsstrecke anschloß. Der Umbau hatte unter anderem den Vorteil, daß Tribünen, manchmal auch Werkstätten und Boxen bereits vorhanden waren.

Der vielleicht bedeutendste Mischkurs war bei Daytona Beach in Florida. Bill France, der führende Kopf der NASCAR, fügte 1959 ein Straßenstück in die vier Kilometer lange Ovalstrecke ein, auf der noch heute internationale 24-Stunden-Rennen ausgetragen werden.

Zu den permanenten Rennstrecken, die sich allmählich in den Bergen und Tälern des ganzen Landes ausbreiteten, gehörten der Lime-Rock-Kurs in Connecticut (1957), initiiert von John Fitch, einem der besten Fahrer des Landes, Elkhart Lake in Wisconsin (1955), der neue Thompson-Kurs (1957), der Virginia International Raceway und – inmitten der Sanddünen im östlichen Teil Long Islands in New York – Bridgehampton (beide 1957).

La transition entre les routes barrées à la circulation durant les courses et la construction de circuits destinés uniquement au sport automobile, ne s'opéra pas brusquement. Les courses ne se déroulèrent pas sur des routes de campagne, puis sur des pistes d'aérodromes et finalement sur des circuits d'une année à l'autre. Les différentes phases se chevauchèrent. Durant une saison, les pilotes étaient confrontés à toutes sortes de parcours dont des tracés hybrides tels que le Marlboro Raceway près de Washington DC et l'ancien Thompson dans le Nord-Est du Connecticut (le circuit actuel de Phoenix en faisait également partie). Ovales au départ, ces parcours avaient pris la forme de véritables circuits après avoir été agrandis d'une boucle sinueuse. En outre, plusieurs d'entre eux possédaient déjà des tribunes et parfois des garages et des stands, ce qui ajoutait à l'avantage de les convertir en circuits permanents.

Daytona Beach en Floride est sans doute le plus important de ces circuits hybrides. En 1959, Bill France, l'éminence grise de la NASCAR, ajouta un segment à la piste ovale de quatre kilomètres qui est, jusqu'aujourd'hui, la scène de courses internationales de 24 heures.

Parmi les circuits permanents qui commencèrent à sinuer par monts et par vaux, citons Lime Rock dans le Connecticut (1957) aménagé sur l'initiative de John Fitch, un des plus brillants pilotes américains, Elkhart Lake dans le Wisconsin (1955), le nouveau Thompson (1957), Virginia International Raceway et Bridgehampton qui s'étend dans les dunes de sable à l'Est de Long Island à New York (ces deux derniers datant de 1957).

Speed was relative. Here, a herd of VWs at Thompson, 1955.

Geschwindigkeit war relativ. Hier ein »Käfer-Rudel« in Thompson, 1955.

Il y en avait pour toutes les vitesses. Ici, une armada de Volkswagen sur le circuit de Thompson, 1955.

THOMPSON 1954, 1955, 1956

1

2

3

(1) A field of 15 stock Volkswagen Beetles in the 11th and final race of the May 1955 meeting.
(2) Don McComb, Jaguar XK120 coupe had fastest lap in his class but finished 4th. 1955.
(3) Fred Proctor, Maserati A6 GCS (#17), and E. "Pup" Pupulidy, VW Special (#40) on the starting grid for a Labor Day race, September 1954.
(4) 3 Austin-Healeys and an Aston Martin in the turn with a car-catching sand bank on the outside. 1955.

(1) Ein Feld von 15 Standard-Käfern beim elften und letzten Rennen im Mai 1955.
(2) Don McComb fuhr im Jaguar XK120 Coupé die beste Rundenzeit seiner Klasse, kam aber nur als Vierter ins Ziel. 1955.
(3) Fred Proctor, Maserati A6 GCS (Nr. 17), und E. »Pup« Pupulidy, VW Special (Nr. 40), in der Startaufstellung eines Labor-Day-Rennens im September 1954.
(4) Drei Austin-Healeys und ein Aston Martin in der Kurve, deren Außenseite durch Sandhügel gesichert ist. 1955.

(1) Un plateau de 15 Volkswagen Coccinelle dans la 11ème et dernière course du meeting de mai 1955.
(2) Don McComb sur le coupé Jaguar XK120 établit le tour le plus rapide dans sa catégorie, mais ne finira que 4ème. 1955.
(3) Fred Proctor, Maserati A6 GCS (n° 17) et E. « Pup » Pupulidy, VW Special (n° 40) sur la grille de départ de la course du Labor Day, septembre 1954.
(4) Trois Austin-Healey et une Aston Martin prennent un virage protégé par des bordures de sable. 1955.

Phil Cade with a Chrysler V8 in his Maserati leads
Russ Boss, C-type Jaguar in the October 1955
meet.

In Phil Cades Maserati steckte ein Chrysler-
V8-Motor. Bei diesem Rennen im Okober 1955
führt er vor Russ Boss' Jaguar C-Type.

Phil Cade au volant de sa Maserati dotée d'un V8
Chrysler devant Russ Boss sur une Jaguar Type C
au meeting d'octobre 1955.

Phil Forno, a mechanic and sometimes-driver for
Briggs Cunningham and Alfred Momo (importer
of Maseratis) tries out a Lotus-Maserati without
much success. 1956.

Phil Forno, Mechaniker und Gelegenheitsfahrer
für Briggs Cunningham und den Maserati-Impor-
teur Alfred Momo, versucht sich – recht erfolglos
– in einem Lotus-Maserati. 1956.

Phil Forno, mécanicien et pilote occasionnel de
Briggs Cunningham et d'Alfred Momo, importa-
teur de Maserati. Il essaie une Lotus-Maserati sans
grand succès. 1956.

1

2

3

(1) A typically varied assortment of competitors, from the Bandini Offenhauser (#50) of David Michaels to a brace of Morgans and Arnolt-Bristols and a BMW 328. 1955.

(2) E. "Pup" Pupulidy was a frequent winner in VW Specials and Porsches at many eastern events. 1955.

(3) Briggs Swift Cunningham (left), in the last year (1955) of campaigning his own Cunningham cars at Le Mans, won Race 7 in his 1500 cc OSCA. His son, Briggs III, here in the Ferrari 225 S in which he finished 2nd in Race 8. Between them is Bill Lloyd, a neighbor, a cousin and fellow driver.

(1) Die typisch bunte Rennmischung: von David Michaels' Bandini Offenhauser (Nr. 50) über eine Reihe von Morgans und Arnolt-Bristols bis hin zu einem BMW 328. 1955.

(2) E. »Pup« Pupulidy gewann mit seinen VW-Spezialanfertigungen und Porsche-Modellen bei vielen Rennereignissen im Osten. 1955.

(3) Briggs Swift Cunningham (links), dessen eigene Rennwagen in diesem Jahr (1955) zum letztenmal in Le Mans an den Start gingen, gewann das siebte Rennen auf einem 1500-cm³-OSCA. Im Ferrari 225 S fuhr sein Sohn Briggs III., der im achten Rennen den zweiten Platz belegte. Dazwischen Bill Lloyd, sein Nachbar, Vetter und Fahrerkollege.

(1) Un plateau typique comprenant la Bandini Offenhauser (n° 50) de David Michaels, un couple de Morgan et Arnolt-Bristol et une BMW 328. 1955.

(2) E « Pup » Pupulidy, remportera de nombreuses courses de la Côte Est au volant de VW Special ou de Porsche. 1955.

(3) Briggs Swift Cunningham (à gauche) remportera la 7ème course sur son OSCA 1,5 litres, après avoir aligné ses voitures pour la dernière fois au Mans (1955). Son fils, Briggs III terminera la 8ème course 2ème au volant de la Ferrari 225 S. Entre eux, Bill Lloyd, leur voisin, cousin et collègue.

(1) America's fastest dentist, Dick Thompson, had a special affinity with Corvettes. His SR-2 at the October 1956 meeting was a precursor of the 1957 car as raced by the factory at Sebring.
(2) The Cadillac-powered John Meyer's Special scored the day's fastest average speed to win the 9th race. 1955.

(1) Amerikas schnellster Zahnarzt, Dick Thompson, hatte eine besondere Vorliebe für Corvettes. Die SR-2, die er im Rennen vom Oktober 1956 fuhr, war ein Vorläufer des 1957er Modells.
(2) Der von einem Cadillac-Motor angetriebene John Meyer's Special erreichte die höchste Durchschnittsgeschwindigkeit des Tages und gewann das neunte Rennen. 1955.

(1) Le plus rapide des dentistes américains, Dick Thompson, avait une affection particulière pour les Corvette. La SR-2 qu'il pilote au meeting d'octobre 1956 est le précurseur de la voiture, d'usine alignée à Sebring en 1957.
(2) La John Meyer's Special, moteur Cadillac, établira la vitesse moyenne la plus rapide de la journée pour remporter la 9ème épreuve. 1955.

2

Len Bastrup, Lotus IX, again won his class/wurde Klassensieger/vainqueur dans sa catégorie. 1955.

George Constantine, Jaguar XK120M was 2nd/wurde Zweiter/se classera 2ème. 1955.

1

1

2

Walt Hansgen, D-type Jaguar, was the big winner in the September 1956 meet.

Walt Hansgen, Jaguar D-Type, war der große Sieger der Veranstaltung vom September 1956.

Walt Hansgen, Jaguar Type D, le grand vainqueur du meeting de septembre 1956.

Charles Cunningham, Lotus Eleven, took a 3rd in class. 1956.

Charles Cunningham, Lotus 11, wurde Dritter seiner Klasse. 1956.

Charles Cunningham, Lotus 11, se classe 3ème du groupe. 1956.

Paul O'Shea and George Tilp's Mercedes-Benz 300SL became frequent victors, winning twice in September 1956.

Paul O'Shea und der Mercedes-Benz 300SL von George Tilp entwickelten sich zum siegreichen Gespann und gewannen im September 1956 zwei Rennen.

Paul O'Shea sur la Mercedes-Benz 300SL de George Tilp est abonné au succès : deux victoires au meeting de septembre 1956.

(1) Fred Proctor, Maserati 150S, was one of the first to tow his race car in a covered trailer. 1956.
(2) Masten Gregory, Ferrari 500 TR, won Sunday's 10-lap race in the Ferrari and a one-hour race on Monday in a Porsche 550 Spyder. 1956.

(1) Fred Proctor, Maserati 150S, transportierte als einer der ersten Fahrer sein Rennfahrzeug in einem geschlossenen Anhänger. 1956.
(2) Masten Gregory, Ferrari 500 TR, gewann das 10-Runden-Rennen vom Sonntag im Ferrari und ein einstündiges Rennen am Montag in einem Porsche 550 Spyder. 1956.

(1) Fred Proctor sur une Maserati 150S. Il est un des premiers à transporter son bolide dans une remorque couverte. 1956.
(2) Masten Gregory, Ferrari 500 TR. Il remportera l'épreuve des dix tours le dimanche sur la Ferrari et la course d'une heure le lundi au volant d'une Porsche 550 Spyder, 1956.

D-type Jaguars, October 1956:
Walter Huggler (#93), George Constantine (#49) and Hansgen finished 4-3-2.
Walter Huggler (Nr. 93), George Constantine (Nr. 49) und Hansgen fuhren in der Reihenfolge 4-3-2 ins Ziel.
Walter Huggler (n° 93), George Constantine (n° 49) et Hansgen franchiront la ligne d'arrivée dans l'ordre 4-3-2.

In the October 1956 races John Fitch (#59) drove a D-type Jaguar with an engine bored out to 3.8 liters and twice beat Walt Hansgen, 3.5-liter D-type Jaguar (#58).

Bei den Rennen vom Oktober 1956 fuhr John Fitch (Nr. 59) einen Jaguar D-Type mit einem auf 3,8 Liter Hubraum aufgebohrten Motor, mit dem er zweimal Walt Hansgens 3,5-Liter-Jaguar D-Type (Nr. 58) schlug.

John Fitch (n° 59) pilote une Jaguar Type D avec moteur suralésé de 3,8 litres aux courses d'octobre 1956 et battra deux fois Walt Hansgen au volant d'une jaguar Type D 3,5 litres (n° 58).

The C Production race. Journalist Denise McCluggage, Jaguar XK140MC (#23) was just starting a racing career.

Rennen der C-Klasse. Die Journalistin Denise McCluggage, Jaguar XK140MC (Nr. 23) begann gerade ihre Rennfahrerkarriere.

La course de groupe C. La journaliste Denise McCluggage, Jaguar XK140MC (n° 23) vient d'entamer une carrière de pilote.

(1) Carroll Shelby, Ferrari 857 S, closely pursued Walt Hansgen, D-type Jaguar in the September 1956 races but was off the road several times with a locking brake and did not finish, breaking a victory streak of 19 races.
(2) The October 1956 grid for the F Production race.

(1) Carroll Shelby, Ferrari 857 S, lag in den September-Rennen 1956 dicht hinter Walt Hansgen, Jaguar D-Type, mußte aber wegen blockierender Bremsen mehrmals aussetzen und schließlich aufgeben, womit seine Serie von 19 Siegen in Reihe endete.
(2) Oktober 1956 – Startaufstellung für die F-Klasse.

(1) Carroll Shelby, au volant d'une Ferrari 857 S, sur les roues de la Jaguar Type D de Walt Hansgen au cours du meeting de septembre 1956. Mais un frein défectueux le fera sortir de la piste plusieurs fois et il devra abandonner après avoir remporté 19 victoires consécutives.
(2) La grille de départ pour l'épreuve de groupe F, octobre 1956.

1

2

Briggs Cunningham (standing) talks with Fred Proctor, Maserati. Between them in the Bandini is Hank Rudkin. September, 1956.

Briggs Cunningham (stehend) redet mit Fred Proctor, Maserati. Dazwischen im Bandini Hank Rudkin. September 1956.

Briggs Cunningham (debout) discute avec Fred Proctor, Maserati. Entre eux, Hank Rudkin assis dans la Bandini. Septembre 1956.

(1) John Fitch smiles from the cockpit of the bored-out D-type Jaguar in which he won two races at the October 1956 race meeting.
(2) A common view of Dick Thompson's Corvette SR-2. The Porsche 356 A was driven by C.F. Fechnel Jr.

(1) John Fitch lächelt aus dem Cockpit des aufgebohrten Jaguar D-Type, mit dem er während der Rennen im Oktober 1956 zwei Siege errang.
(2) Ein Blick auf Dick Thompsons Corvette SR-2. Den Porsche 356 A fuhr C.F. Fechnel Jr.

(1) John Fitch avec un sourire radieux dans la Jaguar Type D au moteur suralésé avec laquelle il a gagné deux courses au meeting d'octobre 1956.
(2) Une vue typique de la Corvette SR-2 de Dick Thompson. La Porsche 356 A est pilotée par C.F. Fechnel Junior.

2

2

3

(1) Lou Brero, A.A. Browne's D-type Jaguar, was 2nd to Carroll Shelby. Road America (the official name) was usually referred to as "Elkhart."
(2) Corner workers watch Frank Baptista, Lotus, lead Jacob Smith, Cooper, through the bend.
(3) Shelby, Ferrari 121 LM, wore his "Texas Tuxedo," the striped bib overalls, to lap all but two in the 28-car field.

(1) Lou Brero wurde in A.A. Brownes Jaguar D-Type Zweiter hinter Carroll Shelby. Den Road-America-Kurs (so sein offizieller Name) bezeichnete man allgemein als »Elkhart«.
(2) Die Streckenposten beobachten Frank Baptista, der in einer Kurve mit seinem Lotus vor Jacob Smith, Cooper, in Führung geht.
(3) Als Shelby auf Ferrari bis auf zwei Fahrzeuge sämtliche 28 Rennteilnehmer überundete, trug er seinen »Texas Smoking«, einen gestreiften Latz-Overall.

(1) Lou Brero. La Jaguar Type D de A.A. Browne se classera 2ème dans la foulée de Carroll Shelby. Le nom officiel du circuit était Road America, mais on l'appelait « Elkhart ».
(2) Des employés du circuit regardent Frank Baptista sur Lotus en train de négocier le virage devant la Cooper de Jacob Smith.
(3) Shelby sur Ferrari 121 LM, a revêtu son « Texas Tuxedo », sa salopette rayée, pour dépasser la totalité du plateau de 28 voitures, sauf deux.

1

M.R.J. (Doc) Wylie (Lotus IX) had a distinctive chin-up style of driving.

M.R.J. (Doc) Wylie (Lotus IX) fuhr in unverkennbarer »Kopf hoch«-Haltung.

M.R.J. (Doc) Wylie sur Lotus IX. Le menton relevé fait partie de son style de conduite.

Hal Ullrich, Excalibur.

John Kilborn, Ferrari 375 MM was 4th in the 150-mile main race.

John Kilborn, Ferrari 375 MM, wurde Vierter im Hauptrennen über 150 Meilen.

John Kilborn sur une Ferrari 375 MM, prendra la 4ème place dans l'épreuve principale de 150 miles.

Ted McGrade, Allard J-2 was 2nd among the B Modifieds.

Ted McGrade, Allard J-2, wurde Zweiter in der Gruppe der modifizierten B-Klasse.

Ted McGrade sur une Allard J-2, classé 2ème du groupe B-modifiés.

VIRGINIA INTERNATIONAL RACEWAY 1957

Paul O'Shea, Mercedes-Benz 300SL Spyder passes the new grandstand of Virginia International Raceway near Danville, August 1957.

Paul O'Shea, Mercedes-Benz 300SL Spyder, passiert die neue Haupttribüne des Virginia International Raceway bei Danville im August 1957.

Paul O'Shea sur Mercedes-Benz 300SL Spyder passe devant la nouvelle tribune du Virginia International Raceway près de Danville, août 1957.

Bob Holbert, Porsche 550 Spyder, in the rain on his way to one of two 1st place finishes.

Bob Holbert fährt mit seinen Porsche 550 Spyder im Regen dem ersten von zwei Rennsiegen entgegen.

Sous une pluie battante, Bob Holbert sur Porsche 550 Spyder va remporter une de ses deux victoires durant ce meeting.

Dick Thompson did not always drive Corvettes. Here he is in a Porsche 356 Carrera GT.

Dick Thompson fuhr nicht ausschließlich Corvettes. Hier sitzt er in einem Porsche 356 Carrera GT.

Dick Thompson ne pilotait pas toujours des Corvette. Ici, il est au volant d'une Porsche 356 Carrera GT.

1

2

3

4

(1) Nose to tail most of the race were these two D-type Jaguars from the Briggs Cunningham stable. Walt Hansgen (#60) and Chuck Wallace (#61) finished 2nd and 3rd behind Shelby's 4.5 Maserati.
(2) Bob Holbert (Porsche 550 Spyder) had reason to smile. He won two races.
(3) Gene Greenspun, Ferrari 857 S, flipped through a ditch and was thrown out relatively unscathed before the car performed a solo flip.
(4) John Kilborn, Ferrari 750 Monza (rebodied), (#10) finished 7th in the 64-lap final race. Rich Lyeth, Ferrari 375 MM (#91) was 5th.

(1) Diese beiden Jaguar D-Types aus dem Stall von Briggs Cunningham fuhren fast das gesamte Rennen dicht an dicht. Walt Hansgen (Nr. 60) und Chuck Wallace (Nr. 61) erreichten hinter Shelbys 4,5-Liter-Maserati die Plätze zwei und drei.
(2) Bob Holbert (Porsche 550 Spyder) hatte allen Grund zu lächeln. Er gewann zwei Rennen.
(3) Gene Greenspun, Ferrari 857 S, wurde bei seinem Ausflug in den Graben relativ unbeschadet aus dem Cockpit geschleudert, bevor der Wagen sich überschlug.
(4) John Kilborn wurde im Ferrari 750 Monza (mit einer neuen Außenverkleidung) (Nr. 10) Siebter im Abschlußrennen über 64 Runden. Rich Lyeth, Ferrari 375 MM (Nr. 91), wurde Fünfter.

(1) Ces deux Jaguar type D de l'écurie de Briggs Cunningham vont pratiquement lutter roue contre roue durant toute la course. Walt Hansgen (n° 60) et Chuck Wallace (n° 61) prendront les 2ème et 3ème places derrière la Maserati 4,5 litres de Shelby.
(2) Bob Holbert (Porsche 550 Spyder) peut se montrer satisfait. Il a gagné deux courses.
(3) Gene Greenspun enverra sa Ferrari 857 S dans le fossé et sera éjecté sans subir de grands dommages, avant que la voiture n'effectue un vol plané.
(4) John Kilborn, Ferrari 750 Monza (n° 10), se classera 7ème dans la course finale de 64 tours. La Ferrari 375 MM de Rich Lyeth (n° 91) arrivera en 5ème position.

BRIDGEHAMPTON 1957, 1958

Briggs Cunningham in his own D-type Jaguar at the September 1957 inaugural of the eastern Long Island course.

Briggs Cunningham in seinem eigenen Jaguar D-Type bei der Einweihung der Rennstrecke im Osten Long Islands. September 1957.

Briggs Cunningham dans le cockpit de sa Jaguar Type D à la course inaugurale de Long Island en septembre 1957.

Walt Hansgen was the day's big winner in another Cunningham D-type Jaguar.

Walt Hansgen, ebenfalls in einem Jaguar D-Type von Cunningham, war der große Sieger des Tages.

Walt Hansgen, le triomphateur de la journée au volant d'une autre Jaguar Type D de Cunningham.

Phil Hill, Ferrari 857 S.

(1) Bob Grossman, NART Ferrari, most likely the 860 Monza. 1958.
(2) The big race prepares to roll over the sand dunes within sight of Peconic Bay, 1957.

(1) Bob Grossman, NART Ferrari, wahrscheinlich der 860 Monza. 1958.
(2) Startaufstellung zum Rennen durch die Sanddünen nahe Peconic Bay, 1957.

(1) Bob Grossman, NART Ferrari, probablement la 860 Monza. 1958.
(2) Départ de la course principale en 1957. Les voitures vont affronter les dunes de sable de la Pecony Bay.

1

(3) George Constantine, Aston Martin DB 2/4 Mark III, was to take a 2nd in class. 1957.
(4) Phil Hill, Tilp's Ferrari 857 S, finished 3rd. 1957.

(3) George Constantine belegte 1957 im Aston Martin DB 2/4 Mark III den zweiten Platz seiner Klasse.
(4) Phil Hill kam in Tilps Ferrari 857 S als Dritter ins Ziel. 1957.

(3) George Constantine sur Aston Martin DB 2/4 Mark III se classera 2ème dans la catégorie. 1957.
(4) Phil Hill termine 3ème au volant de la Ferrari 857 S de Tilp. 1957.

2

3

4

(1) Lake Underwood, Porsche 550 Spyder, one of the smoothest and fastest of Americans came from behind to win one race and finished 2nd in another on this, his retirement weekend, 1957.
(2) Rod Carveth, Aston Martin DB3S (#154); John Norwood, Lister-Bristol (#70). 1957.
(3) Porsches were always popular on Eastern circuits. These 356s raced in 1958.

(1) Lake Underwood, Porsche 550 Spyder, einer der souveränsten und schnellsten US-Fahrer, nahm an diesem Wochenende im Jahr 1957 Abschied vom Rennsport. Von ganz hinten startend, gewann er das Rennen und belegte in einem weiteren den zweiten Platz.
(2) Rod Carveth, Aston Martin DB3S (Nr. 154); John Norwood, Lister-Bristol (Nr. 70). 1957.
(3) Auf den Rennstrecken im Osten waren die Porsche stets gern gesehen. Diese 356er waren 1958 im Rennen.

(1) Lake Underwood, un des meilleurs pilotes américains (Porsche 550 Spyder). Il récupérera son retard pour franchir la ligne d'arrivée en pole position et terminera 2ème dans une autre course. C'était son week-end d'adieu. 1957.
(2) Rod Carveth, Aston Martin DB3S (n°154) ; John Norwood, Lister-Bristol (n° 70). 1957.
(3) Les Porsche étaient des habituées des circuits de la Côte Est. Ces Porsche 356 ont couru durant la saison 1958.

1

2

3

Gordon MacKenzie, Jaguar C-type (#52); Walt Hansgen, Jaguar D-type (#60). 1958.

Major Gil Geitner, Ferrari 500 TRC. 1958.

John Giubardo, Maserati 300S. 1958.

NASSAU 1955

Nassau was a string of colored lights across a tropical night, the liquid sound of steel drums through the palm trees. Nassau was the sharp blip of racing engines on a sun-drenched dock, the soft boiling-fudge speech of the Bahamians selling straw hats along Bay Street. Nassau was an umbrella-drink concoction of star-dipped nights, white sands, conch fritters, a sea rimmed in turquoise (and as clear as gasoline) and racing, racing, racing.

The brain child of Sherman (Red) Crise, the early December Nassau Speed Weeks were initiated to jump-start the winter tourist season, traditionally beginning December 15, by filling empty hotel rooms and restaurants early with invited drivers and car owners from the Americas and Europe. The guests were given free passage for themselves and their cars from Florida and free accommodations and a string of parties. International drivers (Stirling Moss had a house in Nassau) were also drawn to the warm splendors of the Bahamas by the days filled with racing and the nights with music, dining and laughter.

The proportions of all the ingredients were in a perfect balance in the mid to late '50s. Racing (growing increasingly commercial, increasingly serious) would never see the likes of it again.

Nassau – das war ein farbiges Lichtband in der Tropennacht, der Klang von Steeldrums zwischen Palmen. Nassau – das war das durchdringende Donnern von Rennmotoren auf einem sonnen-überfluteten Pier, die weiche, langgezogene Sprache der Bahamaer, die entlang der Nay Street ihre Strohhüte feilboten. Nassau – das war eine Cocktailphantasie aus sternenübersäten Nächten, weißen Stränden, Schnecken im Teigmantel, türkisfarbenem (und benzinklarem) Meer und Rennfahren, Rennfahren, Rennfahren...

Die Anfang Dezember in Nassau ausgetragenen Nassau Speed Weeks, deren geistiger Vater Sherman (Red) Crise war, dienten ursprünglich als Auftakt für die touristische Wintersaison, die traditionell am 15. Dezember beginnt. Die eingeladenen amerikanischen und europäischen Rennwagenfahrer und -besitzer sollten die leeren Hotelzimmer und Restaurants füllen. Den Gästen und ihren Fahrzeugen bot man im Gegenzug eine kostenlose Überfahrt von Florida, dazu freie Unterkunft und jede Menge Parties. Auch international bekannte Rennfahrer (Stirling Moss hatte ein Haus in Nassau) ließen sich von den Rennen am Tage und den musikerfüllten Nächten, von Essen und Gelächter für die sonnige Pracht der Bahamas begeistern.

Von Mitte bis Ende der fünfziger Jahre ergänzten sich all diese Zutaten zu perfekter Harmonie. In der Welt des Rennsports (die zunehmend kommerzieller und ernsthafter wurde) gab es nie wieder etwas Vergleichbares.

Nassau, c'était un collier de lumières colorées dans la nuit tropicale, des sons liquides de tambours dans les palmiers, des moteurs de bolides vrombissant sur les docks inondés de soleil, le doux parler traînant des vendeurs de chapeaux de paille sur la Bay Street. Nassau était un cocktail de nuits étoilées, de sable blond, de beignets de fruits de mer, de flots turquoise (aussi clairs que l'essence) et de courses automobiles.

Conçues par Sherman (Red) Crise, la Nassau Speed Week avait lieu début décembre. A l'origine, elle avait été créée pour démarrer la saison touristique d'hiver qui commence traditionnellement le 15 décembre. Les pilotes et propriétaires de bolides américains et européens venaient remplir les hôtels et restaurants encore déserts. On les avait invités et on leur offrait la traversée (pour leurs voitures aussi) à partir de la Floride, le logement et une multitude de fêtes. Les délices ensoleillés des Bahamas attiraient également des pilotes internationaux (Stirling Moss possédait une maison à Nassau) qui savouraient les journées vouées au sport et les nuits remplies de musique, de festins et de rires.

Tous ces ingrédients constituaient un mélange parfait et harmonieux dans la deuxième moitié des années 50. Le monde du sport automobile (qui devenait de plus en plus commercial et sérieux) ne devait plus jamais connaître une telle époque.

Sherwood Johnston, D-type Jaguar, won one race, 3rd in the Governor's Trophy.

Sherwood Johnston gewann ein Rennen im Jaguar D-Type und wurde Dritter im Rennen um die Governor's Trophy.

Sherwood Johnston, Jaguar Type D, vainqueur d'une course, 3ème au Governor's Trophy.

(1) Sherwood Johnston (white shirt at far right) watches his car arrive.
(2) The Johnston car's tail.
(3) Out of the hold comes an Austin-Healey.
(4) The cars parade down Bay Street; at the center is Jim Orr's Austin-Healey.

(1) Sherwood Johnston (ganz rechts im weißen Hemd) beobachtet die Ankunft seines Fahrzeugs.
(2) Das Heck von Johnstons Wagen.
(3) Ein Austin-Healey wird an Land gebracht.
(4) Autocorso über die Bay Street. In der Mitte Jim Orrs Austin-Healey.

(1) Sherwood Johnston (chemise blanche à l'extrême droite) observe l'arrivée de sa voiture.
(2) L'arrière du bolide de Johnston.
(3) Une Austin-Healey apparaît.
(4) Cortège des voitures dans Bay Street.
Au milieu : l'Austin-Healey de Jim Orr.

Bill Lloyd, Maserati 300S.

(1) Sue and Sherwood Johnston, Dale Duncan (driver, airline pilot, Masten Gregory's brother-in-law).
(2) Roy Jackson-Moore, Louise King, Donald Healey's Austin-Healey.
(3) Inspection. #79 is the Maserati 150S of Isabelle Haskell.

(1) Sue und Sherwood Johnston mit Dale Duncan (Fahrer, Flugzeugpilot und Schwager von Masten Gregory).
(2) Roy Jackson-Moore, Louise King und Donald Healeys Austin-Healey.
(3) Besichtigung. Nummer 79 ist der Maserati 150S von Isabelle Haskell.

(1) Sue et Sherwood Johnston, Dale Duncan (coureur automobile, pilote d'avions et beau-frère de Masten Gregory).
(2) Roy Jackson-Moore et Louise King dans l'Austin-Healey de Donald Healey.
(3) Inspection. Le numéro 79 est la Maserati 150S d'Isabelle Haskell.

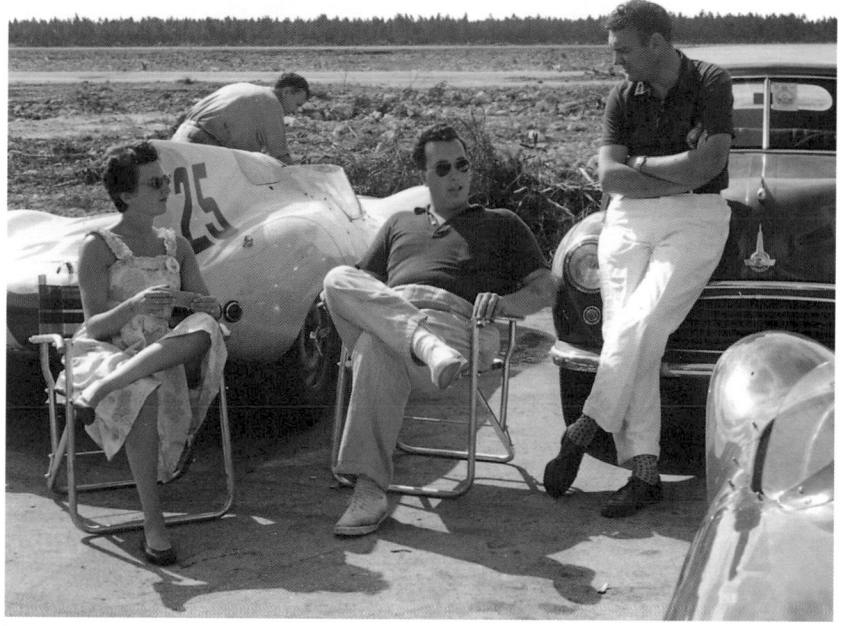

1

2

3

(1) The Marquis Alfonso de Portago (left), photographer/driver Gleb Derujinsky (right).
(2) Phil Hill, Ferrari 857 S (#33); Jim Kimberly, Ferrari 121 LM (#5). Hill won the Nassau Trophy race, Kimberly was 6th. Fon de Portago, who had won nearly everything else during the week, was 2nd.
(3) John Shakespeare's Ferrari 340 America.

(1) Links der Marquis Alfonso de Portago, rechts der Photograph und Rennfahrer Gleb Derujinsky.
(2) Phil Hill, Ferrari 857 S (Nr. 33) vor Jim Kimberly, Ferrari 121 LM (Nr. 5). Hill gewann das Rennen um die Nassau Trophy, Kimberly wurde Sechster. Fon de Portago, der im Laufe der Woche beinahe alle anderen Rennen gewonnen hatte, wurde hier nur Zweiter.
(3) John Shakespeares Ferrari 340 America.

(1) Le marquis Alfonso de Portago (à gauche), Gleb Derujinsky, photographe et pilote (à droite).
(2) Phil Hill, Ferrari 857 S (n° 33), Jim Kimberly, Ferrari 121 LM (n° 5). Hill décrochera le Nassau Trophy ct Kimberly sera 6ème. Fon de Portago qui avait remporté presque toutes les autres courses de la semaine, arrivera deuxième.
(3) La Ferrari 340 America de John Shakespeare.

1

2

3

1

2

3

4

5

6

(1) Jim Kimberly, Ferrari 121 LM.
(2) Gleb Derujinsky driving Fon de Portago's new Ferrari 250 Europa GT Berlinetta rolled the car but did little damage.
(3) Roy Jackson-Moore, Donald Healey's Austin-Healey.
(4) Porfirio Rubirosa's name was usually preceded by "Playboy." Nonetheless he drove this Ferrari 500 Mondial to a 1st in class in the Governor's Cup.
(5) The Louis Breros, father and son, did well by the Ferrari 375 MM. Louis Brero, Sr. was a fixture in West Coast racing and showed the East Coast drivers at Nassau why. The car was the winning Farina/Ascari mount at the 1953 1000 kilometer race at the Nurburgring and Phil Hill's at the 1954 Carrera.
(6) The de Portago Ferrari 735 S (#13) rearranged its nose on the tail of the Sherwood Johnston D-type (#25). Phil Hill's Ferrari 750 Monza (#33) was 2nd to de Portago, Johnston was 3rd in the Governor's Cup.

(1) Jim Kimberly, Ferrari 121 LM.
(2) Gleb Derujinsky überschlug sich mit Fon de Portagos neuem Ferrari 250 Europa GT Berlinetta, verursachte jedoch nur geringfügigen Schaden.
(3) Roy Jackson-Moore, Donald Healeys Austin-Healey.
(4) Porfirio Rubirosa nannte man für gewöhnlich auch den »Playboy«. Dennoch wurde er mit diesem Ferrari 500 Mondial Sieger seiner Klasse im Governor's Cup.
(5) Die beiden Louis Breros, Vater und Sohn, triumphierten mit ihrem Ferrari 375 MM. Brero Senior war bei Rennen an der Westküste und in Nassau unverzichtbar und zeigte den Ostküsten-Piloten, warum das so war. Der Wagen soll Farina/Ascari 1953 beim 1000-Kilometer-Rennen auf dem Nürburgring zum Sieg verholfen haben. Phil Hill holte sich 1954 damit die Carrera Panamericana.
(6) Der Ferrari 735 S (Nr. 13) von de Portago knapp vor Sherwood Johnstons Jaguar D-Type (Nr. 25). Phil Hills Ferrari 750 Monza (Nr. 33) fuhr hinter de Portago als Zweiter ins Ziel, Johnston wurde im Governor's Cup Dritter.

(1) Jim Kimberly, Ferrari 121 LM.
(2) Gleb Derujinsky a sorti la nouvelle Ferrari 250 GT Europa Berlinetta de Fon de Portago de la piste, mais les dégâts seront minimes.
(3) Roy Jackson-Moore, l'Austin-Healey de Donald Healey.
(4) Porfirio Rubirosa avait une réputation de « play boy ». Cela ne l'empêchera pas de remporter une épreuve de groupe de la Governor's Cup dans cette Ferrari 500 Mondial.
(5) Les Louis Brero, père et fils, ont engrangé de beaux succès sur la Ferrari 375 MM. A Nassau, Louis senior montrera aux pilotes de la Côte Est pourquoi il était si populaire sur la Côte Ouest. La voiture pilotée par Farina/Ascari était arrivée première au 1000 km du Nurburgring en 1953 et avait conduit Phil Hill à la victoire à la Carrera Panaméricaine de 1954.
(6) La Ferrari 735 S de Portago (n° 13) s'installe devant la Type D de Sherwood Johnston (n° 25). La Ferrari 750 Monza de Phil Hill (n° 33) se classera 2ème derrière de Portago ; Johnston sera 3ème dans la Governor's Cup.

1

2

3

4

(1) Stirling Moss, Austin-Healey 100S (# 29)
overtakes Bob Williams, Ferrari 225 S (# 8).
(2) Triumph TR3 leads MG A, TR2 and Siata
across the flat expanse of Nassau's airport course.
(3) Jack Rutherford, D-type Jaguar, hit 150 mph in
Saturday's speed trials.
(4) Duncan Black, Ferrari 375 MM, leads Leech
Cracraft, Cooper-Climax.

(1) Stirling Moss, Austin-Healey 100S (Nr. 29)
überholt Bob Williams, Ferrari 225 S (Nr. 8).
(2) Ein Triumph TR3 vor einem MG A, einem
TR2 und einem Siata auf der ausgedehnten Fläche
des Flughafenkurses von Nassau.
(3) Jack Rutherford, Jaguar D-Type, erreichte
samstags im Zeittraining eine Geschwindigkeit
von 240 km/h.
(4) Duncan Black, Ferrari 375 MM, führt vor
Leech Cracraft, Cooper-Climax.

(1) Stirling Moss, Austin-Healey 100S (n° 29)
double Bob Williams, Ferrari 225 S (n° 8).
(2) Une Triumph TR3 fonce devant une MG A,
une TR2 et une Siata sur le tracé plat de l'aérodrome de Nassau.
(3) Jack Rutherford, Jaguar Type D, fera une pointe à 240 km/h dans les essais du samedi.
(4) Duncan Black, Ferrari 375 MM, devant Leech
Cracraft, Cooper-Climax.

1

2

3

4

(1, 3, 5) Small sailboats, beach chairs, palm
fronds and motorscooters were props for Nassau
fun for Stirling Moss.
(2) Stirling, Roy Jackson-Moore (figured shirt)
and Donald Healey.
(4) Stirling gives sister Pat a ride during one of
Nassau's quick rain showers.
(6) Stirling, Roy Jackson-Moore and a small
Bahamian investigate the under-pinnings on the
rental scooter.

(1, 3, 5) Mit kleinen Segelbooten, Strandliegen,
Palmwedeln und Motorrollern vertrieb sich
Stirling Moss die Zeit am Strand von Nassau.
(2) Stirling, Roy Jackson-Moore (im bedruckten
Hemd) und Donald Healey.
(4) Stirling und seine Schwester Pat fahren durch
einen von Nassaus kurzen Regenschauern.
(6) Stirling, Roy Jackson-Moore und ein kleiner
Insulaner untersuchen das Fahrgestell des Miet-
rollers.

(1, 3, 5) Bateaux à voile, transats, palmiers et
scooters agrémentent le séjour de Stirling Moss à
Nassau.
(2) Stirling, Roy Jackson-Moore (chemise
bigarrée) et Donald Healey.
(4) Stirling ramène sa sœur Pat à l'abri durant une
des nombreuses averses qui s'abattent soudaine-
ment sur Nassau.
(6) Stirling, Roy Jackson-Moore et un jeune Baha-
mien vérifient la fiabilité d'un scooter de louage.

5

NASSAU 1956

Again came the singular mix of bright beaches, velvet nights, cocktail parties and motor racing that was Nassau Speed Week. Invitations were eagerly sought from both sides of the Atlantic. Red Crise's week of racing in the sun had become the place to be in early December.

Always known for a rather laissez faire approach to organization, the Nassau races outdid themselves for 1956. For instance, the start of practice was delayed by five hours because the communications system, installed that morning, was not working. They finally discovered the source of the problem: Two cables had been joined by tying them in a knot rather than splicing them together.

Disappointments and dramatic recoveries abounded. Stirling Moss was due to drive a factory Maserati but had it sold out from under him. He then arranged to borrow Bill Lloyd's 3-liter Maserati which Bill proceeded to drive rather forcefully into one of the oil drums marking the course. But not to worry: Bill, being a body-shop operator, and his crew burned some midnight oil and had the car bandaged and ready after all. And Stirling won the 60-lap Nassau Trophy Race.

Carroll Shelby, set to drive John Edgar's 4.9-liter Ferrari in the Governor's Cup, the big race of the final day, had suffered his own sort of body damage – a broken shoulder in a touch football game inspired by a football-shaped coconut found on the beach. But Carroll, like Moss's car, was taped up and ready to go.

Shelby had to deal with a determined Fon de Portago, who was a hard-charging crowd-pleaser the entire week. The race, starting late of course, was finished in darkness as the tropical sun, like a Fourth of July sparkler dunked in water, went out as soon as it hit the sea. Darkness descended almost audibly as Shelby groped his way to victory.

Und wieder begann die Nassau Speed Week – diese einzigartige Mischung aus leuchtenden Stränden, samtigen Nächten, Cocktailparties und Autorennen. Die Einladungen waren auf beiden Seiten des Atlantiks heißbegehrt. Red Crises Rennwoche in der Sonne war das Ereignis zum Dezemberanfang.

Die schon für ihre legere Organisation bekannten Rennveranstaltungen in Nassau übertrafen sich 1956 selbst. So begannen die Trainingsläufe mit fünfstündiger Verspätung, weil das erst am Morgen installierte Kommunikationssystem nicht funktionierte. Schließlich entdeckte man den Fehler dann doch: Man hatte zwei Kabel verknotet statt sie zusammenzuspleißen.

Enttäuschungen und dramatische Notreparaturen häuften sich. Stirling Moss sollte einen Maserati-Werkswagen fahren, der jedoch vor dem Rennen verkauft wurde. Daraufhin sollte er sich Bill Lloyds 3-Liter-Maserati leihen, den Bill jedoch vorher forsch gegen eines der Ölfässer fuhr, die als Streckenmarkierung fungierten. Aber kein Grund zur Sorge: Bill, selbst Karosseriebauer, und sein Team schlugen sich die Nacht um die Ohren, bis der Wagen schließlich gut »bandagiert« und fahrbereit war. Stirling gewann die 60 Runden des Rennens um die Nassau Trophy.

Carroll Shelby, der im Governor's Cup, dem großen Abschlußrennen am letzten Tag, John Edgars 4,9-Liter-Ferrari pilotieren sollte, erlitt ebenfalls eine Art »Karosserieschaden« – er brach sich die Schulter bei einem Footballspiel, zu dem ihn eine am Strand liegende Kokosnuß verführt hatte. Aber Carroll wurde, wie Moss' Wagen, verpflastert und war wieder startbereit.

Shelby trat gegen den zu allem entschlossenen Fon de Portago an, der bereits die ganze Woche mit seiner spektakulären Fahrweise begeistert hatte. Das Rennen, das natürlich mit Verspätung begann, endete im Dunkeln, da die Tropensonne wie eine ins Wasser gefallene Feuerwerksrakete erlosch, sobald Sie den Meereshorizont berührt hatte. Die Dunkelheit brach fast hörbar plötzlich herein, als Shelby sich seinen Weg zum Ziel ertastete.

De nouveau, on retrouvait cette mixture particulière de plages lumineuses, de nuits de velours, de cocktails et de sport automobile qu'est la Nassau Speed Week. Les cartes d'invitations s'arrachaient des deux côtés de l'Atlantique. La semaine de courses au soleil, initiée par Red Crise, était devenue l'événement incontournable à inscrire sur son calendrier, sur la ligne de la première semaine de décembre.

Déjà réputés pour leur gestion désinvolte, les organisateurs de la course se surpassèrent en 1956. Les essais par exemple furent retardés de cinq heures parce que le système de communications, installé le matin-même, refusait de fonctionner. On finit par découvrir la source du problème : deux câbles électriques avaient été joints par un nœud au lieu d'une épissure.

La course eut son compte de déceptions et d'actions de sauvetage dramatiques. Stirling Moss aurait dû piloter une Maserati d'usine...qui fut vendue juste avant la course. Bill Lloyd accepta volontiers de lui prêter sa Maserati 3 litres, mais il alla auparavant la défoncer contre un des tonneaux d'huile qui marquaient le parcours. Nul besoin de s'inquiéter : Bill qui était carrossier et son équipe brûlèrent de l'électricité pendant toute la nuit pour panser la voiture et la remettre sur roues. Stirling termina les 60 tours de la Nassau Trophy Race à la première place.

Carroll Shelby, pilote de la Ferrari 4,9 litres de John Edgar dans la Governor's Cup, avait subi lui aussi quelques dommages corporels. Il s'était fracturé l'épaule en jouant au football avec une noix de coco trouvée sur la plage qui lui avait donné des idées de ballon rond. Mais à l'instar de la voiture de Moss, Carroll avait été raccommodé et pouvait prendre le départ.

Shelby eut à lutter contre un Fon de Portago acharné dont les attaques vigoureuses avaient enthousiasmé le public. La course, commencée bien sûr avec du retard, s'acheva dans l'obscurité lorsque le soleil des tropiques s'abîma soudain dans la mer, tel un feu d'artifice du 4 juillet. Shelby avança à tâtons vers la victoire dans la nuit que l'on entendait pratiquement tomber.

Phil Hill, Ferrari 857 S, had bad luck all week. He left the Governor's Cup when a piece of coral pierced his goggles and left the Nassau Trophy with a broken gas tank after tangling with some course-marking barrels.

Phil Hill, Ferrari 857 S, war die ganze Woche vom Pech verfolgt. Im Governor's Cup gab er auf, weil ein Stück Koralle seine Rennfahrerbrille beschädigt hatte, und bei der Nassau Trophy fiel er aus, nachdem er seinen Benzintank an den als Streckenmarkierung dienenden Fässern beschädigt hatte.

La déveine poursuivra Phil Hill sur une Ferrari 857 S durant toute la semaine. Il doit abandonner la Governor's Cup quand un morceau de corail perce ses lunettes de protection, et quitte le Nassau Trophy avec un réservoir d'essence abîmé, après avoir heurté un mur de tonneaux qui marquait le tracé.

1

3

4

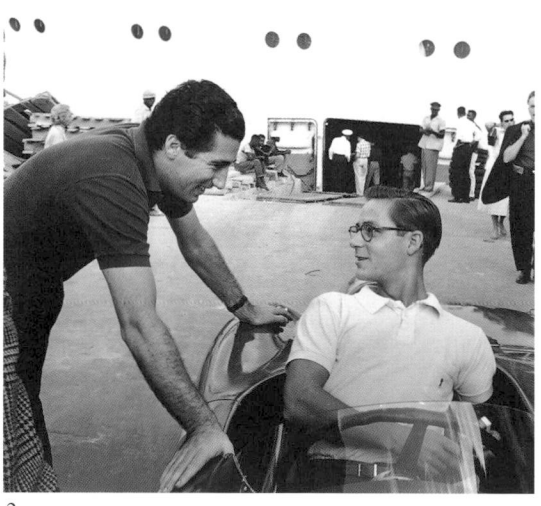

2

(1) Masten Gregory (draped with goggles) and John Edgar.
(2) Fon de Portago and Masten Gregory at the docks, Temple Buell's Ferrari 500 TR.
(3) Sherman (Red) Crise (originator of Nassau Speed Week) with de Portago.
(4) John Fitch, Carroll Shelby.

(1) Masten Gregory (mit Helm) und John Edgar.
(2) Fon de Portago und Masten Gregory an den Kaianlagen mit Temple Buells Ferrari 500 TR.
(3) Sherman (Red) Crise (der Initiator der Nassau Speed Week) mit de Portago.
(4) John Fitch, Carroll Shelby.

(1) Masten Gregory (avec casque) et John Edgar.
(2) Fon de Portago et Masten Gregory discutent au paddock ; la Ferrari 500 TR appartient à Temple Buell.
(3) Sherman (Red) Crise (initiateur de la Nassau Speed Week) et de Portago.
(4) John Fitch, Carroll Shelby.

Porsche 356s/Mehrere Porsche 356/Armada de Porsche 356.

Fashion photographer/driver Bill Helburn and
friend.
Modefotograf und Rennfahrer Bill Helburn mit
einem Freund.
Bill Helburn, photographe de mode et pilote, avec
un ami.

1

3

2

(1) Stirling Moss between his sister Pat (left) and a guest at one of the many island parties.
(2) Even driver's meetings were social events in Nassau. The man seated in the front row with glasses is Alfred Moss, Stirling's father. Aileen Moss, his mother, sits behind Alf.
(3) Stirling checks the day's results.
(4) Moss won the Nassau Trophy in Bill Lloyd's wounded and bandaged Maserati 300S. Eddie Crawford, Porsche 550 Spyder, finished 6th overall, 2nd in class.

4

(1) Stirling Moss zwischen seiner Schwester Pat (links) und einem Partygast auf einer der vielen Inselparties.

(2) In Nassau wurden selbst die Zusammenkünfte der Fahrer zu gesellschaftlichen Ereignissen. Der Mann mit Brille in der vorderen Reihe ist Alfred Moss, Stirlings Vater. Seine Mutter, Aileen Moss, sitzt hinter Alf.

(3) Stirling studiert die Ergebnisse des Tages.

(4) Moss gewann die Nassau Trophy in Bill Lloyds angeschlagenem und »bandagiertem« Maserati 300S. Eddie Crawford, Porsche 550 Spyder, erreichte insgesamt den sechsten Platz und wurde Zweiter seiner Klasse.

(1) Assis entre sa sœur Pat (à gauche) et une invitée, Stirling Moss à une des nombreuses soirées de la semaine.

(2) Les pilotes viennent en famille à la semaine de Nassau. L'homme à lunettes assis au premier plan est Alfred Moss, le père de Stirling. Aileen, sa mère, est assise derrière son mari.

(3) Stirling regarde les résultats de la journée.

(4) Moss remporte le Nassau Trophy sur la Maserati 300S de Bill Lloyd. la voiture endommagée avait été réparée durant la nuit. Eddie Crawford, Porsche 550 Spyder, finira 6ème au classement général et 2ème en épreuve de groupe.

1

2

3

4

(1) Bob Goldich, Ferrari 500 Mondial (#80); Sam Weiss, Porsche 550 Spyder (#74).
(2) Timers atop Jim Kimberly's truck watch a Corvette and a Mercedes-Benz 300SL go by.
(3) Bill Lloyd welcomes Stirling Moss to his Maserati 300S after the car Moss was to drive did not arrive.
(4) Red Crise and journalist/driver Denise McCluggage get the scoop from Moss on how the car is behaving.

(1) Bob Goldich, Ferrari 500 Mondial (Nr. 80); Sam Weiss, Porsche 550 Spyder (Nr. 74).
(2) Von Jim Kimberlys Lkw-Dach aus beobachten die Zeitnehmer eine vorbeifahrende Corvette und einen Mercedes-Benz 300SL.
(3) Bill Lloyd heißt Stirling Moss an Bord seines Maserati 300S willkommen, nachdem das Fahrzeug, mit dem Moss ursprünglich fahren sollte, nicht angekommen war.
(4) Red Crise und die Journalistin und Rennfahrerin Denise McCluggage erhalten von Moss Exklusivnews über das Fahrverhalten des Wagens.

(1) Bob Goldich, Ferrari 500 Mondial (n° 80) ; Sam Weiss, Porsche 550 Spyder (n° 74).
(2) Des chronométreurs perchés sur la camionnette de Jim Kimberly, regardent passer une Corvette et une Mercedes-Benz 300SL.
(3) La voiture de Stirling Moss n'est pas arrivée à Nassau. Bill Lloyd lui prête sa Maserati 300S.
(4) Red Crise et la journaliste/pilote Denise McCluggage demandent à Stirling Moss comment la voiture s'est comportée.

Stirling Moss in the battered Bill Lloyd Maserati 300S. Bill had clobbered an oil drum with it in a preliminary race then stayed up all night making repairs. Stirling went on to win the Nassau Trophy.

Stirling Moss in Bill Lloyds beschädigtem Maserati 300S. Bill hatte in einem Rahmenrennen ein Ölfaß gerammt und die ganze Nacht mit Reparaturen verbracht. Stirling hielt durch und gewann die Nassau Trophy.

En route pour la victoire du Nassau Trophy : Stirling Moss au volant de la Maserati 300S endommagée de Bill Lloyd. Bill a heurté un tonneau d'huile au cours d'une épreuve précédente et a passé la nuit entière à réparer le bolide.

(1) Fon de Portago, Ferrari 860 Monza (2nd, Governor's Cup; 3rd, Nassau Trophy).
(2) Marion Lowe, Frazer Nash Targa Florio; Masten Gregory, Ferrari 500 TR (2nd, Nassau Trophy; 1st all-Ferrari race).

(1) Fon de Portago, Ferrari 860 Monza (Zweiter im Governor's Cup, Dritter in der Nassau Trophy).
(2) Marion Lowe, Frazer Nash Targa Florio vor Masten Gregory, Ferrari 500 TR (Zweiter in der Nassau Trophy, Gesamtsieger des Ferrari-Rennens).

(1) Fon de Portago, Ferrari 860 Monza (2ème à la Governor's Cup, 3ème au Nassau Trophy).
(2) Marion Lowe, Frazer Nash Targa Florio ; Masten Gregory, Ferrari 500 TR (2ème au Nassau Trophy, 1er à l'épreuve des Ferrari).

1

2

(3) Ken Miles in the Pooper/Miles R3, von Neumann's ultra-fast Porsche-engined Cooper (4th overall in the Governor's Cup).
(4) Johnny von Neumann, Ferrari 860 Monza.
(5) Carroll Shelby, Ferrari 410 Sport Scaglietti Spyder, just nosed out Fon de Portago for the Governor's Cup.

(3) Ken Miles im Pooper/Miles R3, von Neumanns sehr schneller Cooper mit Porsche-Motor (vierter Platz Gesamtwertung im Governor's Cup).
(4) Johnny von Neumann, Ferrari 860 Monza.
(5) Carroll Shelby, Ferrari 410 Sport Scaglietti Spyder, hat gerade von de Portago die Führung im Governor's Cup übernommen.

(3) Ken Miles dans la Pooper/Miles R3, la Cooper de von Neumann equipée d'un moteur Porsche (4ème au classement général de Governor's Cup).
(4) Johnny von Neumann, Ferrari 860 Monza.
(5) Carroll Shelby sur une Ferrari 410 Sport Scaglietti Spyder sera vainqueur de la Governor's Cup. Il vient d'arracher la pole position à Fon de Portago.

3

4

5

1

(1) David Darrin, C-type Jaguar (4th behind three
D-types in a race for Jaguars only).
(2) George Reed, Porsche 550 Spyder (#107);
Paul Gougelman, AC Bristol (#81). Gougelman
(3rd overall, 1st in class in 15-lap race for production cars up to 3-liters) drove with a back brace
because of a broken shoulder.
(3) John Fitch's D-type Jaguar (#25); Warren
Flickinger, Corvette.
(4) Lou Brero drove his usual fierce race in the
D-type Jaguar and the car showed it. He was the
first D-type in the Governor's Trophy (3rd overall).

(1) David Darrin, Jaguar C-Type (Vierter hinter
drei Jaguar D-Types in einem nur von Jaguars ausgetragenen Rennen).
(2) George Reed, Porsche 550 Spyder (Nr. 107)
vor Paul Gougelman, AC Bristol (Nr. 81). Gougelman (Dritter in der Gesamtwertung, Sieger im 15-
Runden-Rennen der Werkswagen bis zu drei
Litern Hubraum) fuhr wegen eines Schulter-
bruchs mit Nackenstütze.
(3) John Fitchs Jaguar D-Type (Nr. 25); Warren
Flickinger, Corvette.
(4) Lou Brero fuhr mit dem Jaguar D-Type ein
gewohnt hartes Rennen – was man dem Wagen
auch ansah. Er fuhr als erster Jaguar D-Type ins
Ziel der Governor's Trophy (Dritter im Gesamtklassement).

(1) David Darrin, Jaguar Type C (4ème derrière trois Type D dans une épreuve réservée aux Jaguars).

(2) George Reed sur une Porsche 550 Spyder (n° 107) et Paul Gougelman sur une AC Bristol (n° 81). Gougelman (3ème au classement général, 1er de groupe dans une course de 15 tours pour voitures de plus de 3 litres) conduit avec un appareil orthopédique dans le dos à cause d'une épaule fracturée.

(3) John Fitch's Jaguar type D (n° 25); Warren Flickinger, Corvette.

(4) Lou Brero montre son acharnement habituel au volant d'une Jaguar Type D qui ne le décevra pas. Elle sera la première Type D du Governor's Trophy (3ème au classement général).

(1) An airborne S. H. "Wacky" Arnolt, Arnolt-Bristol (4th place, 2nd in class in the under-3-liter production car race).
(2) Stirling Moss, Bonneville speed-record Austin-Healey.
(3) Jim Jeffords, one of the best Corvette drivers anywhere, failed to finish the Nassau Trophy race.
(4) Lance Reventlow (overall winner in later Speed Weeks in his own Scarab race cars) here in a Cooper-Climax. Masten Gregory, Ferrari 500 TR, overtakes.
(5) Chet Flynn, Mercedes-Benz 300SL (#146); John Fitch, D-type Jaguar (#25); Loyal Katskee, Ferrari 750 Monza (#12); John Kilborn, Ferrari 121 LM (#105); Walt Hansgen, D-type Jaguar (#96). Fitch did the best of any of them finishing 4th in the second heat of the Governor's Cup.

(1) S. H. »Wacky« Arnolts Arnolt-Bristol im Tief-flug. (Vierter Platz, Klassenzweiter der Werkswa-gen bis zu drei Litern Hubraum).
(2) Stirling Moss im rekordschnellen Austin-Healey Bonneville.
(3) Jim Jeffords, einer der besten Corvette-Fahrer überhaupt, mußte bei der Nassau Trophy frühzei-tig aufgeben.
(4) Lance Reventlow (der später bei den Speed Weeks in seinen eigenen Scarab-Rennwagen Gesamtsieger wurde) hier in einem Cooper-Climax. Masten Gregory auf Ferrari 500 TR setzt zum Überholen an.
(5) Chet Flynn, Mercedes-Benz 300SL (Nr. 146); John Fitch, Jaguar D-Type (Nr. 25); Loyal Katskee, Ferrari 750 Monza (Nr. 12); John Kilborn, Ferrari 121 LM (Nr. 105); Walt Hansgen, Jaguar D-Type (Nr. 96). Fitch fuhr von allen das beste Rennen und wurde Vierter im zweiten Lauf des Governor's Cup.

(1) S. H. « Wacky » Arnolt sur Arnolt-Bristol s'essaie à la haute voltige (4ème place, 2ème du groupe des moins de 3 litres).
(2) Stirling Moss sur l'Austin-Healey des records de vitesse à Bonneville.
(3). Jim Jeffords, un des meilleurs pilotes de Cor-vette, ne franchira pas la ligne d'arrivée au Nassau Trophy.
(4) Lance Reventlow sur une Cooper-Climax (il sera 1er au classement général lors de Speed Weeks ultérieures au volant de ses propres voitu-res Scarab). Ici, Masten Gregory le double sur sa Ferrari 500 TR.
(5) Chet Flynn, Mercedes-Benz 300SL (n° 146) ; John Fitch, Jaguar Type D (n° 25) ; Loyal Katskee, Ferrari 750 Monza (n° 12) ; John Kilborn, Ferrari 121 LM (n° 105) ; Walt Hansgen, Jaguar Type D (n° 96). Fitch sera le meilleur du lot en terminant 4ème dans la 2ème manche de la Governor's Cup.

1

2

3

4

5

(1, 2) Carl Haas, now a partner with actor Paul Newman in Indy cars, driving his Porsche 550 Spyder to 13th place in the Nassau Trophy race. He lent the car to McCluggage for the first heat of the Ladies Race which she won, placing 2nd in the combined to Sammy Chapin.

(1, 2) Carl Haas, heute als Partner des Schauspielers Paul Newman im Indy-Car-Rennsport aktiv, steuert seinen Porsche 550 Spyder auf den dreizehnten Platz der Nassau Trophy. Er lieh McCluggage den Wagen für das erste Damenrennen, das sie gewann. In der Gesamtwertung kam sie hinter Sammy Chapin als Zweite ins Ziel.

(1, 2) Carl Haas, aujourd'hui partenaire de l'acteur Paul Newman sur des voitures Indy, prendra la 13ème place du Nassau Trophy sur sa Porsche 550 Spyder. Il prêta la voiture à McCluggage pour la première épreuve de la course des dames. Elle la gagnera et se classera 2ème dans le combiné derrière Sammy Chapin.

Jim Kimberly (in cap) pushes his OSCA MT4-2AD out for Denise McCluggage to drive in the 2nd heat of the Ladies Race. She promptly spun the unfamiliar car and finished 6th.

Jim Kimberly (mit Schirmmütze) schiebt für Denise McCluggage seinen OSCA MT4-2AD an den Start zum zweiten Rennen der Damen. Prompt kam sie mit dem ungewohnten Fahrzeug ins Schleudern und rollte als Sechste durchs Ziel.

Jim Kimberly (avec casquette) pousse son OSCA MT4-2AD que Denise McCluggage va aligner dans la 2ème épreuve de la course des dames. Elle terminera 6ème bien que la voiture ne lui soit pas familière.

"Gentleman Jim" himself in the/höchstpersönlich im/au volant de OSCA MT4-2AD.

2

1

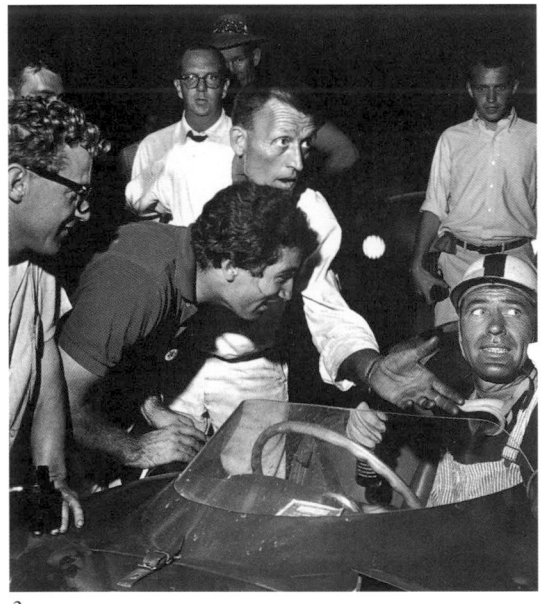

2

3

(1) Stirling Moss with Zora Arkus-Duntov (father of the Corvette).
(2) De Portago leans in to congratulate Carroll Shelby, winner of the Governor's Cup in John Edgar's Ferrari 410 S. Shelby nipped de Portago by three seconds as darkness fell.
(3) Shelby in his "Texas Tuxedo" driving suit and de Portago after they finished 1-2 in the Governor's Cup. Shelby drove with a broken shoulder.

(1) Stirling Moss mit Zora Arkus-Duntov (dem Vater der Corvette).
(2) De Portago gratuliert Carroll Shelby, der in John Edgars Ferrari 410 S bei Einbruch der Dunkelheit mit drei Sekunden Vorsprung vor de Portago den Governor's Cup gewonnen hatte.
(3) De Portago und Shelby in seiner »Texas Smoking«-Fahrermontur, nach ihrem 1-2-Finish im Governor's Cup. Shelby fuhr mit gebrochener Schulter.

(1) Stirling Moss et Zora Arkus-Duntov (père de la Corvette).
(2) De Portago se penche pour féliciter Carroll Shelby qui vient de remporter la Governor's Cup sur la Ferrari 410 S de John Edgar. La nuit tombait quand Shelby a devancé de Portago de 3 secondes.
(3) Shelby dans sa célèbre salopette « Texas Tuxedo » et de Portago après la Governor's Cup qu'ils ont remportée 1er et 2ème. Shelby a conduit avec une épaule fracturée.

The glint of crystal, the sound of laughter marked Nassau by night. Sir Harry and Lady Greta Oakes on the left.

Schimmerndes Kristall und klingendes Lachen prägten die Nächte in Nassau. Links Sir Harry und Lady Greta Oakes.

Cristaux, lumières et rires imprègnent les nuits de Nassau. A gauche : Sir Harry et Lady Greta Oakes.

VENEZUELA 1957

Maserati as a racing power died with the 1957 Grand Prix of Venezuela.

The race was in Caracas over a course that, Phil Hill suggested, was designed by Salvador Dalí: "All those surreal ramps and cloverleaves." Fast, straight stretches of superhighways and their tightly wound access roads made up a hazardous 6.16-mile circuit. It ran between those ornate street lamps, odd obelisks and huge slabs that seem to serve as monuments to totalitarian societies.

All season Ferrari and Maserati had battled neck and neck for the sports car racing championship and this, the last race of the season, would decide which of the Italian teams would wear the crown. Both teams wheeled in their biggest guns, including two 4.5-liter V-8 Maseratis from the factory (for Stirling Moss/Tony Brooks and Jean Behra/Harry Schell) and a 4.7-liter version owned by the American, Temple Buell, to be driven by Masten Gregory and his brother-in-law, Dale Duncan.

Ferrari had two 4.1-liter cars (Phil Hill/Peter Collins and Mike Hawthorn/Luigi Musso) plus a strong team of 3-liter machines.

An American contingent brought Corvettes, Porsche Spyders and AC Bristols.

Maserati was clearly the fastest on the circuit (in practice, Moss cut a lap at an average speed of more than 100 mph and quickly made up twenty-two spots after a poor Le Mans start to build a healthy lead in the race), but the team was methodically hounded by an assortment of crashes and fires. By race end, nearly every factory driver was stitched, bandaged or burned, though still upright. A locally-entered Maserati 300S claimed fifth place but factory Ferraris swept the first four places and won the championship handily. A few weeks later Maserati announced its withdrawal from sports car racing.

Nach dem Grand Prix von Venezuela im Jahre 1957 zog sich Maserati aus dem Rennsport zurück.

Das Rennen wurde in Caracas ausgetragen, auf einer Strecke, die von Salvador Dalí hätte stammen können, wie Phil Hill meinte: »Diese ganzen surrealen Straßenwellen und Kreuzungen in Kleeblattform«. Rasante gerade Autobahnstrecken und enge, kurvige Zufahrten bildeten einen gefährlichen, zehn Kilometer langen Kurs zwischen verschnörkelten Straßenlampen, seltsamen Obelisken und gigantischen Steinplatten, die totalitären Staaten anscheinend als Denkmäler dienen.

Während der gesamten Saison hatten sich Ferrari und Maserati ein Kopf-an-Kopf-Rennen um die Sportwagenmeisterschaft geliefert, und dieses letzte Rennen sollte entscheiden, welches der beiden italienischen Teams gewinnen würde. Beide Mannschaften boten ihre schnellsten Geschosse auf, darunter zwei 4,5-Liter-V8 Maserati-Werkswagen (für die Teams Stirling Moss/Tony Brooks und Jean Behra/Harry Schell) und ein 4,7-Liter-Modell des Amerikaners Temple Buell, das Masten Gregory und sein Schwager Dale Duncan fahren sollten.

Ferrari hatte zwei 4,1-Liter-Boliden (für Phil Hill/Peter Collins und Mike Hawthorn/Luigi Musso) und eine starke Abordnung von 3-Liter-Fahrzeugen.

Das amerikanische Kontingent war mit Corvettes, Porsche Spyders und AC Bristols vertreten.

Die Maseratis waren eindeutig die Schnellsten (im Training fuhr Moss Rundendurchschnitte von über 160 km/h und machte so nach einem schwachen Le-Mans-Start rasch 22 Plätze gut, was für eine sichere Führungsposition ausreichte), aber das Team wurde systematisch von einer Reihe von Unfällen und Feuerausbrüchen heimgesucht. Gegen Ende des Rennens waren die Werksfahrer zwar noch tapfer dabei, aber praktisch alle genäht, verbunden oder brandverletzt. Zwar erreichte ein Einheimischer mit seinem Maserati 300S den fünften Platz, aber die Ferrari-Werkswagen belegten die ersten vier Plätze und gewannen mühelos die Meisterschaft. Wenige Wochen später gab Maserati seinen Rückzug aus dem Rennsport bekannt.

Maserati a abandonné le cirque du sport automobile après le grand Prix du Venezuela de 1957.

La course se déroula à Caracas sur un parcours qui, selon Phil Hill, avait dû être tracé par Salvador Dalí : « Toutes ces dénivellations surréelles et ces sinuosités en feuilles de trèfle. » Un circuit hasardeux déroulait ses 10 km de lignes droites rapides raccordées à des virages serrés, entre les réverbères kitsch, les obélisques bizarres et les dalles gigantesques auxquels les sociétés totalitaires semblent donner une valeur symbolique.

Durant la saison entière, Ferrari et Maserati avaient lutté, roue dans roue, pour décrocher le championnat. Cette course, la dernière de la saison, allait déterminer laquelle des écuries italiennes porterait la couronne. Les plus puissants bolides des deux équipes étaient sur la grille de départ, dont deux Maserati d'usine 4,5 litres V–8 (pour Stirling Moss/Tony Brooks et Jean Behra/Harry Schell) ainsi qu'un modèle de 4,7 litres, appartenant à l'Américain Temple Buell et destiné à Masten Gregory et Dale Duncan, son beau-frère.

Ferrari aligna deux voitures de 4,1 litres (pour Phil Hill/Peter Collins et Mike Hawthorn/Luigi Musso) et une flottille de trois litres.

Le contingent américain comprenait des Corvette, des Porsche Spyder et des AC Bristol.

Les Maserati furent incontestablement les plus rapides : aux essais, Stirling Moss tourna à une moyenne de plus de 160 km/h et à la course, remonta rapidement 22 positions après un faible départ style Le Mans pour s'assurer une place en tête. Hélas, l'équipe subit une série d'accidents et d'incendies durant toute la course. Si aucun ne fut gravement blessé, presque tous les pilotes de l'écurie durent être recousus ou soignés pour plaies et brûlures. La Maserati 300S d'un pilote local arriva cinquième, mais les Ferrari d'usine s'octroyèrent les quatre premières places, emportant ainsi le championnat haut la main. Quelques semaines plus tard, Maserati annonçait son retrait de la compétition automobile.

Jean Behra, Maserati 450S, leads the Crawford/Hugus Porsche 550 Spyder through the streets of Caracas lined with bags filled with rock-hard dirt.

In den von Sandsäcken gesäumten Straßen von Caracas übernimmt Jean Behra im Maserati 450S die Führung vor dem Porsche 550 Spyder von Crawford/Hugus.

Jean Behra sur une Maserati 450S devant la Porsche 550 Spyder de Crawford/Hugus dans les rues de Caracas bordées de sacs remplis de gravats.

At play in Caracas:

(1) Huschke von Hanstein makes poolside movies of Wolfgang Seidel, Stirling Moss, Denise McCluggage and Wolfgang "Taffy" von Trips.

(2) Fair-haired Mike Hawthorn protected from the sun. Foreground: Peter Collins, Harry Schell. At wall: Giorgio Scarlatti, Jo Bonnier.

(3) Ruth Levy, Luigi Musso, Ubaldo Bucci (Italian race organizer, standing), Giorgio Scarlatti, Phil Hill.

Spiel und Spaß in Caracas:

(1) Fritz Huschke von Hanstein filmt Wolfgang Seidel, Stirling Moss, Denise McCluggage und Wolfgang »Taffy« von Trips am Pool.

(2) Der blonde Mike Hawthorn sucht Schutz vor der Sonne. Vorne: Peter Collins, Harry Schell. An der Mauer: Giorgio Scarlatti, Jo Bonnier.

(3) Ruth Levy, Luigi Musso, Ubaldo Bucci (ein italienischer Rennveranstalter, stehend), Giorgio Scarlatti, Phil Hill.

Détente à Caracas :

(1) Au bord de la piscine. Huschke von Hanstein filme Wolfgang Seidel, Stirling Moss, Denise McCluggage et Wolfgang « Taffy » von Trips.

(2) Mike Hawthorn protège sa peau de blond du soleil. Devant : Peter Collins, Harry Schell. Sur le mur : Giorgio Scarlatti, Jo Bonnier.

(3) Ruth Levy, Luigi Musso, Ubaldo Bucci (organisateur italien de la course, debout), Giorgio Scarlatti, Phil Hill.

1

2

3

The Gendebiens, Marie-Claire and Olivier.

Luigi Musso surrounded by admirers/im Kreise seiner Fans/entouré d'admirateurs.

Wolfgang von Trips and friend/und Freundin/avec une amie.

Masten Gregory, Tony Brooks, journalist Hans Tanner in the foreground/im Vordergrund/au premier plan. Behind/Hinter/derrière Masten: Giorgio Scarlatti.

The Hap Dressel/Frank Pohanka AC Bristol (later involved in a crash with Stirling Moss) followed by the de Tomaso/Haskell OSCA.

Der AC Bristol von Hap Dressel und Frank Pohanka (später in einen Unfall mit Stirling Moss verwickelt) vor dem OSCA von de Tomaso und Haskell.

L' AC Bristol de Hap Dressel/Frank Pohanka (avant l'accrochage avec Stirling Moss) suivie de l'OSCA de Tomaso/Haskell.

Corvettes. Dick Thompson (#22) was 12th, Fred Windridge (#26) threw a wheel on the 43rd lap.

Zwei Corvettes. Dick Thompson (Nr. 22) wurde Zwölfter, Fred Windridge (Nr. 26) verlor in der 43. Runde ein Rad.

Deux Corvette. Dick Thompson (n° 22) terminera 12ème. Fred Windridge (n° 26) perdra une roue au 43ème tour.

2

(1) Maseratis on the way from the dock.
(2) Mechanic Bertocchi and co-driver Dale Duncan with Masten Gregory in the Temple Buell Maserati 450S which Gregory upset on the first lap.
(3) Denise McCluggage, Porsche 550 Spyder (#70) leaves room for the flying Stirling Moss Maserati 450S (#4) and Maurice Trintignant, Ferrari 250 TR (#18).

(1) Maseratis auf dem Weg vom Hafen.
(2) Mechaniker Bertocchi und Beifahrer Dale Duncan zusammen mit Masten Gregory in Temple Buells Maserati 450S, den Gregory schon in der ersten Runde außer Gefecht setzte.
(3) Denise McCluggage, Porsche 550 Spyder (Nr. 70) macht Platz für Stirling Moss' vorbei-rasenden Maserati 450S (Nr. 4) und Maurice Trintignants Ferrari 250 TR (Nr. 18).

(1) Les Maserati sortent du dock.
(2) Le mécanicien Bertocchi et le copilote Dale Duncan discutent avec Masten Gregory au volant de la Temple Buell Maserati 450S qu'il démolira au 1er tour.
(3) Denise McCluggage au volant d'une Porsche 550 Spyder (n° 70) s'écarte devant l'étoile filante de Stirling Moss (Maserati 450S, n°4) et la Ferrari 250 TR (n° 18) de Maurice Trintignant.

1

5

Moss in conference with Bertocchi/Moss diskutiert mit Bertocchi/Moss confère avec le mécanicien Bertocchi.

(1) Maserati 200S, Venezuelan team Santiago
Gonzalez/Felipe Gutierrez.
(2) Jean Behra, Maserati 450S. His arms were
burned in a refueling fire.
(3) Factory mechanics prepare the Jo Bonnier/
Giorgio Scarlatti Maserati 300S.

(1) Der Maserati 200S des venezolanischen Teams
Santiago Gonzalez/Felipe Gutierrez.
(2) Jean Behra, Maserati 450S. Er verbrannte sich
seine Arme bei einem Feuerunfall während des
Nachtankens.
(3) Die Werksmechaniker machen den Maserati
300S von Jo Bonnier/Giorgio Scarlatti startbereit.

(1) Masarati 200S, tandem Santiago Gonzalez/
Felipe Gutierrez de Vénézuéla.
(2) Jean Behra, Maserati 450S. Behra s'est brûlé
les bras quand l'essence a pris feu pendant un
ravitaillement.
(3) Des mécaniciens d'usine préparent la Maserati
300S de Jo Bonnier/Giorgio Scarlatti.

2

1

1

(1) Jo Bonnier's 300S Maserati (#6) and Harry Schell's 450S (#2) collided when Bonnier experienced tire failure. He was thrown clear before the car felled the lamp post. Schell ended in flames against the wall.
(2) Masten Gregory with some stitches after crashing his Maserati 450S on the first lap. Behind him, car owner Temple Buell.
(3, 4) Schell with bandaged arms, Bonnier with injured head.

(1) Jo Bonniers 300S Maserati (Nr. 6) und Harry Schells 450S (Nr. 2) kollidierten, als an Bonniers Wagen ein Reifen platzte. Bevor das Fahrzeug den Laternenpfahl fällte, wurde Bonnier herausgeschleudert. Schells Wagen endete brennend vor einer Wand.
(2) Nach einem Unfall mit seinem Maserati 450S in der ersten Runde, mußte Masten Gregory genäht werden. Hinter ihm Temple Buell, der Besitzer des Wagens.
(3, 4) Schell mit bandagierten Armen, Bonnier mit Kopfverletzung.

(1) L'éclatement d'un pneu de la Maserati 300S (n° 6) de Jo Bonnier a provoqué une collision avec la 450S (n° 2) de Harry Schell. Bonnier est éjecté avant que la voiture ne percute la lanterne. Schell s'écrase en flammes contre le mur.
(2) Masten Gregory s'en tire avec quelques points de suture après avoir démoli sa Maserati 450S au 1er tour. Derrière lui : Temple Buell, propriétaire de la voiture.
(3, 4) Schell a les bras bandés ; Bonnier s'est blessé à la tête.

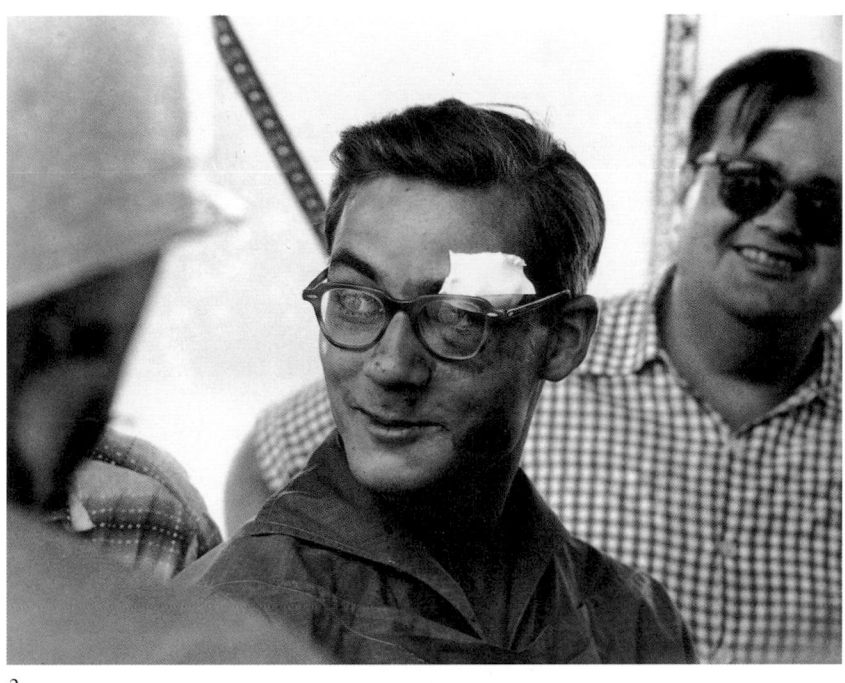

2

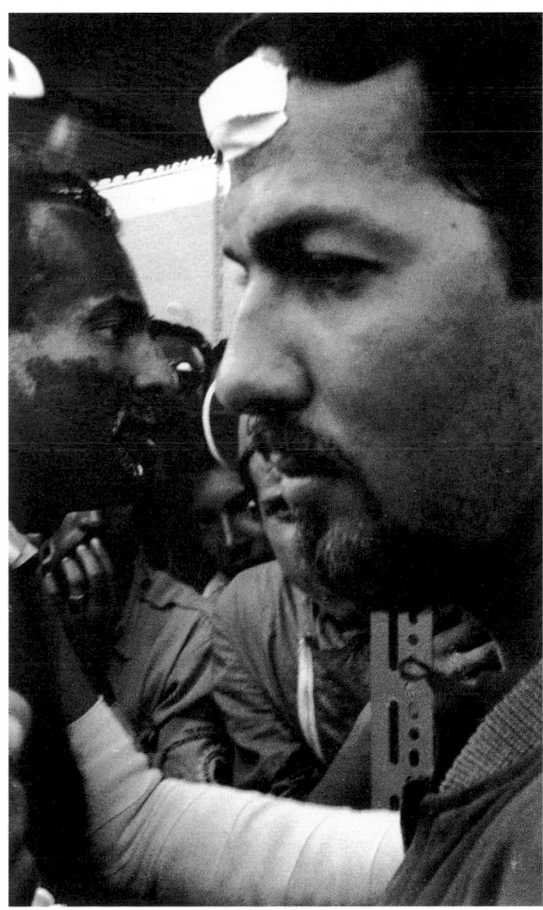

3

4

Harry Schell, flash burned in one of the fiery crashes that ended Maserati's championship hopes and being escorted back to the pits after his arms were bandaged.

Harry Schell mit Verbrennungen nach einem der Unfälle, die Maseratis Hoffnungen auf die Meisterschaft beendeten, und auf dem Weg zurück zur Box, nachdem seine Arme bandagiert wurden.

Harry Schell s'est brûlé dans l'accident spectaculaire qui met fin aux espoirs de Maserati de remporter le championnat. Il est escorté au stand après avoir reçu les premiers soins.

Maurice Trintignant, co-driver/Beifahrer/copilote d'Olivier Gendebien.

Phil Hill waits patiently while Ferrari Team Manager Romolo Tavoni and co-driver Peter Collins are given directions.

Phil Hill wartet geduldig, während Ferraris Team-Manager Romolo Tavoni und Beifahrer Peter Collins instruiert werden.

Phil Hill attend patiemment tandis que Romolo Tavoni, directeur de l'écurie Ferrari et Peter Collins, copilote, donnent des instructions.

1

2

3

(1) Luigi Musso in the Ferrari 335 S he shared with Mike Hawthorn.
(2) The two Wolfgangs: von Trips leans over to confer with Seidel. They shared a Ferrari 250 TR and finished 3rd.
(3) In the Ferrari pits: Luigi Musso in helmet, Olivier Gendebien pointing.

(1) Luigi Musso im Ferrari 335 S, den er sich mit Mike Hawthorn teilte.
(2) Die beiden Wolfgangs: von Trips berät sich mit Seidel. Die beiden teilten sich einen Ferrari 250 TR und wurden Dritte.
(3) In der Ferrari-Box: Luigi Musso mit Helm und Olivier Gendebien, der auf etwas zeigt.

(1) Luigi Musso de la Ferrari 335 S qu'il partage avec Mike Hawthorn.
(2) Les deux Wolfgang : von Trips se penche vers Seidel. Ils partagent une Ferrari 250 TR et arriveront 3èmes.
(3) Aux stands Ferrari : Luigi Musso casqué, Olivier Gendebien pointe un doigt.

The Ferrari pits:
(1) Peter Collins takes over for Phil Hill (behind him).
(2) The undulating shapes of the Ferraris.
(3) Phil Hill prepares to go out for practice.
(4) Front to back: Peter Collins (335 S), Mike Hawthorn (335 S), Olivier Gendebien (250 TR).

Die Ferrari Box:
(1) Peter Collins übernimmt das Lenkrad von Phil Hill (hinten).
(2) Die geschwungenen Silhouetten der Ferrari-Renner.
(3) Phil Hill macht sich für den Trainingslauf bereit.
(4) Von vorne nach hinten: Peter Collins (335 S), Mike Hawthorn (335 S), Olivier Gendebien (250 TR).

Les stands Ferrari:
(1) Peter Collins remplace Phil Collins (derrière lui).
(2) Les lignes ondulées des Ferrari.
(3) Phil Hill s'apprête à commencer les essais.
(4) De l'avant à l'arrière : Peter Collins (335 S), Mike Hawthorn (335 S), Olivier Gendebien (250 TR).

4

1

2

3

Wolfgang von Trips, Ferrari 250 TR. The Jeffords/Windridge Corvette is passing the wall where the Schell Maserati burned.

Wolfgang von Trips, Ferrari 250 TR. Die Corvette von Jeffords und Windridge fährt gerade an der Mauer vorbei, an der Schells Maserati ausbrannte.

Wolfgang von Trips sur une Ferrari 250 TR. La Corvette de Jeffords/Windridge passe devant le mur où la Maserati de Schell a pris feu.

Mike Hawthorn, Ferrari 335 S, and his typical chin-high driving style/und sein unverkennbarer »Kopfhoch«-Fahrstil/montre son style typique de conduite : menton relevé !

1

2

(1) A Ferrari mechanic treats a hot car gingerly. Gendebien/Trintignant drove the 250 TR to 4th place.
(2) Peter Collins and Phil Hill get news of another crash.

(1) Ein Ferrari-Mechaniker arbeitet vorsichtig an einem heißgelaufenen Motor. Gendebien und Trintignant erreichten im 250 TR den vierten Platz.
(2) Peter Collins und Phil Hill erfahren von einem weiteren Unfall.

(1) Un mécanicien de Ferrari s'approche avec précaution du bolide surchauffé. Gendebien/Trintignant ont conduit la 250 TR à la 4ème place.
(2) Peter Collins et Phil Hill apprennent qu'un nouvel accident vient de se produire.

1

(1) Peter Collins in the winning Ferrari 335 S .
(2) Mike Hawthorn wore a rain shield whatever the weather and a green battle jacket.
(3) Maurice Trintignant, Ferrari 250 TR (4th with Gendebien).
(4) Mike Hawthorn, Ferrari 335 S (2nd with Musso).

(1) Peter Collins im Siegerfahrzeug, einem Ferrari 335 S.
(2) Mike Hawthorn trug bei jedem Wetter Helmvisier und grüne Windjacke.
(3) Maurice Trintignant, Ferrari 250 TR (Vierter mit Gendebien).
(4) Mike Hawthorn, Ferrari 335 S (Zweiter mit Musso).

(1) Peter Collins au volant de la Ferrari 335 S qui remportera la course.
(2) Qu'il pleuve ou qu'il fasse du soleil, Mike Hawthorn porte toujours un casque à visière et un blouson vert.
(3) Maurice Trintignant, Ferrari 250 TR (4ème en compagnie de Gendebien).
(4) Mike Hawthorn, Ferrari 335 S (2ème avec Musso).

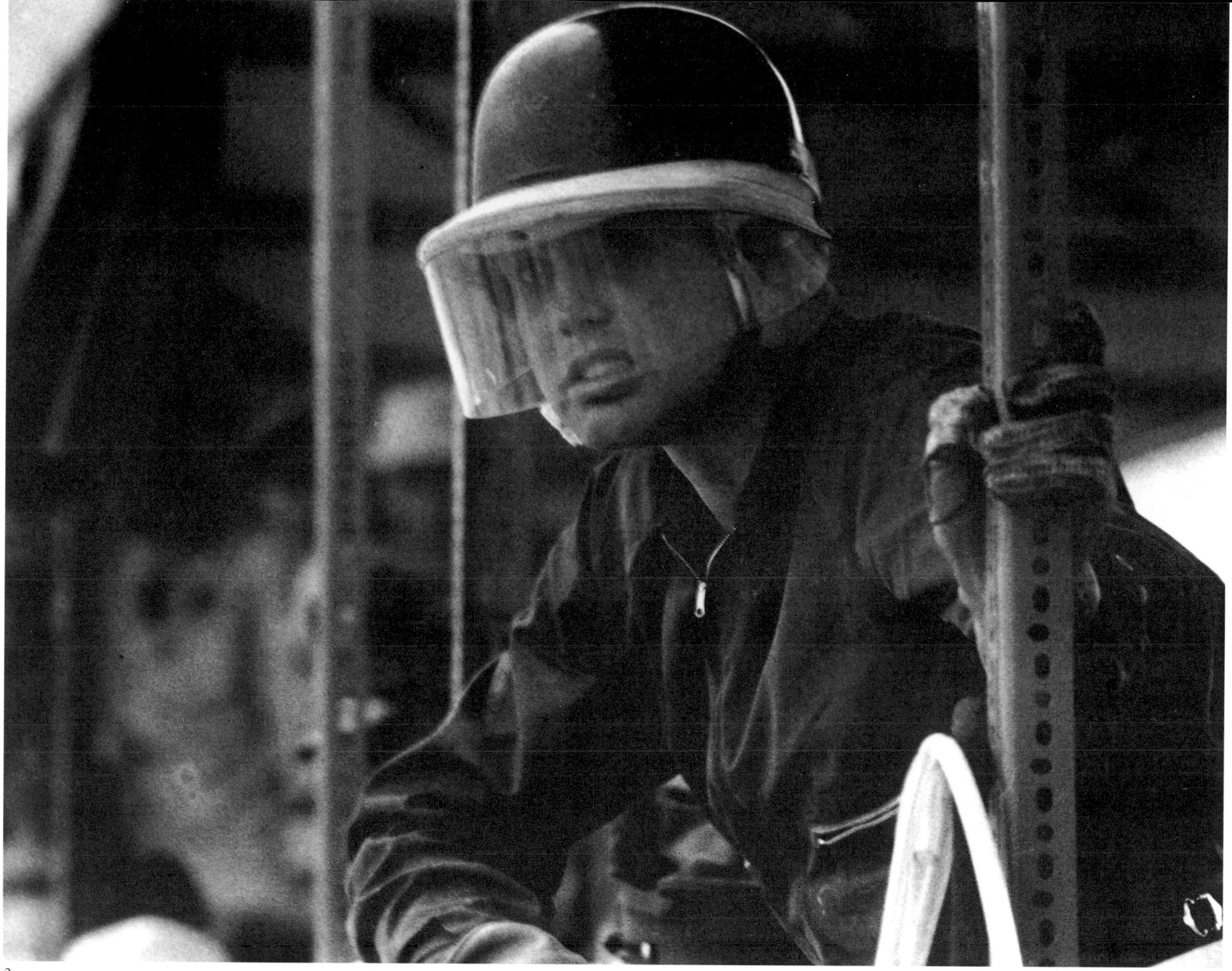

2

3

4

Jan de Vroom, Ferrari 500 TRC (9th with/Neunter mit/9ème avec Julio Batista).

Art Bunker, Porsche 550 Spyder (10th with/Zehnter mit/10ème avec Carel Godin de Beaufort).

Dick Thompson, Corvette (12th with/Zwölfter mit/12ème avec Dick Doane).

Edgar Barth, Porsche 550 Spyder (6th with/Sechster mit/6ème avec Huschke von Hanstein).

Denise McCluggage, Porsche 550 Spyder (13th with/13. mit/13ème avec Ruth Levy).

Umberto Masetti/André Testut, 1500 cc OSCA (11th)/1500-cm3-OSCA (11.)/OSCA 1,5 litre (11ème).

Piero Drogo, Ferrari 500 TR (8th with/Achter mit/8ème avec Julio Pola).

Refueling:
(1) The latest factory Porsche 550 A with a
1600 cc engine, driven by Edgar Barth and Huschke
von Hanstein.
(2) Spilled gas gets washed off Porsche 550
Spyder, Denise McCluggage in signature polka-dot
helmet.

Auftanken:
(1) Der neueste Werksporsche 550 A mit 1600-
cm3-Motor, Fahrer waren Edgar Barth und
Huschke von Hanstein.
(2) Übergelaufener Treibstoff wird von einem
Porsche 550 Spyder abgewaschen. Denise Mc-
Cluggage in ihrem charakteristischen gepunkteten
Helm.

Ravitaillement :
(1) La nouvelle Porsche 550 A d'usine avec un
moteur 1,6 litre, pilotée par Edgar Barth et Huschke von Hanstein.
(2) De l'essence s'est renversée sur le capot. On
nettoie la Porsche 550 Spyder de Denise McCluggage. Le casque à pois est l'emblème de cette pilote.

1

1

2

4

(1) Victorious Phil Hill waves, with co-driver Peter Collins.
(2) Edgar Barth (bottom left) and Huschke von Hanstein (center) chat with fellow Porsche pilot Denise McCluggage.
(3) Armed protection for a line-up of Ferraris.
(4) A pensive Stirling Moss.

(1) Sieger Phil Hill winkt, daneben Beifahrer Peter Collins.
(2) Edgar Barth (unten links) und Huschke von Hanstein (Mitte) plaudern mit Porsche-Team-kollegin Denise McCluggage.
(3) Militärschutz für eine Reihe von Ferraris.
(4) Ein nachdenklicher Stirling Moss.

(1) Phil Hill salue la victoire avec son copilote Peter Collins.
(2) Edgar Barth (en bas à gauche) et Huschke von Hanstein (au centre) bavardent avec Denise McCluggage, leur collègue chez Porsche.
(3) Des soldats armés protègent les Ferrari.
(4) Perdu dans ses pensées – Stirling Moss.

3

CUBA 1957

Juan Manuel Fangio once said of himself "I was never spectacular." Alfonso Cabeza de Vaca, Marquis de Portago, was always spectacular. This pair with their contrasting styles kept the spectators along Havana's Malecon on a fine edge all afternoon, although it was a mechanical problem that finally decided the race.

De Portago, driving a 3.5-liter Ferrari, had nipped into the lead on the second lap when Carroll Shelby almost lost his 4.9 Ferrari on the always slippery seaside course. Fangio followed in close pursuit. The 45-year-old Fangio in a 3-liter Maserati pressed de Portago lap after lap, but the young Spaniard never faltered and, indeed, stretched his lead until he had lapped every car on the course, save Fangio.

With the race three-quarters run a sputtering engine brought de Portago's Ferrari to the pits for five minutes of fuel-line repair. Thus Fangio led the way under the checkered flag with Shelby second. De Portago, delighting the crowd with his efforts, recovered several places to take third. At the awards ceremony when Fangio was presented as the victor he, typically, acknowledged de Portago's performance. "Here, gentlemen, is the real winner of the race," he said.

The next year, 1958, the Cuban Gran Prix was far different for Fangio. He watched the race on television as an unwilling guest of Fidel Castro's revolutionaries. Fangio later said that the kidnappers might well have done him a favor. The race was crash-ridden and the inherent dangers of the fast Malecon course with spectators at curbside were realized when a car went into the crowd and killed several people.

The Third Cuban Grand Prix, set for February, 1959, was not to be. The political upheaval, which put Castro in power for decades to come, intervened.

Juan Manuel Fangio sagte einmal von sich selbst: »Ich war nie spektakulär.« Alfonso Cabeza de Vaca, Marquis de Portago, war immer spektakulär. Diese beiden stilistisch so unterschiedlichen Fahrer hielten die Zuschauer entlang Havannas Malecon-Rennstrecke den ganzen Nachmittag in Atem, wenn auch schließlich ein mechanisches Problem das Rennen entschied.

De Portago hatte mit seinem 3,5-Liter-Ferrari in der zweiten Runde die Führung übernommen, als Carroll Shelby auf der stets schlüpfrigen Küstenpiste fast seinen 4,9-Liter-Ferrari aus der Gewalt verlor. Aber Fangio war dem heißblütigen Adligen im Nacken. Mit seinem 3-Liter-Maserati hatte der 45jährige den jungen Spanier bereits über viele Runden bedrängt, aber de Portago ließ sich nicht verunsichern, baute seine Führungsposition sogar noch aus und überrundete schließlich alle Fahrzeuge auf der Strecke – mit Ausnahme von Fangio.

Nach etwa Dreiviertel des Rennens mußte de Portago mit stotterndem Motor an die Box fahren, und verlor fünf Minuten durch eine Reparatur der Benzinleitung. So erreichte Fangio als Erster die schwarzweiße Zielflagge, Shelby fuhr als Zweiter ins Ziel. De Portago begeisterte die Zuschauer mit Kampfesmut, machte mehrere Plätze gut und erreichte den dritten Platz. Während der Preisverleihung würdigte Fangio auf die für ihn so typische Art de Portagos Leistung, indem er sagte: »Hier, Gentlemen, steht der wahre Sieger des Rennens«.

Im folgenden Jahr verlief der Grand Prix von Kuba für Fangio vollkommen anders. Er verfolgte das Rennen auf dem Bildschirm – als unfreiwilliger Gast der Revolutionstruppen Fidel Castros. Später sagte er, daß die Revolutionäre ihm damit womöglich sogar einen Gefallen erwiesen hätten. Das Rennen wurde nämlich von zahlreichen Unfällen heimgesucht, und die horrende Gefährlichkeit des schnellen Malecon-Kurses, bei dem die Zuschauer direkt am Rande der Rennstrecke standen, wurde besonders deutlich, als ein Wagen ins Publikum raste und mehrere Menschen tötete.

Der für Februar 1959 geplante dritte Grand Prix von Kuba fand aufgrund der Revolution, die Fidel Castro für die nächsten Jahrzehnte an die Macht brachte, nie statt.

Juan Manuel Fangio dit un jour : « Je n'ai jamais été spectaculaire. » Alfonso Cabeza de Vaca, marquis de Portago, était toujours spectaculaire. Ces deux pilotes, à la personnalité et au style si opposés, tinrent les spectateurs en haleine durant toute l'après-midi à la course Malecon de La Havane. C'est un problème mécanique qui décida du dénouement.

De Portago au volant d'une Ferrari 3,5 litres s'était faufilé en pole position au deuxième tour alors que Carroll Shelby faillit perdre sa Ferrari 4,9 litres sur le trajet toujours glissant du bord de mer. La Maserati 3 litres de Fangio était sur ses roues. Le vétéran de 45 ans pourchassa sans relâche le jeune Espagnol qui, loin de se laisser démonter, accentua même son écart, laissant tous ses concurrents à un tour – sauf Fangio.

Aux trois-quarts de la course, un moteur défaillant imposa à de Portago cinq minutes d'arrêt au stand, le temps de réparer la conduite d'essence. C'est ainsi que le drapeau à damiers noirs et blancs s'abaissa en premier devant Fangio suivi de Shelby. De Portago se battit comme un lion devant un public enthousiasmé pour remonter jusqu'à une troisième position qu'il conserva jusqu'à la fin. Sur le podium, Fangio, toujours gentleman, rendit hommage à la prouesse de Portago. « Messieurs, voici le vrai vainqueur de la course », annonça-t-il.

L'année suivante, en 1958, Fangio vécut le Grand Prix de Cuba dans un contexte fort différent. Il regarda la course à la télévision – hôte involontaire des révolutionnaires de Fidel Castro. Il déclara plus tard que ses kidnappeurs lui avaient sans doute rendu service. La course fut semée d'accidents et on réalisa enfin les dangers du parcours rapide où les spectateurs se tenaient directement sur les bords, quand une voiture fonça dans le public, faisant plusieurs victimes.

Le troisième Grand Prix de Cuba, fixé à février 1959, ne devait pas avoir lieu. Le pays vivait la période troublée de la révolution qui porta Castro au pouvoir.

Juan Manuel Fangio, Maserati 300S (winner/ Sieger/vainqueur).

1

(1) A rainstorm during practice. Masten Gregory/
Wolfgang von Trips Ferrari 500 TR (#42); Carroll
Shelby Ferrari 410 S (#18); Olivier
Gendebien/Bill Helburn Ferrari 500 TR (#36).
(2) Fon de Portago in his Ferrari 857 S takes on
refreshment while Stirling Moss fiddles with his
movie caméra.

(1) Regenguß beim Training. Masten Gregory/
Wolfgang von Trips auf Ferrari 500 TR (Nr. 42);
Carroll Shelby auf Ferrari 410 S (Nr. 18); Olivier
Gendebien/Bill Helburn auf Ferrari 500 TR (Nr. 36).
(2) Fon de Portago erfrischt sich in seinem Ferrari
857 S, während Stirling Moss an seiner Film-
kamera herumbastelt.

(1) Pluie battante durant les essais. Ferrari 500 TR
(n° 42) de Masten Gregory/Wolfgang von Trips ;
Ferrari 410 S (n° 18) de Carroll Shelby ; Ferrari
500 TR (n° 36) d'Olivier Gendebien/Bill Helburn.
(2) Fon de Portago au volant de sa Ferrari 857 S
Monza, il se désaltère pendant que Stirling Moss
joue avec sa caméra.

Stirling Moss with the Gary Coopers/mit Gary Cooper und Frau/avec Gary Cooper et son épouse.

Fon de Portago improvises a shelter by Shell/mit einem Shell-Schild als improvisiertem Regenschutz/improvise un abri chez Shell.

Modesto Bolanos, Mercedes-Benz 300SL, 2nd in class in the all-Cuban race but set fastest lap.

Modesto Bolanos, Mercedes-Benz 300SL, wurde nur Klassenzweiter im Rennen der Kubaner, setzte aber den Rundenrekord.

Modesto Bolanos sur une Mercedes-Benz 300SL ; 2ème de groupe dans l'épreuve réservée aux Cubains, mais établira le record du tour.

1

2

(1) Actress Linda Christian, Fon de Portago.
(2) Juan Manuel Fangio was always willing to sign autographs.

(1) Schauspielerin Linda Christian, Fon de Portago.
(2) Juan Manuel Fangio war immer für Autogramme zu haben.

(1) L'actrice Linda Christian, Fon de Portago.
(2) Juan Manuel Fangio reste toujours aimable avec les chasseurs d'autographes.

Porsche 356 Speedster.

Cuban 300SLs. Santiago Gonzales (#24) and Bolanos/Kubanische 300SL von Santiago Gonzales (Nr. 24) und Bolanos/300SL cubaines. Santiago Gonzales (n° 24) et Bolanos.

Enthusiasm for Santiago Gonzales, the "M.O.P." (Ministry of Police) entrant/Jubel für Santiago Gonzales, der für das »M.O.P.« (Ministry of Police) teilnahm/Un public enthousiaste encourage Santiago Gonzales, qui court pour le M.O.P. (Ministère de la Police).

Cuban Manolo Pacheco, MG A, on the Malecon where sea spray often made the way slippery.

Der Kubaner Manolo Pacheco, MG A, auf der durch Seewasserspritzer oft rutschigen Malecon-Piste.

Le Cubain Manolo Pacheco, MG A, sur le Malecon en bord de mer. La chaussée était souvent glissante à cause des embruns.

(1) A Cuban Jaguar XK 120 motors down the Malecon.

(2) Paul O'Shea in George Tilp's Ferrari 857 S, in practice. Phil Hill, who was to drive this car, was disqualified as the race began because of a push start.

(3) Carroll Shelby in his distinctive driving togs.

(4) Eugenio Castelotti in de Portago's "spare" Ferrari 860 Monza being pushed to the starting grid by Ferrari mechanics. He did not finish.
In the background Alejandro de Tomaso leans against his OSCA.

(1) Ein kubanischer Jaguar XK 120 rast den Malecon hinab.

(2) Paul O'Shea während des Trainings in George Tilps Ferrari 857 S. Phil Hill, der den Wagen eigentlich fahren sollte, wurde schon zu Rennbeginn wegen eines Frühstarts disqualifiziert.

(3) Carroll Shelby in seiner unverwechselbaren Arbeitskleidung.

(4) Eugenio Castelotti, der hier in de Portagos »Ersatz«-Ferrari 860 Monza von Ferrari-Mechanikern an den Start geschoben wird, erreichte das Ziel nicht. Im Hintergrund Alejandro de Tomaso an seinem OSCA.

(1) Une Jaguar XK 120 cubaine descend le Malecon.

(2) Paul O'Shea sur la Ferrari 857 S de George Tilp durant les essais. Phil Hill qui pilotait la voiture, sera disqualifié dès le début de la course pour faute au départ.

(3) Carroll Shelby en tenue de travail.

(4) Des mécaniciens de l'équipe poussent Eugenio Castelotti sur la grille de départ. Il pilote la Ferrari 860 Monza de « réserve » de Portago, mais ne finira pas la course. A l'arrière plan : Alejandro de Tomaso s'appuie contre son OSCA.

1

2

3

4

Juan Manuel Fangio, Maserati 300S, biding his time. He won.

Juan Manuel Fangio, Maserati 300S, wartet auf den rechten Augenblick. Er gewann das Rennen.

Juan Manuel Fangio, Maserati 300S, attend son heure. Il triomphera.

Fon de Portago, Ferrari 857 S, followed by, most likely, Ferrari 121 LM, Jean Lucas. De Portago led most of the race.

Fon de Portago, Ferrari 857 S, wahrscheinlich vor Jean Lucas, Ferrari 121 LM. De Portago lag fast das gesamte Rennen in Führung.

Fon de Portago mène avec une Ferrari 857 S probablement devant Jean Lucas sur une Ferrari 121 LM. De Portago restera en tête durant presque toute la course.

Olivier Gendebien, Ferrari 500 TR (5th/Fünfter/ 5ème place).

Carroll Shelby, Ferrari 410 S (2nd behind/Zweiter hinter/2ème dans la foulée de Fangio).

1

2

3

(1, 2) Fon de Portago urging his pit crew to find
the problem with his fuel supply, then resigned
that solving it will take time.
(3) Peter Collins, Ferrari 500 TR (4th, 1st in
class).

(1, 2) Fon de Portago drängt seine Crew, einen
Fehler bei der Treibstoffzufuhr zu beheben,
erkennt dann aber resigniert, daß die Reparatur
Zeit braucht.
(3) Peter Collins, Ferrari 500 TR (Vierter, Klassenerster).

(1, 2) L'alimentation du moteur est défaillante. de
Fon de Portago exhorte son équipe à se hâter de
régler le problème. Mais il devra prendre son mal
en patience.
(3) Peter Collins, Ferrari 500 TR (4ème, 1er de
catégorie).

(4, 5) Stirling Moss with Harry Schell who turned his trouble-ridden Maserati 300S over to Moss.
(6) Castellotti, Ferrari 121 LM, in practice. Crowds lined the curb on straights and turns, an invitation to disaster that was realized the next year when several spectators were killed.

(4, 5) Stirling Moss mit Harry Schell, der seinen von Defekten geplagten Maserati 300S an Moss übergab.
(6) Castellotti, Ferrari 121 LM, während des Trainings. Die Schaulustigen an Geraden und Kurven forderten die Katastrophe förmlich heraus – und tatsächlich wurden im folgenden Jahr mehrere Zuschauer getötet.

(4, 5) Stirling Moss avec Harry Schell qui passera à Moss sa Maserati 300S, source de maints problèmes.
(6) Castellotti sur une Ferrari 121 LM aux essais. La foule borde les deux côtés du virage, une incitation à la catastrophe qui deviendra triste réalité l'année suivante lorsque plusieurs spectateurs seront tués.

4

5

6

(1) Alfonso Gomez Mena, D-type Jaguar, finished 6th to the delight of his countrymen.
(2) Luigi Chinetti (in foreground) was responsible for assembling the Ferraris that raced in Cuba after a US dock strike sent the factory cars back to Italy unloaded.

(1) Alfonso Gomez Mena, Jaguar D-Type, erreichte zur Freude seiner Landsleute als Sechster das Ziel.
(2) Luigi Chinetti (vorne) organisierte den Ferrari-Einsatz für das Rennen in Kuba, nachdem die Werkswagen aufgrund eines US-Hafenstreiks nach Italien zurückgeschickt worden waren.

(1) Alfonso Gomez Mena sur une Jaguar Type D. Il terminera 6ème à la grande joie de ses concitoyens.
(2) Luigi Chinetti (au premier plan) sera chargé de réunir les Ferraris pour la course de Cuba parce que les voitures d'usine ont été renvoyées en Italie à cause de la grève des dockers aux Etats-Unis.

Fangio during his 15-second pit stop/während seines 15sekündigen Boxenstopps/s'arrête 15 secondes au stand.

Most likely/wahrscheinlich/probablement Ferrari
121 LM, Jean Lucas.

Jo Bonnier (a driver without a ride) and friend/
(ein Fahrer ohne Fahrzeug) und seine Freundin/
(pilote sans voiture) avec une amie.

Harry Schell tries a local cigar/probiert eine
Havanna/savoure un havane.

Peter Collins and Louise King Collins, newly-
weds/frisch vermählt/des jeunes mariés.

Jo Bonnier, Fon de Portago, Carroll Shelby and
Wolfgang "Taffy" von Trips, El Presidente Hotel.

Fernandez Miranda presents Prix de Cuba trophy
to Alfonso Gomez Mena, "the best driver Cuba
ever had."

Fernandez Miranda überreicht Alfonso Gomez
Mena – dem »besten Fahrer, den Kuba je hatte« –
die Prix-de-Cuba-Trophäe.

Fernandez Miranda remet le trophée du Prix de
Cuba à Alfonso Gomez Mena, « le meilleur pilote
que Cuba ait jamais eu ».

At the awards ceremony: Alfonso de Portago, Linda Christian, Jo Bonnier (in second row).

Während der Preisverleihung: Alfonso de Portago, Linda Christian, Jo Bonnier (zweite Reihe).

A la remise des prix : Alfonso de Portago, Linda Christian et Jo Bonnier au deuxième rang.

CUBA 1960

The Twenty-Sixth of July Movement, Fidel Castro's revolutionaries, had been opposed to motor racing, papering Havana with entreaties to boycott the first Grand Prix in 1957 and disrupting the second in 1958 by kidnapping Fangio. But 1960, and power, saw a change of heart and the promotion of a week-long festival of racing, the *Primer Gran Premio Libertad* – The First Freedom Grand Prix.

The dramatic race circuit of previous years along the Malecon was abandoned for an airport and its support roads where crowd control could be more easily affected. It was a relatively fast circuit and the drivers liked it.

Lucky Casner's Camoradi (CAsner MOtor RAcing DIvision) had a most successful time of it in 1960. Stirling Moss, driving a Camoradi Type 61 2.8-liter Birdcage Maserati, got away first in the Le Mans start for the week's main event, the *Gran Premio de Cuba*, and stayed there, lapping all but the second place Pedro Rodriguez in a 3-liter Ferrari Testa Rossa.

Camoradi USA drivers also won the 2–liter class with Masten Gregory (Porsche RSK) and the Grand Touring class with Jim Jeffords (Chevrolet Corvette). Dan Gurney and Carroll Shelby also drove for Camoradi although the promised Birdcages did not materialize and they had to settle for some rather tired lesser machines.

Three drivers from the Indianapolis circuit – Rodger Ward, Jim Rathmann and Eddie Sachs – turned their talents away from the high-speed ovals to try some international road racing.

Although Spanish-speaking heroes of previous years were absent (Fangio had largely retired and de Portago had lost his life in the Mille Miglia) the enthusiastic crowd did not lack for new Latinos to cheer. The young Rodriguez brothers, Pedro and Ricardo, were immediate favorites.

Die Bewegung des 26. Juli, die Revolutionstruppe Fidel Castros, war ein entschiedener Gegner des Autorennsports. Bereits 1957 pflasterte sie Havanna mit Aufrufen zum Boykott des ersten Grand Prix, 1958 sabotierte sie den zweiten mit der Entführung Fangios. Aber mit dem Regierungswechsel kam 1960 auch ein Sinneswandel, und man rief zu einem einwöchigen Festival des Autorennsports auf, dem *Primer Gran Premio Libertad* – dem ersten Grand Prix der Freiheit.

Die am Malecon gelegene gefährliche Rennstrecke der vergangenen Jahre wurde aufgegeben. Man wich auf einen Flugplatz und dessen Anlieferstraßen aus, wo sich Ordnungsmaßnahmen leichter realisieren ließen. Es war ein relativ schneller Kurs, den die Fahrer mochten.

Lucky Casners Camoradi (CAsner MOtor RAcing DIvision) war hier 1960 äußerst erfolgreich. Stirling Moss übernahm in seinem 2,8-Liter-Maserati Tipo 61 Birdcage des Camoradi-Teams unmittelbar nach dem Le-Mans-Start die Führung im *Gran Premio de Cuba*, dem wichtigsten Rennen dieser Woche. Er hielt diese Position und überrundete das gesamte Feld mit Ausnahme von Pedro Rodriguez, der mit seinem 3-Liter Ferrari Testa Rossa in zweiter Position fuhr.

Mit Masten Gregory (Porsche RSK) in der 2-Liter-Klasse und Jim Jeffords (Chevrolet Corvette) in der Grand-Touring-Klasse fuhren die amerikanischen Fahrer von Camoradi weitere Siege ein. Dan Gurney und Carroll Shelby starteten ebenfalls für Camoradi, obwohl sie die ursprünglich zugesagten Birdcages dann doch nicht bekamen, und sie sich mit langsameren Fahrzeugen begnügen mußten.

Rodger Ward, Jim Rathmann und Eddie Sachs, drei erfolgreiche Indianapolis-Piloten, verabschiedeten sich von den ovalen Hochgeschwindigkeitskursen, um sich bei internationalen Straßenrennen zu beweisen.

Zwar fehlten in diesem Jahr die Spanisch sprechenden Helden der vergangenen Jahre (Fangio hatte sich fast völlig zurückgezogen, und de Portago war bei der Mille Miglia tödlich verunglückt), die begeisterten Zuschauer jubelten jedoch schon bald zwei neuen Lateinamerikanern zu. Die jungen Brüder Pedro und Ricardo Rodriguez wurden sofort zu Publikumslieblingen.

Le Mouvement du 26 juillet, les révolutionnaires de Castro, étaient des adversaires du sport automobile. En 1957, ils avaient exhorté les Cubains à boycotter le premier Grand Prix à La Havane et avaient perturbé le second Grand Prix de 1958 en kidnappant Fangio. Mais la prise du pouvoir changea les esprits et les révolutionnaires décidèrent en 1960 de promouvoir sept jours de fête du sport automobile, le *Primer Gran Premio Libertad* – le Premier Grand Prix de la Liberté.

Le circuit Malecon des années précédentes, trop dangereux, fut abandonné pour un aéroport et ses voies d'accès où il était plus facile d'assurer la sécurité du public. Les pilotes apprécièrent d'emblée le nouveau circuit qui était relativement rapide.

1960 fut une année en or pour l'écurie Camoradi de Lucky Casner (CAsner MOtor RAcing DIvision). Stirling Moss, au volant d'une Camoradi de type 61 2,8 litres Birdcage Maserati, prit la pole position au départ style Le Mans de la principale épreuve de la semaine, le *Gran Premio de Cuba*. Il la conserva, laissant le plateau entier à un tour, hormis Pedro Rodriguez qui s'acharna à lui coller aux roues dans sa Ferrari Testa Rossa 3 litres.

Les pilotes américains de l'écurie Camoradi s'imposèrent également dans la catégorie 2 litres avec Masten Gregory (Porsche RSK) et dans la catégorie Grand Touring avec Jim Jeffords (Corvette Chevrolet). Dan Gurney et Carroll Shelby défendaient aussi les couleurs de Camoradi, mais les Birdcages qu'on leur avait promises n'étant pas arrivées, ils durent se contenter de véhicules de moindre puissance.

Trois pilotes qui avaient fait leurs preuves à Indianapolis – Rodger Ward, Jim Rathmann et Eddie Sachs – abandonnèrent les pistes ovales rapides pour se lancer dans la compétition automobile internationale.

Les héros de langue espagnole des années précédentes n'étaient plus de la partie cette année-là (Fangio avait pratiquement pris sa retraite et de Portago s'était tué aux Mille Miglia). Mais une jeune relève de Latino-Américains enthousiasmait d'ores et déjà le public, les favoris étant les frères Pedro et Ricardo Rodriguez.

Ricardo Rodriguez practices Le Mans starts in his Porsche 1600 RSK.

Ricardo Rodriguez übt mit seinem Porsche 1600 RSK den Le-Mans-Start.

Ricardo Rodriguez s'entraîne au départ style Le Mans sur sa Porsche 1600 RSK.

2

(1) Lloyd (Lucky) Casner (in cap), founder of the Camoradi USA race team, talks with Carroll Shelby, a Camoradi driver.
(2) The Camoradi garage. Team cars included Corvettes, Maseratis and Porsches.
(3) Race cars from around the world. The Ferrari 250 TR 59 in the foreground was driven to 2nd place by Pedro Rodriguez.

(1) Lloyd (Lucky) Casner (mit Schirmmütze), der Begründer des Camoradi-USA-Rennteams, diskutiert mit Carroll Shelby, einem Camoradi-Fahrer.
(2) Die Camoradi-Werkstatt. Zu den Teamfahrzeugen zählten Corvettes, Maseratis und Porsche.
(3) Rennwagen aus aller Welt. Mit dem Ferrari 250 TR 59 im Vordergrund erreichte Pedro Rodriguez den zweiten Platz.

(1) Lloyd (Lucky) Casner (en casquette), fondateur de l'écurie Camoradi USA, discute avec Carroll Shelby qui défend ses couleurs.
(2) Le garage de Camoradi. L'écurie comprend des Corvette, des Maserati et des Porsche.
(3) Des bolides venus du monde entier. Pedro Rodriguez se classera 2ème avec la Ferrari 250 TR 59 (au premier plan).

3

Arms were everywhere. A soldier perches on Jack
Brabham's Cooper Monaco, another rests in the
pits.

Das Militär war allgegenwärtig. Ein Soldat sitzt
auf Jack Brabhams Cooper Monaco, ein anderer
bleibt in den Boxen.

Les militaires montent la garde partout. Un soldat
armé s'est installé sur la Cooper Monaco de Jack
Brabham, un autre se repose dans un stand.

1

2

3

4

5

6

7

8

9

The Le Mans start:
(1-6) Stirling Moss in the Camoradi Birdcage Maserati, first away and never headed. Jack Brabham runs to his Cooper Monaco.
(7, 8) Joakim Bonnier, Porsche RSK (#35) retired with two laps to go; Ricardo Rodriguez, Porsche RSK (#39) ran 3rd before clutch trouble; Pedro Rodriguez, Ferrari 250 TR 59 (#10) finished 2nd, the only car not lapped by Moss; Huschke von Hanstein, Porsche RSK (#36) finished 4th; George Constantine, Cooper Monaco (#25) finished 9th.
(9) Brabham's Cooper Monaco still sits as Moss charges off.

Der Le-Mans-Start:
(1-6) Stirling Moss im Camoradi Birdcage Maserati ging von Start an in Führung. Jack Brabham rennt zu seinem Cooper Monaco.
(7, 8) Joakim Bonnier, Porsche RSK (Nr. 35), schied zwei Runden vor dem Ziel aus; Ricardo Rodriguez, Porsche RSK (Nr. 39), war Dritter, hatte dann aber Probleme mit der Kupplung; Pedro Rodriguez, Ferrari 250 TR 59 (Nr. 10), wurde als einziger nicht von Moss überrundeter Fahrer Zweiter; Huschke von Hanstein, Porsche RSK (Nr. 36), wurde Vierter und George Constantine, Cooper Monaco (Nr. 25), Neunter.
(9) Brabhams Cooper Monaco steht noch am Start, während Moss losrast.

Départ style Le Mans :
(1-6) Stirling Moss sur la Camoradi Birdcage Maserati, premier parti et jamais rattrapé. Jack Brabham court vers sa Cooper Monaco.
(7, 8) Joakim Bonnier, Porsche RSK (n° 35) abandonnera à deux tours de la fin ; Ricardo Rodriguez, Porsche RSK (n° 39) conservera une 3ème position jusqu'à des ennuis d'embrayage; Pedro Rodriguez, Ferrari 250 TR 59 (n° 10) se classera 2ème, le seul pilote que Moss n'a pas distancé d'un tour ; Huschke von Hanstein, Porsche RSK (n° 36) prendra la 4ème et George Constantine, Cooper Monaco (n° 25) la 9ème place.
(9) Moss attaque alors que la Cooper Monaco de Brabham est encore immobile.

(1) Jean-Louis Bonnet of France, Porsche 550 Spyder (12th).
(2) George Constantine, Cooper Monaco, diced with Maurice Trintignant's 3-liter Maserati much of the race, finished three spots behind him in 9th.

(1) Der Franzose Jean-Louis Bonnet im Porsche 550 Spyder (Zwölfter).
(2) George Constantine, Cooper Monaco, kämpfte während des Rennens lange gegen Maurice Trintignants 3-Liter-Maserati und kam drei Plätze hinter ihm als Neunter ins Ziel.

(1) Le Français Jean-Louis Bonnet sur une Porsche 550 Spyder (12ème).
(2) George Constantine, Cooper Monaco et Maurice Trintignant, Maserati 3 litres, se livreront un duel durant presque toute la course. Constantine finira 9ème, à trois places de Trintignant.

2

Rodger Ward, Dr. Lane/Camoradi Ferrari 250 TR (13th/13./13ème).

Maurice Trintignant, Maserati 300S (6th/Sechster/6ème).

Jim Jeffords, Camoradi Corvette (8th/Achter/8ème).

Masten Gregory's Porsche RSK, owned by Dr. David Lane and managed by Camoradi, is refueled. Carroll Shelby leans in. Masten got off to a slow Le Mans start having put his leg through the steering wheel.

Der Porsche RSK – Fahrer Masten Gregory, Besitzer Dr. David Lane, eingesetzt von Camoradi – wird aufgetankt. Carroll Shelby beugt sich in den Wagen. Masten hatte einen schwachen Le-Mans-Start, weil er mit einem Bein ins Lenkrad geraten war.

Carroll Shelby parle à Masten Gregory pendant qu'on ravitaille la Porsche RSK qui appartient au Dr David Lane et fait partie de l'écurie Camoradi. Masten retardera son départ style Le Mans en s'accrochant la jambe dans le volant.

Harry Schell, Maserati 200S.

Der Spanier/L'Espagnol/Francisco Godia of Spain, OSCA F2/S (11th/11./11ème).

1

2

(1) Pedro Rodriguez, Ferrari 250 TR 59, proved he had put his wild days behind him with his smooth drive to 2nd place.
(2) Dan Gurney, Maserati 200S, was to have had a new Birdcage but had to settle for an older, smaller car.

(1) Pedro Rodriguez, Ferrari 250 TR 59, fuhr souverän auf den zweiten Platz und bewies, daß er seine wilden Tage hinter sich gelassen hatte.
(2) Dan Gurney, Maserati 200S, hätte einen neuen Birdcage fahren sollen, mußte sich aber mit einem älteren und kleineren Wagen begnügen.

(1) Pedro Rodriguez, Ferrari 250 TR 59, prouve qu'il a assagi sa conduite avec une course sans à-coups qui le mènera à la 2ème place.
(2) Dan Gurney, Maserati 200S, aurait dû piloter une nouvelle Birdcage. Mais il devra se contenter d'une voiture plus ancienne et moins puissante.

Cuban driver F.G. Chaves, Jaguar XKSS.
Der kubanische Pilot F.G. Chaves, Jaguar XKSS.
Le pilote cubain F.G. Chaves, Jaguar XKSS.

Ada Pace, OSCA MT4 (14th/14./14ème).

Stirling Moss drove the Camoradi USA Birdcage Maserati impeccably to lap all cars but the Pedro Rodriguez Ferrari.

Stirling Moss überrundete mit seinem Camoradi USA Birdcage Maserati alle Fahrzeuge mit Ausnahme von Pedro Rodriguez' Ferrari.

Stirling Moss accomplit un parcours impeccable au volant d'une Camoradi USA Birdcage Maserati qui laisse toutes les voitures à un tour, sauf la Ferrari de Pedro Rodriguez.

Ada Pace of Italy drove her OSCA MT4 to 14th place without so much as breaking a finger nail. She also drove in the Formula Junior race.

Die Italienerin Ada Pace erreichte mit ihrem OSCA MT4 den 14. Platz, ohne sich dabei auch nur einen Fingernagel abzubrechen. Sie fuhr auch in der Formel Junior.

L'Italienne Ada Pace conduira son OSCA MT4 à la 14ème place sans même se casser un ongle. Elle s'alignera également dans l'épreuve Formule Junior.

Colin Davis of England, often an OSCA team
driver, here in a Cooper-Maserati (5th).

Colin Davis aus England, oft als OSCA-Werksfah-
rer aktiv, hier in einem Cooper-Maserati (Fünfter).

L'Anglais Colin Davis sur une Cooper-Maserati
(5ème). On le voit aussi fréquemment au volant
d'une OSCA.

(1) Stirling Moss has an armed escort through the crowd.
(2) Moss, the overwhelming victor in the First (and last) Cuban Grand Prix of Freedom, interviewed on radio.
(3) The Formula Junior race was a popular part of the week-long celebration of "Libertad."

(1) Stirling Moss mit Polizeieskorte im Publikum.
(2) Moss, überragender Sieger des ersten (und letzten) Cuban Grand Prix of Freedom, beim Radiointerview.
(3) Die Formel Junior war ein beliebter Bestandteil des einwöchigen »Libertad«-Festes.

(1) Stirling Moss fend la foule, entouré d'une escorte armée.
(2) Un journaliste de la radio interviewe Moss, le triomphateur du premier (et dernier) Grand Prix Cubain de la Liberté.
(3) L'épreuve Formule Junior était une des manifestations les plus populaires de la semaine qui consacrait la « Libertad ».

1

2

3

PUERTO RICO 1962

Another Caribbean Island adopting motor racing as a tourist attraction, reminiscent of Nassau Speed Weeks, was Puerto Rico, with a week of racing set for early November, 1962. The course was a scenic circuit of under two miles not far from San Juan and the organization – headed by American David Ash – was impeccable, but the field was sparse and the main race, the Grand Prix of Puerto Rico, proved to be a run-away-and-hide romp for the winner.

However, in retrospect the race acquires new interest because that winner was a 25-year-old named Roger Penske. By the time he had doubled his age his race cars were dominating the Indianapolis racing circuit.

Roger was already bent on overwhelming, not just beating, his competition. His race car, winning its third decisive international victory in a row, was a controversial Cooper Special with a seat in the center. A vestigial passenger seat, concealed by body work, hardly met the FIA requirements for a sports car but it did appear to satisfy the Sports Car Club of America. Roger had started with a former Formula I Cooper complete with rear-mounted 2.7-liter Climax engine. The result was handsome and fast and he drove it well. That, and the lack of competition, gave Penske a three-lap victory over a 12-car field, all of which were finishers. In second place was Corporal Tim Mayer in a Cooper Monaco. Auguring yet another common occurrence in decades to come, the also-ran was an ex-Penske car.

Many racing teams and name drivers which were expected did not come to Puerto Rico. Some blamed political uncertainty because of the Cuban missile crisis, but more directly affecting attendance was the recent death of Ricardo Rodriguez. The 20-year-old had been killed in practice for the Mexico Grand Prix. At least one team whose cars had already reached Puerto Rico withdrew because of that.

Mit der für Anfang November 1962 geplanten Rennwoche war Puerto Rico eine weitere Karibikinsel, die den Rennsport in Anlehnung an die Nassau Speed Weeks als Touristenattraktion einsetzte. Als Rennstrecke diente ein knapp drei Kilometer langer Berg- und Talkurs. Die Organisation unter der Leitung des Amerikaners David Ash war erstklassig, aber das Teilnehmerfeld so klein, daß sich der Sieg im Hauptrennen, dem Grand Prix von Puerto Rico, als Kinderspiel erwies.

Rückblickend ist das Rennen dennoch von einigem Interesse, denn der Sieger war ein damals 25jähriger Fahrer namens Roger Penske, dessen Wagen später, als er doppelt so alt war, das Oval von Indianapolis dominierten.

Schon damals war Roger entschlossen, seine Gegner nicht nur zu schlagen, sondern förmlich zu überrollen. Sein Wagen – mit dem er bereits den dritten entscheidenden internationalen Sieg in Reihe einfuhr – war ein umstrittener Cooper Special mit Mittelsitz. Der rudimentäre, unter dem Fahrzeugaufbau fast verschwindende Beifahrersitz entsprach kaum den Sportwagen-Vorschriften der FIA, aber dem Sports Car Club of America schien er zu genügen. Roger hatte einen ehemaligen Formel-1-Cooper mit 2,7-Liter-Climax-Mittelmotor umgebaut. Das Ergebnis war ein schöner, schneller Wagen, den er ausgezeichnet beherrschte. Mit diesem Auto und wenig Konkurrenz am Start siegte Penske mit drei Runden Vorsprung über ein Feld von zwölf Teilnehmern, die allesamt das Ziel erreichten. Corporal Tim Mayer belegte in einem Cooper Monaco den zweiten Platz. Daß der zweitplazierte Wagen zuvor Penske gehört hatte, war ein Omen für ein in späteren Jahrzehnten völlig normales Bild.

Viele der in Puerto Rico erwarteten Rennteams und namhaften Fahrer blieben aus. Manche machten hierfür die politische Instabilität aufgrund der kubanischen Raketenkrise verantwortlich, der akutere Grund für die mangelnde Teilnahme war aber wohl der tragische Tod des hochbegabten, erst 20jährigen Ricardo Rodriguez, der bei den Trainingsläufen für den Grand Prix von Mexiko verunglückt war. Zumindest ein Team, dessen Wagen bereits in Puerto Rico angekommen waren, sagte aus diesem Grund die Teilnahme ab.

Porto Rico, une autre île caraïbe, suivit l'exemple de Nassau et créa une nouvelle attraction touristique en instaurant une semaine de sport automobile qui eut lieu début novembre 1962. Le parcours était un beau circuit sinueux de quelque trois kilomètres près de San Juan et l'organisation gérée par l'Américain David Ash s'avéra impeccable. Cependant, en raison du maigre plateau, la course principale – le Grand Prix de Porto Rico – fut remportée au bout de ce qu'on pourrait qualifier de partie de cache-cache enfantine.

Néanmoins, considérée en rétrospective, cette course eut un aspect intéressant car le vainqueur en était un jeune pilote de 25 ans, nommé Roger Penske. Il avait à peine doublé son âge que ses voitures régnaient sur le circuit d'Indianapolis.

A cette époque déjà, Roger ne voulait pas seulement gagner, mais aussi établir sa supériorité. Sa voiture avec laquelle il remportait une troisième victoire internationale consécutive, était une Cooper Special dotée d'un siège central qui fit l'objet de nombreuses contestations. Le siège rudimentaire du coéquipier, dissimulé dans la carrosserie, ne répondait guère aux conditions requises de la FIA, mais le Sports Car Club of America semblait avoir moins d'exigences. Roger s'alignait donc sur une Cooper de Formule I équipée d'un moteur Climax de 2,7 litres monté à l'arrière. Le résultat était une belle voiture rapide qu'il maniait à la perfection. Cet avantage associé à la pénurie de concurrents lui valut une victoire, avec trois tours d'avance, sur un plateau de 12 voitures qui franchirent toutes la ligne d'arrivée. Le caporal Tim Mayer décrocha la deuxième place dans une Cooper Monaco. Sa voiture avait auparavant appartenu à Penske. C'était un présage annonciateur de ce qui allait devenir une situation courante dans les décennies à venir.

Des écuries de courses et des pilotes renommés étaient attendus à Porto Rico. Plusieurs retirèrent leur participation. Certains en virent la cause dans la situation politique incertaine due à la crise des missiles cubains. Or, la véritable raison fut sans doute la mort récente de Ricardo Rodriguez. Le pilote de 20 ans s'était tué durant les essais du Grand Prix du Mexique. Toujours est-il qu'une écurie dont les voitures étaient déjà arrivées à Porto Rico, invoqua cette raison pour se retirer de la compétition.

Corvettes had a race of their own, the Carrera Corvette.

Die Corvettes fuhren ihr eigenes Rennen, die Carrera Corvette.

Les Corvette ont leur propre course : la Carrera Corvette.

Dick Thompson drove the new Grady Davis Stingray to a one-lap victory in the Carrera Corvette and also won the Columbus Cup for Grand Touring cars.

Dick Thompson gewann in Grady Davis' neuem Stingray die Carrera Corvette mit einer Runde Vorsprung und triumphierte außerdem im Columbus Cup für GT-Fahrzeuge.

Dick Thompson conduira la nouvelle Grady Davis Stingray avec un tour d'avance dans l'épreuve Carrera Corvette et remportera également la Columbus Cup pour voitures Grand Tourisme.

The Candy Higuera Stingray in the lead.
Der Stingray von Candy Higuera in Führung.
La Candy Higuera Stingray est en tête.

The Don Yenko Corvette, 2nd in the Columbus Cup.
Die Corvette von Don Yenko wurde Zweite im Columbus Cup.
La Don Yenko Corvette, 2ème de la Columbus Cup.

George Rand with Dan Gurney (center) and Huschke von Hanstein of the Porsche team (right).

George Rand mit Dan Gurney (Mitte) und Huschke von Hanstein vom Porsche-Team (rechts).

George Rand avec Dan Gurney (au centre) et Huschke von Hanstein de l'équipe Porsche (à droite).

1

(1) The Heart Trophy for Formula Jrs. Peter Revson (#3, 3rd) and Corporal Tim Mayer (#1, 1st) both in Coopers.
(2) Honorary Starter, Juan Manuel Fangio, gives a thumbs up. Airline Pilot Hugh Dibley, Lola, drove much of the 45-minute race with a sheared bolt in his steering mechanism and did not finish.
(3) Fangio with the Chuck Dietrich Elva in the pits to cope with overheating.

(1) Die Heart Trophy der Formel Junior. Peter Revson (Nr. 3, Dritter) und Corporal Tim Mayer (Nr. 1, Erster) beide auf Coopers.
(2) Der ehrenamtliche Starter, Juan Manuel Fangio, gibt grünes Licht. Der Flugzeugpilot Hugh Dibley, Lola, fuhr den Großteil des 45minütigen Rennens mit einem abgescherten Bolzen in der Lenkung und kam doch nicht ins Ziel.
(3) Fangio mit Chuck Dietrich Elva wegen Motorüberhitzung an der Box.

(1) Le Heart Trophy pour Formule Junior. Peter Revson (n° 3, 3ème) and Corporal Tim Mayer (n° 1, 1er) sur des Coopers.
(2) Honneur suprême : Juan Manuel Fangio donne le départ. Le pilote d'avion Hugh Dibley, Lola, conduira durant presque toute la course de 45 minutes avec un boulon défectueux dans la direction de sa voiture et devra abandonner.
(3) Fangio avec Chuck Dietrich doit faire un arrêt au stand. Son Elva a surchauffé.

2

The Caguas Cup Race for smaller cars. Howard Hanna (4th) in front in his Deutsch-Bonnet, followed by a Morgan Plus 4 then a Lotus Elite between two Porsches.

Das Caguas-Cup-Rennen für kleinere Fahrzeuge. Howard Hanna (Vierter) führt mit seinem Deutsch-Bonnet, gefolgt von einem Morgan Plus 4 und einem Lotus Elite zwischen zwei Porsche.

La Caguas Cup est une course pour plus petites cylindrées. Howard Hanna (4ème) mène avec sa Deutsch-Bonnet, suivi d'une Morgan Plus 4 et d'une Lotus Elite entre deux Porsche.

(1) Herb Swan, Porsche RS-61 Spyder (#99), and Bob Hurt, Ferrari 250 TR 59 (#36), did not have enough tires for the abrasive course and drifted back to finish 9th and 11th.
(2) Ludwig Heimrath of Canada, Porsche RS-60 Spyder (5th).
(3) Jack Ryan, Porsche RSK Spyder, won a battle with the Luis Merino Elva to take 7th.

(1) Herb Swan, Porsche RS-61 Spyder (Nr. 99), und Bob Hurt, Ferrari 250 TR 59 (Nr. 36), hatten nicht genügend Reifen für die rauhe Strecke und fielen auf den neunten bzw. elften Platz zurück.
(2) Der Kanadier Ludwig Heimrath, Porsche RS-60 Spyder (Fünfter).
(3) Jack Ryans Porsche RSK Spyder gewann ein Duell mit Luis Merinos Elva um den siebten Platz.

(1) Herb Swan, Porsche RS-61 Spyder (n° 99) et Bob Hurt, Ferrari 250 TR 59 (n° 36). Leurs pneus ne tiendront pas le coup sur le parcours ; ils reculeront aux 9ème et 11ème places.
(2) Le Canadien Ludwig Heimrath, Porsche RS-60 Spyder (5ème).
(3) La Porsche RSK Spyder de Jack Ryan remportera le duel qui l'a opposée à l'Elva de Luis Merino et prendra la 7ème place.

1

2

3

Corporal Tim Mayer, stationed in Puerto Rico, made the first tire change in the ex-Penske Cooper Monaco. Then a 2nd stop for rear tires only, and an assist. He finished 2nd, 3 laps behind the Penske Zerex Special.

Der in Puerto Rico stationierte Corporal Tim Mayer beim ersten Reifenwechsel im Ex-Penske Cooper Monaco. Es folgte ein zweiter Boxenstopp zum Wechsel der Hinterreifen samt Starthilfe. Er wurde Zweiter, drei Runden hinter Penskes Zerex Special.

Le Caporal-Chef Tim Mayer, stationné à Porto Rico, fait un arrêt au stand pour changer les pneus de la Cooper Monaco qui a appartenu à Penske. Il s'arrêtera une seconde fois pour changer les pneus arrière et terminera 2ème, avec trois tours de retard sur la Penske Zerex Special.

Tires were everyone's concern. Rafi Rosales,
Elva Mark VI, stops at his pits and helps with
a tire change. He finished 8th.

Die Reifen wurden für alle zum Problem. Rafi
Rosales, Elva Mark VI, hilft beim Reifenwechsel
in der Box. Er wurde Achter.

L'usure des pneus est un problème général qui
conditionnera de nombreux arrêts aux stands.
Rafi Rosales met la main à la pâte pour changer les
pneus de son Elva Mark VI. Il terminera 8ème.

Bob Hurt, Ferrari 250 TR 59, was bothered by overheating and lack of spare wheels for the tire-hungry course. He finished next to last.

Bob Hurts Ferrari 250 TR 59 hatte Überhitzungs-probleme. Außerdem gab es nicht genügend Ersatzreifen für den reifenfressenden Kurs. Er wurde Vorletzter.

Bob Hurt n'aura que des ennuis : le moteur de sa Ferrari 250 TR 59 est surchauffé et il n'a pas assez de pneus de rechange. Il terminera avant-dernier.

(1) Dan Gurney in the factory 8-cyl 2-liter Porsche W-RS Spyder restrained his usual eye-of-the-tiger driving style to conserve tires. He finished 3rd, 1st in class.
(2) Porsche Team Manager von Hanstein keeps his stop watches on the restrained Gurney.

(1) Dan Gurney in einem Zweiliter-Achtzylinder-Werksporsche W-RS Spyder verzichtete auf seinen üblichen Kamikaze-Fahrstil, um die Reifen zu schonen. Er wurde Dritter und Klassenerster.
(2) Porsches Team-Manager von Hanstein stoppt die Zeit des äußerst beherrscht fahrenden Gurney.

(1) Dan Gurney au volant d'une Porsche W-RS Spyder deux litres d'usine. Il n'effectuera pas sa course folle habituelle pour ménager ses pneus et terminera 3ème et 1er du groupe.
(2) Von Hanstein, directeur de l'équipe Porsche, chronomètre les temps pour faire ralentir Gurney.

A 10-second stop for a look-see – don't get out,
they're OK!

Zehn-Sekunden-Stopp für einen Reifencheck –
bleib sitzen, sie sind OK!

Une vérification de 10 secondes au stand. Reste au
volant, tout est OK !

1

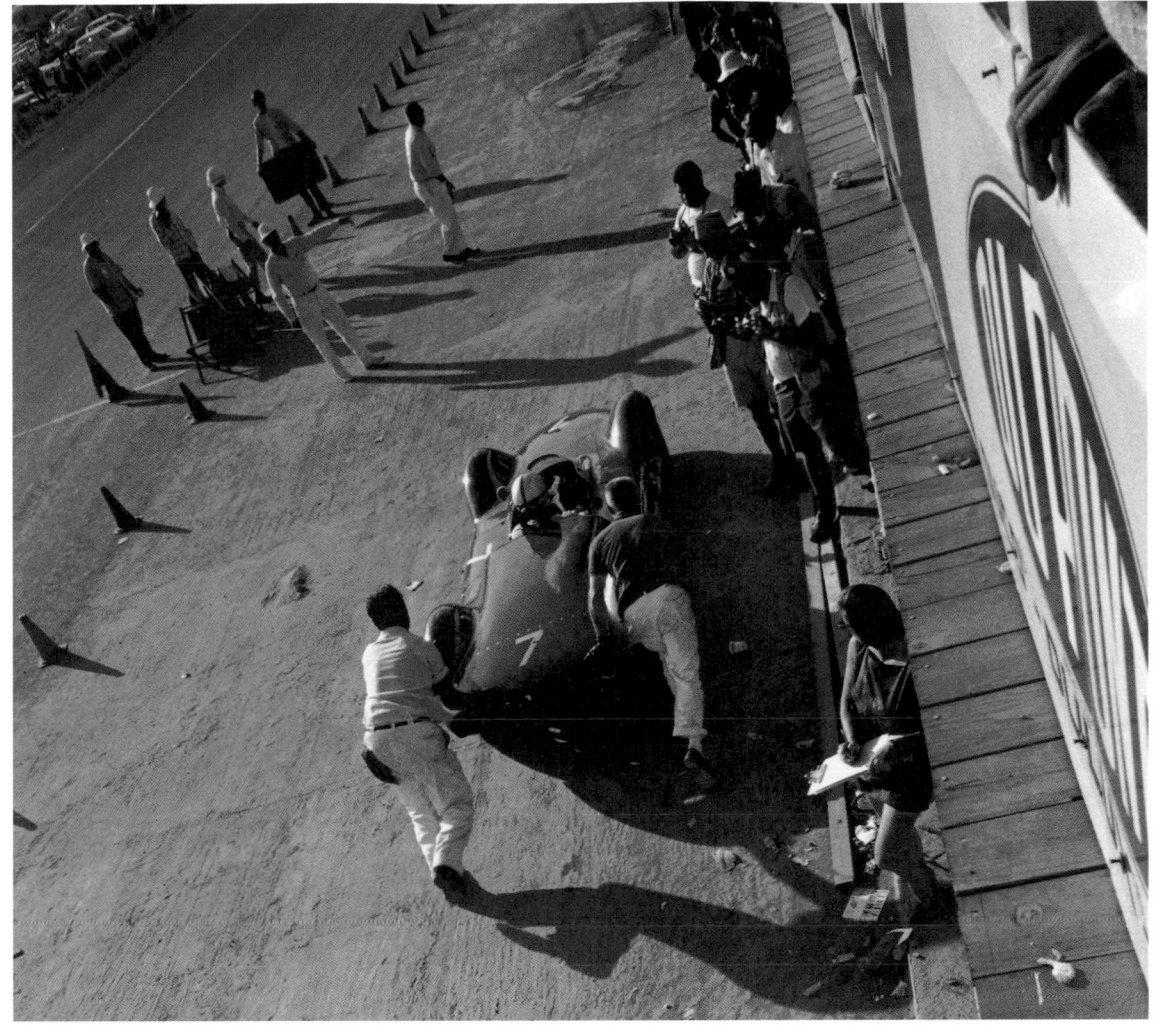

Helpful hands get the Zerex Special underway again.
Starthilfe für den Zerex Special.
La Zerex Special repart vers la victoire.

The winning Roger Penske effort. Designed by Penske, the controversial center-seated Cooper won 3 major races in a row. The FIA frowned on it, the SCCA approved. It was banned after this race.
(1) Chief mechanic Roy Gane suggests a tire check.
(2) Roger won by three laps.

Das Siegerfahrzeug von Roger Penske. Der von Penske entworfene, umstrittene Mittelsitz-Cooper gewann drei große Rennen hintereinander. Trotz der Zweifel der FIA akzeptierte der SCCA den Wagen, der nach diesem Rennen allerdings nicht mehr zugelassen wurde.
(1) Chefmechaniker Roy Gane rät zum Reifenwechsel.
(2) Roger gewann mit drei Runden Vorsprung.

Roger Penske veut la victoire. Il a conçu la Cooper dotée du fameux siège central, objet de nombreuses contestations, qui remportera trois victoires importantes consécutives. La FIA la réprouvait, mais la SCCA l'acceptait. Elle sera bannie des circuits après cette course.
(1) Le mécanicien-chef Roy Gane suggère un changement de pneus.
(2) Triomphe de Roger Penske ; il a achevé la course avec trois tours d'avance.

2

SEBRING

Sebring, a small town in central Florida, seemed an unlikely spot to attract the international motor racing world. But it did. Over time, its name joined that of Monte Carlo, Le Mans, Spa, the Nurburgring, as immediately recognizable. In 1950, however, it was a sleepy burg with, at its perimeter, a little–used airport lumbered with aging aircraft and dilapidated warehouses. Nonetheless, Alec Ulmann, an urbane European-born American, saw it as a place to stage an endurance race in the vein of Le Mans.

And thanks to the unstinting faith of Alec and the diligent labors of his wife, Mary, and an assortment of local visionaries, Sebring did become a spot on the international calendar.

From almost the beginning, the Twelve Hours of Sebring was a mix of the world's finest drivers from both the old world and the new along with a scattering of American weekend racers. Factory teams and family transport came together in a small southern town which swelled each March to accommodate this influx. For a short while the throb of racing engines occupied the garages of the town's car dealerships and noisy strangers thronged the square and filled the restaurants. And then, as if a plug had been pulled, all the hubbub quickly drained away and Sebring was again left to the retirees playing shuffleboard in the parks.

Oddly, nearly every race at Sebring was rumored to be the last one for any number of reasons: the aviation people were going to forbid use of the runways, an integral part of the circuit; the FIA was going to withdraw its sanction; an all–new course was going to be built elsewhere. Still, the race went on, surviving its own success (crowds grew larger and rowdier) and the increased use of the airport as an airport. The race was never moved.

Sebring, the race, in its fifth decade, is alive and well. And Sebring, the small town, is larger now, and more worldly. And quite used to the international racing world orbiting through its streets each March.

Sebring, ein kleiner Ort mitten in Florida, schien nicht unbedingt prädestiniert, das Interesse des internationalen Autorennsports zu erwecken. Aber genau das geschah. Sebring wurde im Laufe der Zeit ebenso populär wie Monte Carlo, Le Mans, Spa und der Nürburgring. Aber 1950 war es noch eine verschlafene Kleinstadt, an deren Rand sich ein wenig frequentierter Flugplatz mit rostenden Flugzeugen und verwahrlosten Lagerhäusern befand. Dennoch hielt Alec Ulmann, ein weltmännischer Amerikaner europäischer Abstammung, den Ort für geeignet zur Austragung eines Langstreckenrennens im Stil von Le Mans.

Und es ist seinem unbeirrbaren Glauben, dem unermüdlichen Einsatz seiner Frau Mary und der Visionskraft einiger Bürger von Sebring zu verdanken, daß der Ort heute seinen festen Platz im internationalen Rennsportgeschehen hat.

Fast von Anfang an war das Teilnehmerfeld des 12-Stunden-Rennens von Sebring eine Mischung aus den besten Piloten der Alten wie der Neuen Welt und einer kleinen Gruppe amerikanischer Wochenendrennfahrer. Werksteams und Familienunternehmen trafen sich so in einer kleinen Südstaaten Stadt, die jeden März über sich hinauswuchs, um den Publikumszustrom unterzubringen. Für eine kurze Zeit erfüllte das Dröhnen der Rennmotoren die Werkstätten der ortsansässigen Autohändler, lärmende Fremde bevölkerten den Marktplatz. Und dann, als hätte man einen Stecker herausgezogen, war der Tumult plötzlich vorbei, und Sebring gehörte wieder den Rentnern, die in den Parkanlagen Shuffleboard spielten.

Seltsam war, daß beinahe jedem Rennen in Sebring das Gerücht vorausging, es werde – aus immer neuen Gründen – das letzte sein: die Flugplatzverwaltung wolle die Nutzung der Rollbahnen, die integraler Teil der Rennstrecke waren, untersagen; die FIA wolle das Rennen nicht mehr sanktionieren, man werde anderswo einen völlig neuen Kurs bauen. Aber das Rennen ging weiter, überlebte den eigenen Erfolg und die zunehmende Nutzung des Flugplatzes für seinen eigentlichen Bestimmungszweck. Das Rennen wurde nie verlegt.

Nach fünf Jahrzehnten ist das Rennen von Sebring unverändert erfolgreich, und auch die Kleinstadt Sebring ist gewachsen, weniger provinziell geworden, längst daran gewöhnt, daß jedes Jahr im März die Größen der internationalen Rennszene ihre Straßen bevölkern.

Sebring, une petite ville du centre de la Floride, ne semblait vraiment pas prédestinée à devenir un fief du sport automobile international. Or, c'est précisément ce qui arriva. Au fil du temps, le nom de Sebring allait devenir aussi populaire que ceux de Monte Carlo, du Mans, de Spa et du Nurburgring. Mais Sebring était encore une petite localité endormie en 1950. A sa périphérie, il y avait un aérodrome à peine utilisé, où sommeillaient des machines rouillées et des hangars en ruines. Cela n'empêcha pas Alec Ulmann de trouver que l'endroit serait idéal pour y organiser des courses d'endurance comme celle du Mans.

C'est ainsi que Sebring s'inscrivit dans le calendrier international du sport automobile grâce à la foi inébranlable d'Alec, à l'énorme travail de sa femme Mary ainsi qu'au soutien d'un certain nombre de visionnaires locaux.

Dès les débuts, le plateau des Douze Heures de Sebring rassembla les meilleurs pilotes du nouveau et de l'ancien monde ainsi que quelques coureurs amateurs américains. Chaque mars, écuries d'usine, équipes familiales et un nombreux public se retrouvaient dans une petite ville du Sud qui ouvraient les bras pour les accueillir. Les vrombissements de moteurs emplissaient les garages locaux et une foule bruyante envahissait le square municipal. Puis, comme si on avait coupé le contact, tout ce tohubohu mourait soudain et Sebring redevenait le fief des retraités qui retrouvaient leurs jeux de palets dans les parcs.

Bizarrement, presque toutes les courses de Sebring étaient précédées de rumeurs annonçant que celle-ci serait la dernière. On racontait que les responsables de l'aérodrome avaient décidé d'interdire l'usage des pistes qui constituaient une partie du circuit, que la FIA voulait retirer son autorisation ou qu'on allait construire un véritable circuit ailleurs. Or, la course a toujours eu lieu régulièrement et n'a jamais été déplacée. Elle a résisté jusqu'à nos jours bien que sa popularité amène des foules toujours plus nombreuses et plus tapageuses et que l'aéroport serve de plus en plus dans sa fonction première.

Les Douze Heures de Sebring abordent leur cinquième décennie avec vigueur et vitalité. Sebring, la petite ville, s'est agrandie et a pris un petit air cosmopolite. Elle trouve aujourd'hui tout à fait normal de voir les champions du sport automobile foncer dans ses rues tous les mois de mars.

Ricardo Rodriguez, NART Ferrari Dino 196 S, Sebring 1960.

SEBRING 1955

Many years after the race ended, the subject came up between Carroll Shelby and Mike Hawthorn, meeting at some European venue. "Who *did* win that race, Mike? " Carroll asked. Mike shook his head.

Throughout the entire 12 hours the Ferrari of Phil Hill and Carroll Shelby had battled with the D-type of Phil Walters and Mike Hawthorn. Toward the end, the track announcer was saying that the Ferrari was in the lead and when the flag dropped it was declared the winner. But that was quickly changed: The Jaguar had won, and Briggs Cunningham, as owner, accepted the trophy – his third in as many years.

It took an official protest and a careful lap by lap recapitulation of the scoring to demonstrate that the Jaguar was indeed 25.4 seconds ahead of the Ferrari. Yes, the Jaguar had won. No matter, everyone agreed that it was a singularly exciting race.

Als Carroll Shelby und Mike Hawthorn sich viele Jahre nach diesem Rennen irgendwo in Europa trafen und auf das Thema kamen, fragte Carroll: »Wer hat das Rennen nun tatsächlich gewonnen, Mike?« Mike schüttelte nur den Kopf.

Während der gesamten zwölf Sunden hatten Phil Hill und Carroll Shelby mit ihrem Ferrari gegen den Jaguar D–Type von Phil Walters und Mike Hawthorn angekämpft. Kurz vor dem Finale verkündete der Streckensprecher, daß der Ferrari in Führung liege. Und als die Zielflagge fiel, wurde er zum Sieger gekürt – eine Entscheidung, die jedoch schnell revidiert wurde: Der Jaguar hatte gewonnen, und Briggs Cunningham nahm als Besitzer die Trophäe entgegen – seine dritte im dritten Jahr.

Erst nach einem offiziellen Protest und einer sorgfältigen Rekapitulation der einzelnen Runden wurde nachgewiesen, daß der Jaguar tatsächlich 25,4 Sekunden vor dem Ferrari durchs Ziel gegangen war. Der Jaguar hatte eindeutig gewonnen. Wie dem auch sei, alle waren sich einig, ein einzigartig spannendes Rennen gesehen zu haben.

Des années plus tard, Carroll Shelby et Mike Hawthorn reparlèrent de la course au cours d'une rencontre sur un circuit européen. A la question de Carroll: « Qui a vraiment gagné cette course, Mike ? », Mike Hawthorn secoua seulement la tête.

La Ferrari de Phil Hill et Carroll Shelby et la Jaguar Type D de Phil Walters et Mike Hawthorn s'étaient battues roues contre roues durant toutes les douze heures de la course. Juste avant la finale, le commissaire responsable des temps annonça que la Ferrari était en tête et elle fut déclarée vainqueur quand le drapeau d'arrivée s'abaissa. Mais ce résultat fut vite annulé. C'était la Jaguar qui avait gagné et Briggs Cunningham, son propriétaire, reçut le trophée, le troisième en trois ans.

Une protestation officielle fut déposée et une récapitulation minutieuse de la course, tour par tour, prouva que la Jaguar avait effectivement 25,4 secondes d'avance sur la Ferrari. La Jaguar avait incontestablement gagné. Quoi qu'il en soit, tout le monde était d'accord sur un point : on avait rarement vu une course aussi exaltante.

Austin-Healey 100S (Stirling Moss/Lance Macklin).

1

2

4

3

5

6

(1) Harry Schell, Ferrari 750 Monza (5th with Piero Taruffi).
(2) The Amoco pedestrian bridge at the start/finish.
(3) Sterling Edwards/Chuck Daigh, Ferrari 750 Monza.
(4) Candy Poole/Bob Davis, Porsche 550 Spyder (11th) and the clock-man.
(5) Through the hairpin and how they finished. Indianapolis 500 driver Sam Hanks, Kurtis Kraft Buick engine (19th); Sherwood Johnston/Bill Spear, Maserati 300S (3rd); Stirling Moss/Lance Macklin, Austin-Healey 100S (6th); Ernie Erickson/ John Panks, Arnolt-Bristol (18th).
(6) Huschke von Hanstein/Herbert Linge, Porsche 550 Spyder (8th).

(1) Harry Schell, Ferrari 750 Monza (Fünfter mit Piero Taruffi).
(2) Die Amoco-Fußgängerbrücke an Start und Ziel.
(3) Sterling Edwards/Chuck Daigh, Ferrari 750 Monza.
(4) Candy Poole/Bob Davis, Porsche 550 Spyder (11.) und der Zeitnehmer.
(5) Durch die Haarnadelkurve zum Ziel. Indy-500-Fahrer Sam Hanks, Kurtis Kraft mit Buick-Motor (19.); Sherwood Johnston/Bill Spear, Maserati 300S (Dritte); Stirling Moss/Lance Macklin, Austin-Healey 100S (Sechste); Ernie Erickson/John Panks, Arnolt-Bristol (18.).
(6) Huschke von Hanstein/Herbert Linge, Porsche 550 Spyder (Achte).

(1) Harry Schell, Ferrari 750 Monza (5ème avec Piero Taruffi).
(2) La passerelle Amoco sur la ligne de départ.
(3) Sterling Edwards/Chuck Daigh, Ferrari 750 Monza.
(4) Candy Poole/Bob Davis, Porsche 550 Spyder (11èmes) et le signaleur à la pendule.
(5) Passage de l'épingle et leur classement final : Le pilote des 500 miles d'Indianapolis Sam Hanks, Kurtis Kraft à moteur Buick (19ème) ; Sherwood Johnston/Bill Spear, Maserati 300S (3èmes) ; Stirling Moss/Lance Macklin, Austin-Healey 100S (6èmes) ; Ernie Erickson/John Panks, Arnolt-Bristol (18èmes).
(6) Huschke von Hanstein/Herbert Linge, Porsche 550 Spyder (8èmes).

(1) Russ Boss/Jake Kaplan, C-type Jaguar (12th).
(2) Former French Champion and New York restaurateur René Dreyfus shared this Arnolt-Bristol with Bob Grier (29th).

(1) Russ Boss/Jake Kaplan, Jaguar C-Type (12.).
(2) Der ehemalige französische Champion und New Yorker Gastwirt René Dreyfus teilte sich diesen Arnolt-Bristol mit Bob Grier (29.).

(1) Russ Boss/Jake Kaplan, Jaguar type C (12èmes).
(2) L'ancien grand champion français, René Dreyfus, devenu restaurateur à New York, partageait cette Arnolt-Bristol avec Bob Grier (29èmes).

1

2

(3) Phil Walters, D-type Jaguar (winner with Mike Hawthorn).
(4) Bill Lloyd, OSCA MT4 (7th, 1st in class with George Huntoon).

(3) Phil Walters, Jaguar D-Type (Sieger mit Mike Hawthorn).
(4) Bill Lloyd, OSCA MT4 (Siebter, Klassensieger mit George Huntoon).

(3) Phil Walters, Jaguar type D (vainqueur avec Mike Hawthorn).
(4) Bill Lloyd, OSCA MT4 (7ème, 1er de sa catégorie avec George Huntoon).

3

4

Stirling Moss, Austin-Healey 100S (6th) breathes down the tailpipe on the William Brewster/ Charles Rutan Austin-Healey 100S (15th).

Stirling Moss, Austin-Healey 100S (Sechster) schnüffelt am Auspuff des Austin-Healey 100S von William Brewster/Charles Rutan (15.).

Stirling Moss, Austin-Healey 100S (6ème) dans les roues de William Brewster/Charles Rutan, Austin-Healey 100S (15èmes).

Tom Friedman/Karl Brocken, 2-liter Maserati A6GCS.

The Gus Ehrman/Fred Allen Austin-Healey 100S spins off the road.

Der Austin-Healey 100S von Gus Ehrman/Fred Allen schleudert von der Strecke.

Tête-à-queue de l'Austin-Healey 100S de Gus Ehrman/Fred Allen.

1

3

2

(2, 3) Carroll Shelby, Ferrari 750 Monza, registers surprise when told he and Phil Hill had won, with good reason. (A recount placed them 2nd, 1st in Index of Performance). Confusion is reflected in the pit sign Phil is holding up.

(2, 3) Carroll Shelby, Ferrari 750 Monza, wirkt überrascht, als er erfährt, daß er und Phil Hill gewonnen haben - mit gutem Grund. (Eine Überprüfung ergab für sie den zweiten Platz im Gesamtklassement und einen Sieg in der »Index of Performance«-Wertung). Die Verwirrung zeigt sich auch auf dem Boxenschild, das Phil hochhält.

(2, 3) Carroll Shelby, Ferrari 750 Monza, s'étonne, à juste titre lorsqu'on lui dit que Phil Hill et lui on gagné. (Une vérification les placera seconds, lers à l'Indice de Performance). La confusion se reflète dans le panneau de signalisation que tient Phil.

(1, 4) Phil Walters makes a late pit stop in the winning D-type Jaguar. Walters, who raced midgets as "Ted Tappet," was one of the best drivers the US produced. He lost his taste for racing after witnessing the 1955 Le Mans disaster.

(1, 4) Phil Walters bei einem späten Boxenstopp mit dem siegreichen Jaguar D-Type. Walters, der als »Ted Tappet« auch »Midget cars« fuhr, war einer der besten Fahrer der USA. Nachdem er 1955 Zeuge der Le-Mans-Katastrophe geworden war, verlor er das Interesse am Rennsport.

(1, 4) Phil Walters procède à un ultime ravitaillement avec la Jaguar type D victorieuse. Walters, qui avait couru en Midgets sous le pseudonyme de « Ted Tappet », fut l'un des meilleurs pilotes américains. Il perdit son goût pour la course automobile après avoir assisté au désastre du Mans en 1955.

4

SEBRING 1957

Sebring as a race marked several rites of passage with the 1957 12-Hours, the sixth in its history: the largest crowd yet (39 000 people); the first two-in-a-row winning driver in Juan Manuel Fangio (he shared the new 4.5 Maserati with Jean Behra); and the first fatality (Bob Goldich died when his Arnolt-Bristol crashed in the esses).

An eye-catching debut was made by the Corvette SS, designed by Zora Arkus-Duntov. John Fitch, one of the few Americans with an international reputation as a driver, shared the car with Piero Taruffi of Italy. Sleek, silver, toothy and with a large bullet shape for a headrest, the Corvette SS drew lots of attention, particularly when Fangio took the practice car out for a test spin and lapped within three seconds of his best time in the 450S Maserati.

Alas, in the race the Corvette SS called at the pits often and was retired after 23 laps.

Beim 12-Stunden-Rennen von 1957, dem sechsten in der Geschichte von Sebring, gab es eine Reihe von Premieren: die bisher höchste Zuschauerzahl von 39 000 Menschen; den ersten Wiederholungssieg, den Juan Manuel Fangio einfuhr (er teilte sich mit Jean Behra den neuen 4,5-Liter-Maserati); und den ersten Todesfall (Bob Goldich starb bei einem Unfall in seinem Arnolt-Bristol in der S-Kurve).

Die von Zora Arkus-Duntov entworfene Corvette SS hatte ihr spektakuläres Debüt. John Fitch, einer der wenigen international renommierten US-Fahrer, teilte sich den Wagen mit dem Italiener Piero Taruffi. Die schnittige, silberfarbene Corvette SS erregte mit ihrem aggressiven Kühlergrill und der großen, halbrunden Kopfstütze viel Aufmerksamkeit, vor allem, nachdem Fangio mit dem Trainingsfahrzeug bei einigen Testrunden nur drei Sekunden unter seinem eigenen, mit dem Maserati 450S aufgestellten Rundenrekord blieb.

Im Rennen mußte die Corvette SS alllerdings häufig an die Box und schied nach 23 Runden aus.

La course de 1957, la sixième dans l'histoire des Douze Heures de Sebring, se distingue par trois nouveaux événements marquants : un chiffre record de 39 000 spectateurs, une victoire consécutive au compte de Juan Manuel Fangio (il partageait la nouvelle Maserati 4,5 litres avec Jean Behra) et le premier accident mortel (Bob Goldich se tua quand sa Arnolt-Bristol dérapa dans le S).

La Corvette SS, conçue par Zora Arkus-Duntov, fit un début spectaculaire. Au volant: John Fitch, un des rares pilotes américains de réputation internationale, et l'Italien Piero Taruffi. Longue, argentée, aux dents de requins et munie d'un large repose-tête arrondi, la corvette SS attira notamment tous les regards lorsque Fangio prit le volant pour un tour d'essai qu'il acheva avec seulement trois secondes d'écart sur son meilleur temps réalisé au volant de la Maserati 450S.

Hélas, la Corvette SS dut faire plusieurs arrêts au stand et abandonna la course après 23 tours.

Gene Greenspun pushes his Ferrari 250 GT through the pits, to no avail. Sharing with Olivier Gendebien they lasted 111 laps.

Gene Greenspun schiebt seinen Ferrari 250 GT durch die Boxengasse, allerdings vergeblich. Er und Olivier Gendebien überstanden nur 111 Runden.

Gene Greenspun pousse sa Ferrari 250 GT devant les stands, mais en vain. Partagée avec Olivier Gendebien, elle ne tiendra que 111 tours.

De Portago in the garage: informed by Team manager Romolo Tavoni he will not be driving the car of his choice; a game of Backgammon on the floor; conferring with Peter Collins; and painting his car.

De Portago in der Werkstatt. Er erfährt von Team-Manager Romolo Tavoni, daß er den gewünschten Wagen nicht fahren kann, spielt auf dem Boden Backgammon, berät sich mit Peter Collins, und lackiert sein Fahrzeug.

De Portago, dans le garage, est informé par le Directeur Sportif Romolo Tavoni qu'il ne pîlotera pas la voiture qu'il souhaitait, un jeu de Backgammon sur le sol, conciliabule avec Peter Collins ; il peint sa voiture.

(1) Ferraris unload at the Pontiac garage.
(2) Kids peer through the window at Phil Hill checking his Ferrari 290 MM with Team Manager Romolo Tavoni (in suit).
(3) Olivier Gendebien, Peter Collins and a delighted de Portago (before his talk with Tavoni).
(4) The Corvette SS makes its debut. Checking the driver's side is GM engineer Frank Burrell.

1

2

3

(1) Ferraris werden an der Pontiac-Werkstatt abgeladen.
(2) Kinder beobachten durch das Fenster, wie Phil Hill zusammen mit Team-Manager Romolo Tavoni (im Anzug) seinen Ferrari 290 MM durchcheckt.
(3) Olivier Gendebien, Peter Collins und ein vergnügter de Portago (vor seinem Gespräch mit Tavoni!).
(4) Das Debüt der Corvette SS. GM-Ingenieur Frank Burrell kontrolliert die Fahrerseite.

(1) On décharge les Ferrari au garage Pontiac.
(2) Des gamins épient par la fenêtre Phil Hill qui vérifie sa Ferrari 290 MM avec le Directeur Sportif Romolo Tavoni (en complet).
(3) Olivier Gendebien, Peter Collins et un de Portago ravi (avant sa conversation avec Tavoni).
(4) La Corvette SS fait ses débuts. Vérifiant du côté du conducteur on voit l'ingénieur Frank Burrell de la GM.

4

1

3

2

(1) De Portago in the less-than-pristine cockpit of the Ferrari 315 S he shared with Luigi Musso.
(2) Pre-race preparations, top to bottom: Cooper-Climax (#58); Maserati 200S (#27); Maserati 150S (#46); Maserati 300S (#22).
(3) Zora Arkus-Duntov (in stripes), father of the Corvette SS, listens as Stirling Moss, who took a practice run in the prototype, yells over the engine noise.

(1) De Portago im nicht mehr ganz tadellosen Cockpit des Ferrari 315 S, den er sich mit Luigi Musso teilte.
(2) Rennvorbereitungen, von oben nach unten: Cooper- Climax (Nr. 58), Maserati 200S (Nr. 27), Maserati 150S (Nr. 46), Maserati 300S (Nr. 22).
(3) Zora Arkus-Duntov (im gestreiften Hemd), Vater der Corvette SS, hört über den Motorenlärm hinweg Stirling Moss zu, der im Prototyp eine Trainingsrunde absolviert hat.

(1) De Portago dans le cockpit plus très impeccable de la Ferrari 315 S qu'il partageait avec Luigi Musso.
(2) Préparation pour la course, de haut en bas : Cooper-Climax (n° 58); Maserati 200S (n° 27), Maserati 150S (n° 46); Maserati 300S (n° 22).
(3) Zora Arkus-Duntov (chemise à rayures), le père de la Corvette SS, écoute Stirling Moss qui vient de faire un tour d'essai avec le prototype, et crie pour couvrir le bruit du moteur.

Masten Gregory, Ferrari 290 MM (4th with/Vierter mit/4ème avec Lou Brero).

2

(1) Juan Manuel Fangio, Maserati 450S (winner with Jean Behra).
(2) Gaston Andrey, Corvette (12th overall, 1st in class with Dick Thompson).
(3) Jack McAfee, Porsche 550 Spyder (165 laps with Hans Herrmann but DNF).

(1) Juan Manuel Fangio, Maserati 450S (Sieger mit Jean Behra).
(2) Gaston Andrey, Corvette (Zwölfter im Gesamtklassement, Klassensieger mit Dick Thompson).
(3) Jack McAfee, Porsche 550 Spyder (165 Runden mit Hans Herrmann, aber letztlich nicht im Ziel).

(1) Juan Manuel Fangio, Maserati 450S (vainqueur avec Jean Behra).
(2) Gaston Andrey, Corvette (12ème au général, 1er de catégorie avec Dick Thompson).
(3) Jack McAfee, Porsche 550 Spyder (165 tours avec Hans Herrmann, mais abandon).

3

1

(1) Phil Hill, Ferrari 290 MM, went out after 6 hours with engine failure.
(2) Evelyn Mull, one of the country's best women drivers, in the AC Bristol she shared with her husband, John (146 laps but DNF).
(3) Joe Sheppard, Lotus Eleven, shared with Colin Chapman and D. Dungan (11th overall, 1st in class).
(4) Stirling Moss, Maserati 300S (2nd overall, 1st in class with Harry Schell).

(1) Phil Hill, Ferrari 290 MM, fiel nach sechs Stunden mit Motorschaden aus.
(2) Evelyn Mull, eine der besten Fahrerinnen des Landes, im AC Bristol, den sie sich mit ihrem Ehemann John teilte (146 Runden, aber nicht im Ziel).
(3) Joe Sheppard teilte sich den Lotus 11 mit Colin Chapman und D. Dungan (11. im Gesamtklassement, Klassensieger).
(4) Stirling Moss, Maserati 300S (Zweiter im Gesamtklassement, Klassensieger mit Harry Schell).

(1) Phil Hill, Ferrari 290 MM, abandonna en panne de moteur après 6 heures.
(2) Evelyn Mull, l'une des meilleures conductrices américaines, dans l'AC Bristol qu'elle partageait avec son mari John (146 tours et abandon).
(3) Joe Sheppard, dans la Lotus 11 qu'il partageait avec Colin Chapman et D. Dungan (11ème au général et 1er de catégorie).
(4) Stirling Moss, Maserati 300S (2ème au général, 1er de catégorie avec Harry Schell).

2

3

1

4

(1) The pit sign has the final order.
(2) Taffy von Trips and Jo Bonnier compare their DNFs.
(3) Luigi Musso and a friend silhouetted by the pit lights.
(4) De Portago and Tavoni share an anxious moment in the Ferrari pits.
(5) Victorious Fangio and Behra, Maserati mechanic Bertocchi.

(1) Die Boxentafel mit der Reihenfolge des Zieleinlaufs.
(2) Taffy von Trips und Jo Bonnier tauschen ihre Erlebnisse aus.
(3) Die Silhouetten von Luigi Musso und einer Freundin im Gegenlicht der Boxenbeleuchtung.
(4) De Portago und Tavoni erleben gemeinsam ängstliche Minuten in der Ferrari-Box.
(5) Die Sieger Fangio und Behra mit dem Maserati-Mechaniker Bertocchi.

(1) La signalisation du stand annonce le classement définitif.
(2) Taffy von Trips et Jo Bonnier comparent leurs abandons respectifs.
(3) La silhouette de Luigi Musso et d'une amie se découpent dans la lumière des stands.
(4) Un moment angoissant partagé par de Portago et Tavoni dans le stand Ferrari.
(5) Fangio et Behra victorieux avec le chef mécanicien de Maserati Bertocchi.

SEBRING 1958

The Martini & Rossi vehicle bridge, which was to frame many a Sebring sunset, was new in 1958. So was the MG footbridge over the esses. And the crowd was up to 45,000 souls. Ferrari was back in full force, but Maserati – first and second the year before – had all but disappeared from the racing scene after the debacle at Venezuela the previous fall. Two private entries, neither of which lasted half the race, constituted the entire Maserati presence.

New, also, was the 3-liter limit for the FIA sports car championship. That played well in the Ferrari camp with several 250 Testa Rossas taking the start. The TR of Phil Hill and Peter Collins finished a lap ahead of that of Luigi Musso and Olivier Gendebien.

A Porsche RS (Harry Schell/Wolfgang Seidel) was third. Three Lotus Elevens, one driven by Colin Chapman himself, placed in the top ten.

Im Jahre 1958 war die Martini & Rossi-Autobrücke, die seither viele Sonnenuntergänge in Sebring eingerahmt hat, ebenso neu wie die MG-Fußgängerüberführung über die S-Kurve. Insgesamt 45 000 Zuschauer sahen das Rennen. Ferrari war wieder voll da, aber Maserati – Sieger und Zweitplazierter des Vorjahres – hatte sich nach dem Venezuela-Debakel im Herbst nahezu vollständig aus dem Renngeschehen zurückgezogen. Die Marke war lediglich durch zwei Privatfahrer vertreten, die beide vor dem Ende der ersten Rennhälfte ausschieden.

Neu war auch die Hubraumbegrenzung auf drei Liter für die FIA-Sportwagenmeisterschaft. Gute Nachrichten für Ferrari, die mit mehreren 250er Testa Rossa an den Start gingen. Der TR von Phil Hill und Peter Collins siegte mit einer Runde Vorsprung vor dem von Luigi Musso und Olivier Gendebien.

Den dritten Platz belegte ein Porsche RS (Harry Schell/Wolfgang Seidel). Unter den ersten zehn Fahrzeugen waren drei Lotus 11, einer von Colin Chapman selbst pilotiert.

Le pont Martini & Rossi qui allait encadrer plus d'un coucher de soleil sur Sebring et la passerelle MG au-dessus du S venaient juste d'être construits en 1958. 45 000 personnes assistaient à la course. Ferrari était de retour en force, mais les Maserati – qui s'étaient classées première et seconde l'année précédente – avaient pratiquement disparu du cirque automobile depuis la débâcle en automne au Venezuela. Seules, deux Maserati privées participaient au départ. Toutes les deux abandonnèrent avant la moitié de la course.

Une autre nouveauté : les cylindrées étaient désormais limitées à trois litres pour les championnats de la FIA. Cela avantageait grandement l'équipe Ferrari qui alignait plusieurs Testa Rossa 250 sur la grille de départ. La TR de Phil Hill/Peter Collins termina avec un tour d'avance sur celle de Luigi Musso/Olivier Gendebien.

Une Porsche RS (Harry Schell/Wolfgang Seidel) enleva la troisième place. Trois Lotus 11, dont une pilotée par Colin Chapman lui-même, se placèrent dans les dix premiers.

Peter Collins, Ferrari 250 TR (winner with Phil Hill/Sieger mit Phil Hill/victorieux avec Phil Hill).

1

2

3

(1) The winning cars: Ferrari 250 TRs.
(2, 3) The gear.
(4) Mary Ulmann's striped tent for club members and drivers. Harry Schell seated at the entry. Porfirio Rubirosa in hat standing by the umbrella.
(5) Three Ferrari mechanics.
(6) Caps are in. Wearing them: John Fitch, Harry Schell, Phil Hill. Hatless in rear: Dave Allen with back to camera, Jim Kimberly in jacket. At right: Luigi Chinetti talking to the hatted Ed Hugus.

(1) Die Siegerfahrzeuge: Ferrari 250 TR.
(2, 3) Fahrerutensilien.
(4) Mary Ulmanns gestreiftes Zelt für Clubmitglieder und Fahrer. Harry Schell sitzt am Eingang. Porfirio Rubirosa (mit Hut) steht am Sonnenschirm.
(5) Drei Ferrari-Mechaniker.
(6) Schirmmützen sind in. Gut behütet: John Fitch, Harry Schell, Phil Hill. Im Hintergrund ohne Kopfbedeckung: Dave Allen (mit dem Rücken zur Kamera) und Jim Kimberly (mit Jacke). Rechts: Luigi Chinetti spricht mit Ed Hugus (mit Hut).

(1) La voiture victorieuse : Ferrari 250 TR.
(2, 3) Le matériel.
(4) La tente à rayures de Mary Ulman réservée aux membres du club et aux pilotes. Harry Schell est assis à l'entrée. Porfirio Rubirosa avec un chapeau est debout près d'un parasol.
(5) Trois mécaniciens de Ferrari.
(6) Les casquettes sont à la mode : John Fitch, Harry Schell et Phil Hill en portent. Dave Allen – sans chapeau – tourne le dos à la caméra. Jim Kimberly porte un veste. A droite, Luigi Chinetti parle avec Ed Hugus, qui a un chapeau.

4

5

6

(1) Ferrari mechanics (Marchetti holding jack handle) work furiously on the Musso/Gendebien 250 TR, technical director Mimo Amarotti behind them.
(2) Technical Inspection. Ed Hugus pushes the John Fitch/E.D. Martin Ferrari 250 TR; under tent, the Norman Scott/Frank Bott Porsche 550 Spyder.
(3) Fiat-Abarth Zagato (Denise McCluggage/Ruth Levy) draws banter from Phil Hill (in cap), George Tilp and Skip Hudson.
(4) Boris "Bob" Said spins the wheels of Ferrari 500 TRC stuck in a muddy paddock.

(1) Ferrari-Mechaniker (Marchetti hält einen »jack handle«) arbeiten wild entschlossen am 250 TR von Musso/Gendebien. Hinter ihnen steht der technische Direktor Mimo Amarotti.
(2) Technische Abnahme. Ed Hugus schiebt den Ferrari 250 TR von John Fitch und E.D. Martin. Im Zelt: der Porsche 550 Spyder von Norman Scott und Frank Bott.
(3) Phil Hill (mit Mütze), George Tilp und Skip Hudson scherzen über den Abarth Zagato von Denise McCluggage und Ruth Levy.
(4) Boris »Bob« Saids Ferrari 500 TRC steckt mit durchdrehenden Rädern im Schlamm fest.

(1) Les mécaniciens (Marchetti tient un levier) travaillent furieusement sur la Ferrari 250 TR de Musso/Gendebien, le directeur technique se trouve derrière lui.
(2) Les vérifications techniques : Ed Hugus pousse la Ferrari 250 TR de John Fitch/E.D. Martin. Sous la tente : la Porsche 550 Spyder de Norman Scott/Frank Bott.
(3) La Fiat-Abarth Zagato (Denise McCluggage/ Ruth Levy) se fait réprimander par Phil Hill (casquette), George Tilp et Skip Hudson.
(4) Boris « Bob » Said fait patiner les roues de la Ferrari 500 TRC dans un paddock boueux.

2

3

4

1

1

2

(1) Roy Salvadori, Aston Martin DBR1 (shared with Carroll Shelby, DNF).
(2) Phil Hill, Ferrari 250 TR (winner with Peter Collins).
(3) Edgar Barth, Porsche RSK (shared with Jean Behra, DNF).

(1) Roy Salvadori, Aston Martin DBR1 (gemeinsam mit Carroll Shelby, nicht im Ziel).
(2) Phil Hill, Ferrari 250 TR (Sieger mit Peter Collins).
(3) Edgar Barth, Porsche RSK (gemeinsam mit Jean Behra, nicht im Ziel).

(1) Roy Salvadori, Aston Martin DBR1 (partagée avec Carroll Shelby, abandon).
(2) Phil Hill, Ferrari 250 TR (vainqueur avec Peter Collins).
(3) Edgar Barth, Porsche RSK (partagée avec Jean Behra, abandon).

3

Stirling Moss, Aston Martin DBR1 (co-driver Tony Brooks, DNF/Beifahrer Tony Brooks, Ausfall/coéquipier Tony Brooks, abandon).

Johnny von Neumann, Ferrari 250 TR (co-driver Richie Ginther, DNF/Beifahrer Richie Ginther, Ausfall/coéquipier Richie Ginther, abandon).

Sam Weiss/Dave Tallakson, Lotus Eleven (4th overall, 1st in class/Vierter im Gesamtklassement, Klassensieger/4ème au général, 1èr de catégorie).

Bill Lloyd, Ferrari 500 TR (co-driver Gus Andrey, DNF/Beifahrer Gus Andrey, Ausfall/coéquipier Gus Andrey, abandon).

2

(1) 750 cc OSCA, Alejandro de Tomaso/Isabelle Haskell de Tomaso/Rick Ferguson. The de Tomasos at right. Finished a remarkable 8th overall and won the Index of Performance.
(2) Ferrari 250 GT (the first Sebring entry of NART (North American Racing Team) driven to 5th overall and 1st in Grand Touring by Paul O'Shea, Bruce Kessler and David Cunningham.

(1) Der 750-cm3-OSCA von Alejandro de Tomaso, Isabelle Haskell de Tomaso und Rick Ferguson (rechts die de Tomasos). Sie erreichten einen bemerkenswerten achten Platz im Gesamtklasse-ment und wurden Sieger der Index-Wertung.
(2) Mit Paul O'Shea, Bruce Kessler und David Cunningham am Steuer wurde der Ferrari 250 GT (der erste Sebring-Teilnehmer des North Ameri-can Racing Teams [NART]) insgesamt Fünfter und Erster im GT-Rennen.

(1) OSCA 750 cm^3, Alejandro de Tomaso/Isabelle Haskell de Tomaso/Rick Ferguson, les de Tomaso sont à droite. Ils ont remporté une remarquable 8ème place au général et l'Indice de Performance.
(2) Ferrari 250 GT (le premier engagement à Sebring de NART-North American Racing Team). Menée à la 5ème place de général et 1ère en GT par Paul O'Shea, Bruce Kessler et David Cunningham.

The outdoor award ceremony:
Preisverleihung im Freien:
La remise des prix en plein air :

2

3

(1) Among those in the center are Denise McCluggage, Phil Hill, Robin and Paul O'Shea, Bruce Kessler, Peter and Louise King Collins, Luigi Musso, Romolo Tavoni, Wolfgang von Trips.
(2) Alejandro de Tomaso, Isabelle de Tomaso, Phil Hill, Peter Collins, Bruce Kessler, Paul O'Shea.
(3) Race founder Alec Ulmann shakes hands with Bruce Kessler (between them, George Arents). Paul O'Shea with cup and arm around Luigi Chinetti.

(1) In der Mitte sind unter anderem zu sehen: Denise McCluggage, Phil Hill, Robin und Paul O'Shea, Bruce Kessler, Peter und Louise King Collins, Luigi Musso, Romolo Tavoni, Wolfgang von Trips.
(2) Alejandro de Tomaso, Isabelle de Tomaso, Phil Hill, Peter Collins, Bruce Kessler, Paul O'Shea.
(3) Renninitiator Alec Ulmann schüttelt die Hand von Bruce Kessler (dazwischen George Arents). Paul O'Shea (mit Cup) legt den Arm um Luigi Chinetti.

(1) Parmi les personnages au centre, on trouve Denise Mc Cluggage, Phil Hill, Robin et Paul O'Shea. Bruce Kessler, Peter et Louise King Collins, Luigi Musso, Romolo Tavoni et Wolfgang von Trips.
(2) Alejandro de Tomaso, Isabelle de Tomaso, Phil Hill, Peter Collins, Bruce Kessler, Paul O'Shea.
(3) Le fondateur de la course, Alec Ulmann, serre la main de Bruce Kessler (entre eux, George Arents), Paul O'Shea tient une tasse et enlace Luigi Chinetti.

SEBRING 1959

And the rains came. In biblical proportions they came. Airports rarely drain well and the Sebring course was no exception. The lighter, more powerful cars buzzed uselessly on top of the standing water, spun in wide circles or threw up rooster tails suitable for unlimited hydrofoils.

Again Phil Hill was the winner in a Ferrari 250 TR along with Olivier Gendebien after they took over the car driven by Dan Gurney and Chuck Daigh. Porsches were strong, taking the next three places with the RSK Spyders.

The rain stopped in time for a resplendent sunset and gave Ricardo Rodriguez a chance to hop in the 750 cc OSCA of Alejandro and Isabelle de Tomaso and Denise McCluggage and make a run at the Deutsch-Bonnet of Paul Armagnac and Gerald Laureau for the Index of Performance. But the D-B had fared too well in the wet to be caught. It was the Index winner.

Es war das Jahr, als der Regen kam – als die Sintflut kam. Die meisten Flugplätze haben schlechte Drainagesysteme, und Sebring machte da keine Ausnahme. Die leichteren, leistungsfähigeren Fahrzeuge schwammen hilflos auf den Wasserlachen, kreiselten reihenweise von der Strecke oder warfen Wasserfontänen auf, die von Tragflächenbooten hätten stammen können.

Wieder gewannen Phil Hill und Olivier Gendebien in einem Ferrari 250 TR, nachdem sie den Wagen von Dan Gurney und Chuck Daigh übernommen hatten. Die starke Porsche-Flotte belegte mit den RSK Spydern die folgenden drei Ränge.

Der Regen machte einem glanzvollen Sonnenuntergang Platz, und Ricardo Rodriguez nutzte die Gunst der Stunde, griff sich den 750 cm³ - OSCA von Alejandro und Isabelle de Tomaso und Denise McCluggage und nahm gegen den Deutsch-Bonnet von Paul Armagnac und Gerald Laureau das Rennen um die Sonderwertung des »Index of Performance« auf. Aber der D-B hatte auf der nassen Strecke ein gutes Rennen gezeigt und war nicht mehr einzuholen. Er gewann letztlich die Index-Wertung.

1959 fut l'année des pluies. Un véritable déluge. Les aérodromes n'ont pas de très bons drainages et Sebring ne faisait pas exception à la règle. Les voitures plus légères et plus puissantes faisaient de l'aquaplaning, des tête-à-queue ou soulevaient des masses d'eau qui auraient supporté des hydroptères.

Phil Hill et Olivier Gendebien furent de nouveau vainqueurs sur une Ferrari 250 TR après avoir pris le relais de Dan Gurney et Chuck Daigh. Porsche s'offrit un beau palmarès en s'octroyant les trois places suivantes dans des Spyder RSK.

La pluie stoppa juste à temps pour laisser la place à un coucher de soleil resplendissant et permettre à Ricardo Rodriguez de prendre le volant de l'OSCA 750 CC d'Alejandro et Isabelle de Tomaso et de Denise McCluggage. Il se mit en chasse de la Deutsch-Bonnet de Paul Armagnac et Gerard Laureau pour l'Indice de Performance. Mais la D-B était imbattable sur la piste mouillée et s'octroya l'Indice de Performance.

Jo Bonnier/Wolfgang von Trips, Porsche RSK (#31, 3rd); Briggs Cunningham/Lake Underwood/Stirling Moss/Russ Boss, Lister Jaguar (#4, 15th).

Jo Bonnier/Wolfgang von Trips, Porsche RSK (Nr. 31, Dritte); Briggs Cunningham/Lake Underwood/Stirling Moss/Russ Boss, Lister Jaguar (Nr. 4, 15.).

Jo Bonnier/Wolfgang von Trips, Porsche RSK (n° 31, 3ème) ; Briggs Cunningham/Lake Underwood/Russ Boss, Lister Jaguar (n° 4, 15ème).

(1) The winning Ferrari 250 TR 59 taken over by Phil Hill and Olivier Gendebien from Dan Gurney (here) and Chuck Daigh. Jean Behra stands by his 250 TR 59 which was 2nd.
(2) Olivier Gendebien mentally rehearses his race much to everyone's amusement.
(3) Jean Behra (in helmet); Team Manager Romolo Tavoni (in sweater) talks with Gendebien.

(1) Phil Hill und Olivier Gendebien übernehmen das Siegerfahrzeug, einen Ferrari 250 TR 59, von Dan Gurney und Chuck Daigh. Jean Behra steht neben seinem 250 TR 59, der als Zweiter durchs Ziel ging.
(2) Olivier Gendebien bereitet sich zur allgemeinen Belustigung geistig auf das Rennen vor.
(3) Jean Behra (mit Helm). Team-Manager Romolo Tavoni (im Pullover) spricht mit Gendebien.

(1) La Ferrari 250 TR 59 victorieuse a été reprise par Phil Hill et Olivier Gendebien de Dan Gurney (ici) et Chuck Daigh. Jean Behra est à côté de sa 250 TR 59 qui se classera 2ème.
(2) A l'amusement général, Olivier Gendebien révise le circuit de tête.
(3) Jean Behra (casqué) ; le directeur sportif Romolo Tavoni (en sweater) parle à Gendebien.

2

1

3

Phil Hill perched on winning Ferrari talks with
Paul O'Shea and Ricardo Rodriguez.

Phil Hill sitzt auf dem Sieger-Ferrari und spricht
mit Paul O'Shea und Ricardo Rodriguez.

Phil Hill, perché sur la Ferrari victorieuse, parle à
Paul O'Shea et Ricardo Rodriguez.

Phil Hill, Dan Gurney, Luigi Chinetti.

Ricardo Rodriguez.

Pedro Rodriguez.

Pedro Rodriguez.

The Rodriguez family in the pits:
(1) Mama Rodriguez times Ricardo as Pedro and friend look on.
(2) The family often prayed in the pits, here Conchita Rodriguez with her son, Pedro.
(3) Family discussion: Ricardo, Pedro, Mama and Papa (Pedro Sr).

Familie Rodriguez in der Box:
(1) Mama Rodriguez stoppt Ricardos Zeit, während Pedro und seine Freundin zusehen.
(2) Die Familie betete oft in der Box, hier Conchita Rodriguez mit ihrem Sohn Pedro.
(3) Familiendiskussion: Ricardo, Pedro, Mama und Papa (Pedro Senior).

La famille Rodriguez dans les stands :
(1) Mama Rodriguez chronomètre Ricardo et Pedro sous l'œil d'une amie.
(2) La famille priait souvent dans les stands, on voit ici Conchita Rodriguez et son fils Pedro.
(3) Discussion familiale : Ricardo, Pedro, Mama et Papa (Pedro Sr.)

3

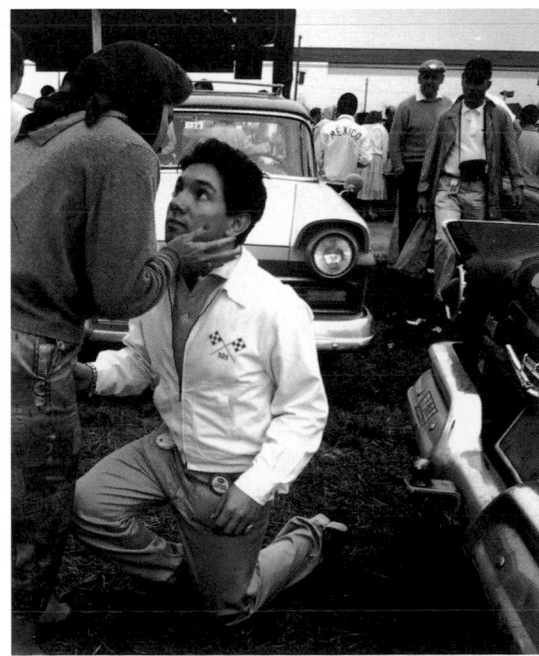

2

(1, 3, 6) OSCA S 950, Ricardo Rodriguez/Bruce
Kessler (DNF): Rodriguez leaps in for the
Le Mans start; leading the Lance Reventlow/
E.D. Martin Ferrari 250 TR (6th); Kessler driving.
(2) Lucky Casner/Jim Hunt, NART Ferrari
500 TR (rebodied like a 250 TR), damaged but
finishing 13th.
(4) Dan Gurney in the winning Ferrari 250 TR 59.
(5) Lined up for the start. Pedro Rodriguez shared
the Ferrari 250 TR (#11) with Paul O'Shea. They
did not finish.

1

(1, 3, 6) OSCA S 950, Ricardo Rodriguez/Bruce
Kessler (Ausfall): Rodriguez beim Le-Mans-Start;
vor dem Ferrari 250 TR von Lance Reventlow und
E.D. Martin (Sechster); Kessler während der Fahrt.
(2) Lucky Casner/Jim Hunt im NART Ferrari 500
TR (mit der Außenverkleidung eines 250 TR)
trotz Beschädigung 13. Platz.
(4) Dan Gurney im Siegerfahrzeug, Ferrari 250
TR 59.
(5) In Startaufstellung. Pedro Rodriguez teilte sich
den Ferrari 250 TR (Nr. 11) mit Paul O'Shea. Sie
kamen nicht ins Ziel.

2

3

4

(1, 3, 6) OSCA S 950, Ricardo Rodriguez, Bruce Kessler (abandon) ; Rodriguez saute pour un départ Le Mans. Il précède la Ferrari 250 TR de Lance Reventlow/E.D. Martin (6ème), Kessler est au volant.

(2) Lucky Casner/Jim Hunt, Ferrari 500 TR (avec la carosserie d'une Ferrari 250 TR) du NART, endommagée mais classée 13ème.

(4) Dan Gurney dans la Ferrari 250 TR 59 victorieuse.

(5) Alignés au départ, Pedro Rodriguez partageait la Ferrari 250 TR (n° 11) avec Paul O'Shea. Ils ne finirent pas.

5

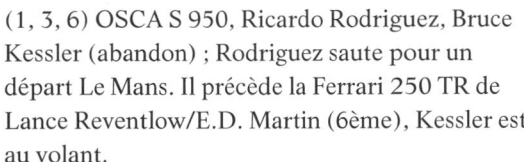

6

1

2

3

4

(1) The William Entwhistle/Robert Hanna Lotus
15 acknowledges pit sign. DNF.
(2) Roy Jackson-Moore/James Cook/Bobbie
Burns, AC Bristol (14th, 1st in class).
(3) OSCA 187S, Alejandro de Tomaso/Isabelle
Haskell de Tomaso/Denise McCluggage. Ricardo
Rodriguez took it over after his car failed.
Finished 18th, 2nd in Index of Performance.
(4) Howard Hively takes over the Ferrari 250 GT
California he shared with Richie Ginther for 9th
place, 1st in class.

(1) William Entwhistle und Robert Hanna auf
Lotus 15 bestätigen eine Boxentafel, kommen aber
nicht ins Ziel.
(2) Roy Jackson-Moore/James Cook/Bobbie
Burns, AC Bristol (14., Klassensieger).
(3) OSCA 187S, Alejandro de Tomaso/Isabelle
Haskell de Tomaso/Denise McCluggage. Ricardo
Rodriguez übernahm das Steuer, nachdem sein
eigener Wagen ausfiel. Er wurde 18. und Zweiter
der Index-Wertung.
(4) Howard Hively übernimmt den Ferrari 250
GT California, den er mit Richie Ginther teilte. Er
wurde insgesamt Neunter und Klassensieger.

(1) La Lotus 15 de William Entwhistle/Robert
Hanna accuse réception d'un signal de son stand.
(2) Roy Jackson-Moore/James Cook/Bobbie
Burns, AC Bristol (14ème, 1er de catégorie).
(3) OSCA 187S, Alejandro de Tomaso/Isabelle
Haskell de Tomaso/Denise McCluggage. Elle fut
reprise par Ricardo Rodriguez après l'abandon de
sa voiture et termina 18ème à l'Indice de Performance.
(4) Howard Hively reprend la Ferrari 250 GT
California qu'il partageait avec Richie Ginther. Ils
terminèrent 9èmes, 1ers de la catégorie.

2

3

4

(1) Walt Hansgen/Dick Thompson, Lister Jaguar.
(2) The first Phil Hill/Olivier Gendebien Ferrari
250 TR 59 before it was retired.
(3) Jo Bonnier/Taffy von Trips, Porsche RSK
shown exiting the flooded pits (3rd, 1st in class).
(4) Chuck Wallace, Elva Mk IV (19th, 1st in cIass
with Frank Baptista and Art Tweedale).

(1) Walt Hansgen/Dick Thompson, Lister Jaguar.
(2) Der erste Phil Hill/Olivier Gendebien Ferrari
250 TR 59, bevor er ausgetauscht wurde.
(3) Der Porsche RSK von Jo Bonnier und Taffy
von Trips verläßt die überflutete Boxengasse
(Dritte und Klassensieger).
(4) Chuck Wallace, Elva Mk IV (19., Klassensieger mit Frank Baptista und Art Tweedale).

(1) Walt Hansgen/Dick Thompson, Lister Jaguar.
(2) La première Ferrari 250 TR 59 de Phil
Hill/Olivier Gendebien avant son remplacement.
(3) Jo Bonnier/Taffy von Trips, Porsche RSK quit-
tant les stands inondés (3èmes, 1ers de catégorie).
(4) Chuck Wallace, Elva MkIV (19ème, 1er de
catégorie avec Frank Baptista et Art Tweedale).

1

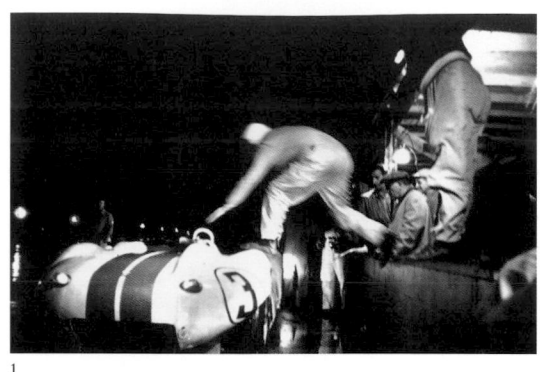

1

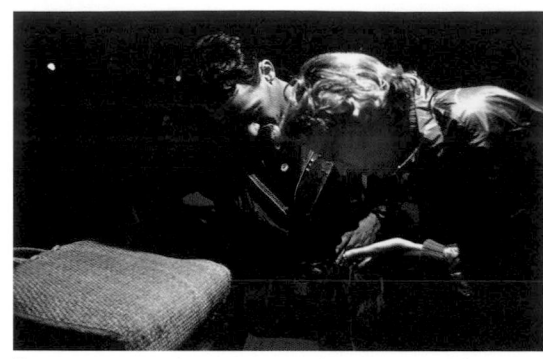

2

3

4

(1) Driver change for the Hansgen/Thompson
Lister Jaguar (12th).
(2) Alejandro and Isabelle de Tomaso.
(3) De Tomaso, Ricardo Rodriguez, Denise
McCluggage in the OSCA pits.
(4) The Cunningham/Underwood/Moss/Boss,
Lister Jaguar (15th).
(5) Pedro Rodriguez consoles Stirling Moss.
(6) Victory! Olivier Gendebien in helmet, Phil Hill
in smiles and Sue Bowden, Miss Florida, in tiara.

5

(1) Fahrerwechsel auf dem Lister Jaguar von
Hansgen und Thompson (12.).
(2) Alejandro und Isabelle de Tomaso.
(3) De Tomaso, Ricardo Rodriguez, Denise
McCluggage in der OSCA-Box.
(4) Cunningham/Underwood/Moss/Boss, Lister-
Jaguar (15.).
(5) Pedro Rodriguez tröstet Stirling Moss.
(6) Sieg! Olivier Gendebien mit Helm, Phil Hill
mit Siegerlächeln und Sue Bowden, Miss Florida,
mit Diadem.

(1) Changement de pilote pour la Lister-Jaguar de
Hansgen/Thompson (12ème).
(2) Alejandro et Isabelle de Tomaso.
(3) De Tomaso, Ricardo Rodriguez, Denise Mc
Cluggage dans le stand OSCA.
(4) Cunningham/Underwood/Moss/Boss, Lister-
Jaguar (15ème).
(5) Pedro Rodriguez console Stirling Moss.
(6) Victoire ! Olivier Gendebien casqué, Phil Hill
souriant et Sue Bowden, Miss Floride, avec sa
tiare.

6

SEBRING GRAND PRIX 1959

Alec Ulmann had pressed to have a true Grand Prix of the United States for Formula 1 cars and in a way he succeeded. The December race was, indeed, sanctioned by the FIA and a championship was decided there in a dramatic fashion, but the crowd was half what it had been for the sports car 12-Hours and the relatively rag-tag 18 starters (including an Offenhauser midget for Rodger Ward) dwindled to seven cars at the finish.

But what a finish!

Jack Brabham appeared to have the race in the bag and with it the championship, particularly after the faster Stirling Moss went out on the sixth lap. But as the checker fell it was the 22-year-old Bruce McLaren scooting across the finish less than a second ahead of the 42-year-old Maurice Trintignant – the youngest and the oldest in the race, both in Coopers, first and second.

Where was Brabham?

Eyes turned toward the Martini & Rossi bridge. There an exhausted Brabham was pushing his white-striped Cooper-Climax toward the line. A leak had drained it of fuel a quarter mile from the finish. The red Ferrari of Tony Brooks took the flag before Brabham put his car across the line and collapsed. He was fourth. The championship was his by 31 points to 27 for Brooks.

Alec Ulmann, der darauf gedrängt hatte, einen echten Formel-1-Grand-Prix der USA auszutragen, erreichte hier gewissermaßen sein Ziel. Das Rennen im Dezember wurde tatsächlich von der FIA sanktioniert und bot eine dramatische Meisterschaftsentscheidung. Es kamen jedoch nur etwa halb so viele Zuschauer wie zu den 12-Stunden-Rennen, und von den ohnehin nur 18 Fahrzeugen im Starterfeld (darunter ein kleiner Offenhauser für Rodger Ward) kamen ganze sieben ins Ziel.

Aber was für ein Finish!

Es schien, als hätte Jack Brabham das Rennen, und damit die Meisterschaft, bereits in der Tasche, insbesondere nachdem der schnellere Stirling Moss in der siebten Runde ausgeschieden war. Aber als die schwarzweiß-karierte Zielflagge fiel, war der 22jährige Bruce McLaren als Erster im Ziel – knapp eine Sekunde vor dem 42jährigen Maurice Trintignant. So belegten der jüngste und der älteste Fahrer im Rennen die Plätze eins und zwei, und beide fuhren einen Cooper.

Wo war Brabham abgeblieben?

Alles blickte zur Martini & Rossi-Brücke. Dort schob ein erschöpfter Brabham seinen weißgestreiften Cooper-Climax auf die Ziellinie zu. Durch ein Leck in der Benzinleitung war sein Wagen runde 400 Meter vor der Ziellinie ohne Treibstoff stehengeblieben. Hinter Tony Brooks' rotem Ferrari schob Brabham sein Fahrzeug schließlich über die Ziellinie und brach zusammen. Er wurde Vierter und hatte am Ende mit 31 zu 27 Punkten vor Brooks die Meisterschaft gewonnen.

Alec Ulmann voulait absolument instaurer un vrai Grand Prix des Etats-Unis, avec des voitures de Formule I. Dans un sens, il atteignit son objectif. La FIA accepta de sanctionner la course de décembre qui offrit tous les grands moments dramatiques attendus d'un championnat de ce niveau. Mais il y avait 50% de moins de spectateurs par rapport aux épreuves de 12 Heures. Et des 18 voitures inscrites – de qualité plutôt moyenne – (Rodger Ward pilotait une petite Offenhauser) 7 seulement franchirent la ligne d'arrivée.

Mais quel finish !

On avait d'abord cru que Jack Brabham allait remporter la course, à savoir qu'il s'assurait le championnat. L'affaire était dans le sac, surtout lorsque Stirling Moss, son adversaire le plus rapide, sortit de la piste au 6ème tour. Or, le drapeau d'arrivée s'abaissa devant Bruce McLaren, jeune pilote de 22 ans, suivi à moins d'une seconde de Maurice Trintignant, un vétéran de 42 ans. Le benjamin et le doyen de la course se classaient premier et second, tous les deux au volant de Cooper.

Mais où était Brabham ?

Tous les regards se tournèrent vers le pont Martini & Rossi où un Brabham en sueur poussait sa Cooper-Climax à raies blanches vers la ligne d'arrivée. Une fuite d'essence avait stoppé la voiture à un quart de mile de l'arrivée. La Ferrari rouge de Tony Brooks le dépassa encore avant que Brabham ne s'écroule derrière la ligne. Il était quatrième et s'adjugeait quand même le championnat avec 31 points, 4 de plus que Brooks.

Jack Brabham, orange blossoms and a championship.
Jack Brabham, Orangenblüten und die Meisterschaft.
Jack Brabham, les fleurs d'oranger et le championnat.

Unfamiliar to Sebring, Formula 1 cars.

Ein ungewohnter Anblick in Sebring:
Formel-1-Wagen.

Les Formule 1, inhabituelles à Sebring.

Stirling Moss, John Cooper, Jack Brabham.

Jack Brabham and his Cooper-Climax.

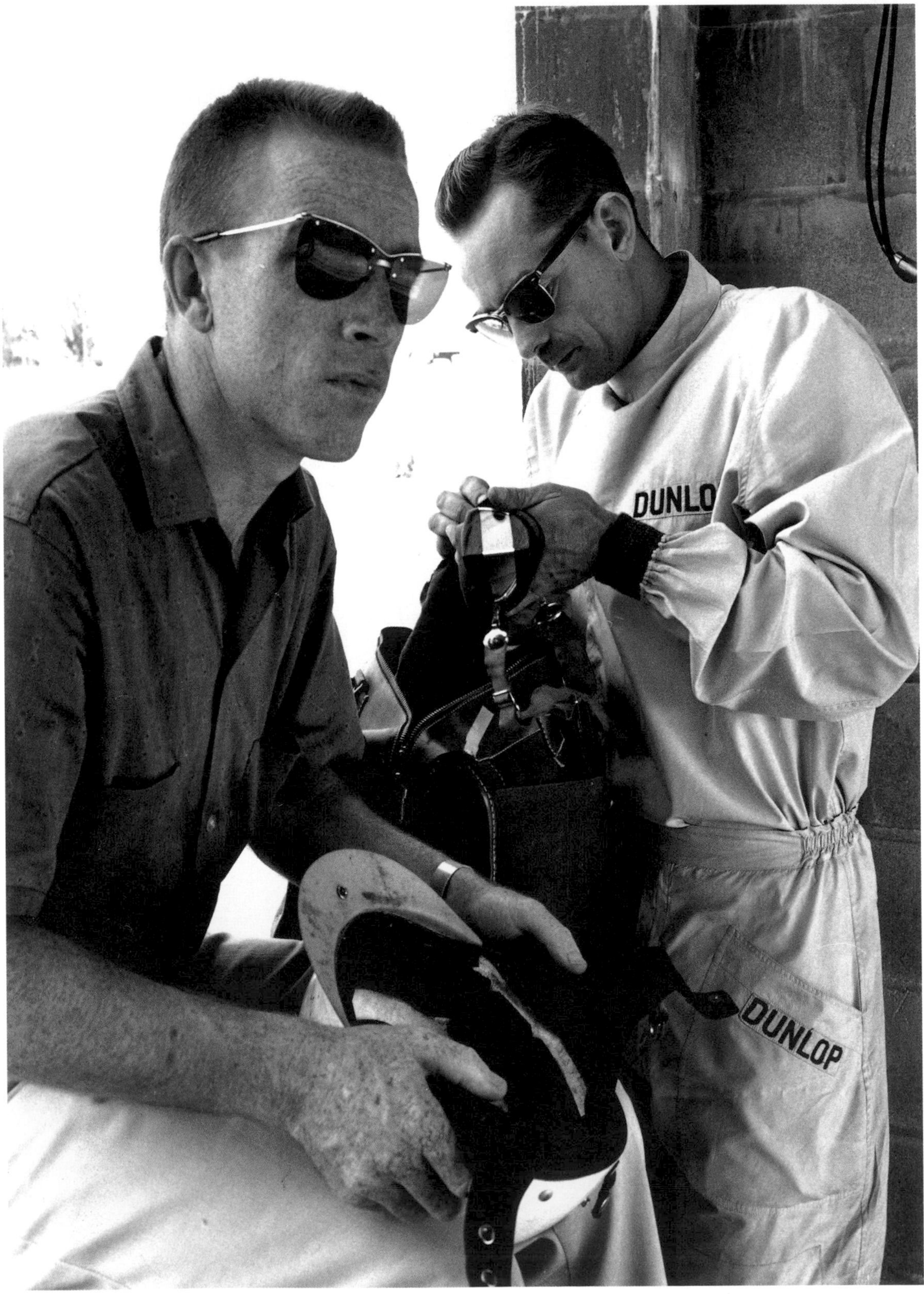

Richie Ginther, Phil Hill.

Jack Brabham and his Cooper-Climax.

(1) The Ferrari team cars. Phil Hill's #6 was blue with a white nose, US racing colors. Pedro Rodriguez peering at #5, Zora Arkus-Duntov in white jacket.
(2) Boris "Bob" Said (standing), out on the first lap in an aging Connaught, waits with Taffy von Trips and his engine-troubled Ferrari.
(3) Stirling Moss, Cooper-Climax, puts in earplugs for a practice session.
(4) The Ferraris.

(1) Die Wagen des Ferrari-Teams. Phil Hills Nummer 6 war blau mit weißer Front – die amerikanischen Rennfarben. Pedro Rodriguez wirft einen prüfenden Blick auf die Nummer 5, Zora Arkus-Duntov in weißer Jacke.
(2) Boris »Bob« Said (stehend), der in der ersten Runde in einem betagten Connaught ausfiel, wartet mit Taffy von Trips, dessen Ferrari einen Motorschaden erlitten hatte.
(3) Stirling Moss, Cooper-Climax, steckt sich vor einem Trainingslauf Wachswatte in die Ohren.
(4) Die Ferraris.

(1) Les voitures de l'équipe Ferrari. Celle de Phil Hill (n° 6) était bleue avec le nez blanc, les couleurs officielles des Etats-Unis. Pedro Rodriguez examine la n° 5. Zora Arkus-Duntov est en veste blanche.
(2) Boris « Bob » Said (debout) qui abandonna au premier tout avec une vieille Connaught, attend avec Taffy von Trips dont la Ferrari a des ennuis de moteur.
(3) Stirling Moss, Cooper-Climax, se protège les oreilles pour participer aux essais.
(4) Les Ferrari.

1

2

4

3

Bruce McLaren, Cooper-Climax (winner/Sieger/
vainqueur).

Innes Ireland, Lotus 16 (5th/Fünfter/5ème).

Bob Said, Connaught. DNF/nicht im Ziel/
abandon.

Phil Hill, Ferrari Dino 246, lost his brakes on the 9th lap. DNF.

Die Bremsen von Phil Hills Ferrari Dino 246 versagten in der neunten Runde – Ausfall.

Phil Hill, Ferrari Dino 246, fut lâché par ses freins au 9ème tour. Abandon.

(1) Cliff Allison, Ferrari Dino 246 , 3rd until out with bad clutch.

(2) Jack Brabham, Cooper, led most of the way, here ahead of the OSCA of Alejandro de Tomaso.

(3) Maurice Trintignant, Cooper-Climax, 2nd.

(4) De Tomaso, OSCA, was out before the 15th lap.

(5) Rodger Ward, Kurtis Kraft Offenhauser midget, was the slowest qualifier but delighted the crowd with his tail-hanging-out technique.

(6) Wolfgang von Trips, Ferrari Dino 246, 3rd until engine failure left him to push the car across the finish to place 6th.

(1) Cliff Allison, Ferrari Dino 246, war an dritter Stelle, bevor er wegen eines Kupplungsschadens ausfiel.

(2) Jack Brabham, Cooper, führte viele Runden lang, hier vor dem OSCA von Alejandro de Tomaso.

(3) Maurice Trintignant, Cooper-Climax, Zweiter.

(4) De Tomaso, OSCA, schied schon vor der 15. Runde aus.

(5) Rodger Ward war in seinem kleinen Kurtis Kraft Offenhauser zwar der langsamste unter den Plazierten, begeisterte aber die Zuschauer mit seinem spektakulären Fahrstil.

(6) Wolfgang von Trips, Ferrari Dino 246, war Dritter, bevor er nach einem Motorschaden den Wagen, an sechster Stelle liegend, über die Ziellinie schieben mußte.

1

2

3

4

5

(1) Cliff Allison, Ferrari Dino 246, 3ème jusqu'à son abandon causé par un embrayage défectueux.
(2) Jack Brabham, Cooper, mena presque toute la course. Il est ici devant l'OSCA d'Alejandro de Tomaso.
(3) Maurice Trintignant, Cooper-Climax (2ème).
(4) De Tomaso, OSCA, abandonna avant le 15ème tour.

(5) Rodger Ward, midget Kurtis Kraft Offenhauser, fut le moins rapide en qualification mais il ravit les spectateurs par sa technique de glissades.
(6) Wolfgang von Trips, Ferrari Dino 246, 3ème jusqu'à une défaillance de moteur qui le contraignit à pousser sa voiture sur la ligne pour se classer 6ème.

6

Roy Salvadori's Cooper-Maserati awaits repairs
under the wing of a decommissioned WW2 cargo
plane.

Roy Salvadoris Cooper-Maserati wartet unter der
Tragfläche eines ausgedienten Transportflugzeugs
aus dem Zweiten Weltkrieg auf seine Reparatur.

La Cooper-Maserati de Roy Salvadori attend
qu'on la répare sous l'aile d'un avion de transport
désaffecté de la dernière guerre.

SEBRING 1964

Except for a Porsche victory in 1960, Ferrari had been the winner in every Sebring 12-Hours since 1958, and 1964 was no exception. Three prototypes from the factory gained the first three spots with Mike Parkes and Umberto Maglioli in the 275 P taking first.

However, one might have thought from the elation in the Carroll Shelby camp that his Ford-powered Cobras were the victors with their fourth through sixth place finishes. And in a sense they were. They were 1-2-3 in the Grand Touring category and that had been Shelby's target: Collect the maximum points possible toward the GT championship. Bob Holbert and Dave MacDonald led the way in the Ford Cobra coupe; Lew Spencer and Bob Bondurant were next with Jo Schlesser and Phil Hill behind them.

For the first time at Sebring, qualifying times determined the order of start instead of engine displacement. The honor of the first earned pole position went to the John Surtees/Lorenzo Bandini Ferrari 330 P.

Mit Ausnahme eines Porsche-Sieges 1960 hatte Ferrari seit 1958 jedes 12-Stunden-Rennen von Sebring gewonnen – und daran änderte sich auch 1964 nichts. Drei Werksprototypen belegten die ersten drei Plätze, Mikes Parkes und Umberto Maglioli fuhren im 275 P zum Sieg.

Aber die Begeisterung im Lager von Carroll Shelby hätte glauben machen können, daß seine von Ford–Motoren angetriebenen Cobras – die die Plätze Vier bis Sechs erreicht hatten – die eigentlichen Sieger des Rennens seien. Und in gewisser Hinsicht waren sie das auch. In der Grand-Touring-Kategorie belegten sie die Plätze 1, 2 und 3 – und genau das hatte Shelby erreichen wollen: möglichst viele Punkte für die GT-Meisterschaft zu sammeln. Bob Holbert und Dave MacDonald im Ford Cobra Coupé lagen vorn, gefolgt von Lew Spencer, Bob Bondurant, Jo Schlesser und Phil Hill.

Erstmalig bestimmten in Sebring anstelle des Hubraums die in den Trainingssitzungen erreichten Rundenzeiten die Startaufstellung. Die Ehre der ersten erkämpften Pole Position ging an den Ferrari 330 P von John Surtees/Lorenzo Bandini.

Hormis une victoire de Porsche en 1960, Ferrari avait remporté toutes les 12 Heures de Sebring depuis 1958. 1964 ne fit pas exception à la règle. Trois prototypes d'usine s'emparèrent des trois premières places, Mike Parkes et Umberto Maglioli courant à la victoire dans la 275 P.

Cependant, l'enthousiasme qui régnait dans le camp de Carroll Shelby aurait pu faire croire que ses Cobra équipées de moteurs Ford – qui avaient pris de la quatrième à la sixième places – étaient en fait les vainqueurs de la course. Et c'était vrai dans un sens. Elle s'étaient octroyé les trois premières places dans la catégorie Grand Tourisme, ce qui avait été l'objectif de Shelby : ramasser le maximum de points pour le championnat GT. Bob Holbert et Dave MacDonald arrivèrent en tête sur la Ford Cobra Coupé, suivis de Lew Spencer et Bob Bondurant que talonnaient Jo Schlesser et Phil Hill.

Pour la première fois à Sebring, les temps de qualifications aux essais et non plus la cylindrée déterminèrent les positions sur la grille de départ. L'honneur de la première pole position méritée revint au tandem John Surtees/Lorenzo Bandini sur une Ferrari 330 P.

The Cobra Garage.
Die Cobra-Werkstatt.
Le garage des Cobras.

Graham Hill in front of his Ferrari 330 P which he drove with Jo Bonnier.

Graham Hill vor seinem Ferrari 330 P, den er gemeinsam mit Jo Bonnier pilotierte.

Graham Hill devant sa Ferrari 330 P qu'il conduisit avec Jo Bonnier.

Umberto Maglioli (dark shirt) confers with a Ferrari mechanic about the 275 P he would share with Mike Parkes. They won.

Umberto Maglioli (im dunklen Hemd) diskutiert mit einem Ferrari-Mechaniker über einen 275 P, den er sich mit Mike Parkes teilen sollte. Sie gewannen das Rennen.

Umberto Maglioli (chemise foncée) discute avec un mécanicien de Ferrari de la 275 P qu'il va partager avec Mike Parkes. Ils ont gagné.

The Pedro Rodriguez/John Fulp Ferrari 330 P (#25).

Der Ferrari 330 P von Pedro Rodriguez und John Fulp (Nr. 25).

La Ferrari 330 P (n° 25) de Pedro Rodriguez/ John Fulp.

The John Surtees/Lorenzo Bandini 330 P (#21). Surtees in white shirt, Graham Hill in dark shirt.

Der 330 P (Nr. 21) von John Surtees/Lorenzo Bandini, Surtees im weißen, Graham Hill im dunklen Hemd.

La 330 P (n° 21) de John Surtees/Lorenzo Bandini. Surtees en chemise blanche, Graham Hill en chemise foncée.

Elation in the Cobra pits. Ken Miles and Carroll
Shelby (on crutches).

Begeisterung in der Cobra-Box. Ken Miles und
Carroll Shelby (auf Krücken).

Joie dans le stand cobra. Ken Miles et Carroll
Shelby (avec béquilles).

Graham Hill.

John Surtees, Ferrari 330 P.

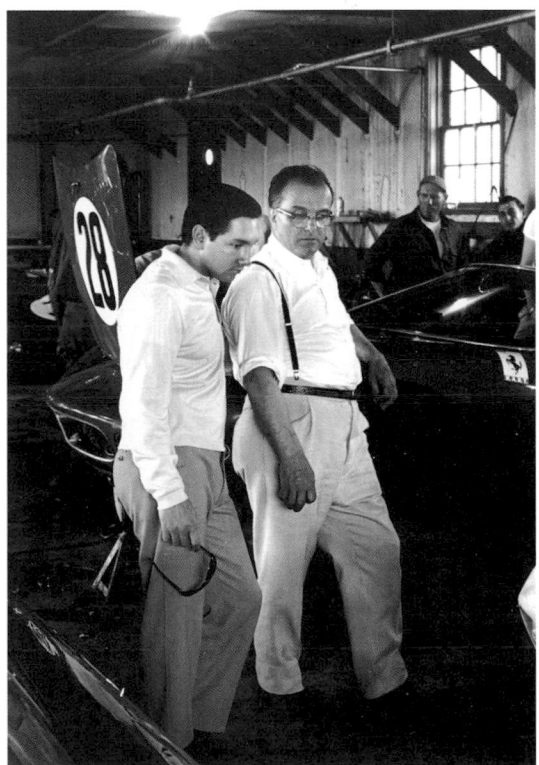

Pedro Rodriguez, Luigi Chinetti.

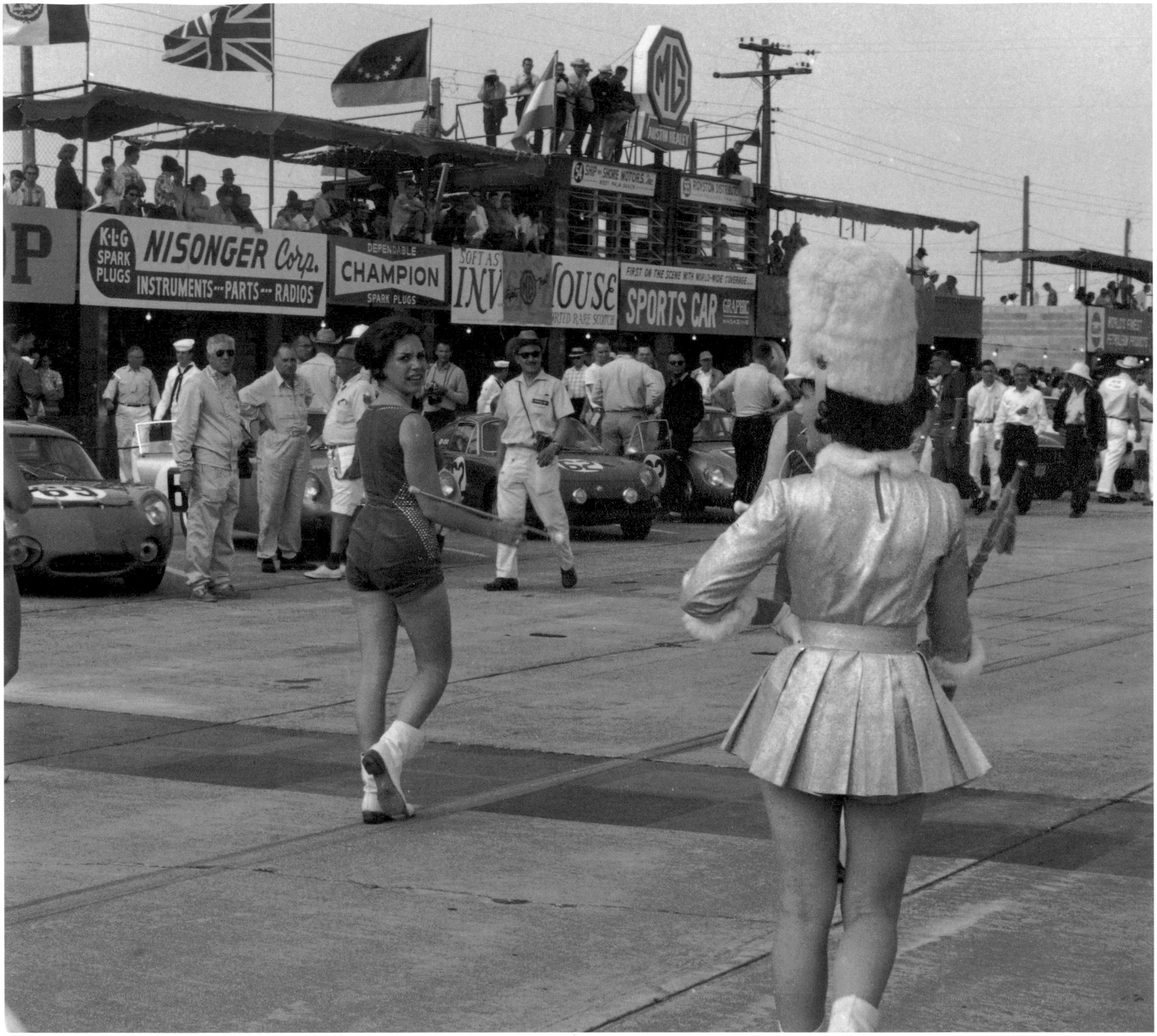
MG
K·L·G
SPARK
PLUGS
NISONGER Corp.
INSTRUMENTS — PARTS — RADIOS
DEPENDABLE
CHAMPION
SPARK PLUGS
FIRST ON THE SCENE WITH WORLD-WIDE COVERAGE
SPORTS CAR
GRAPHIC

1

keep your eyes on the
cortina
Gulf
Gulfprid
WORLD'S FINEST MOTOR

2

MARTINI & ROSSI

3

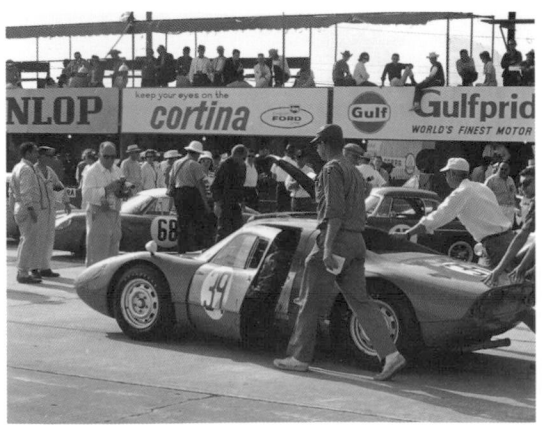

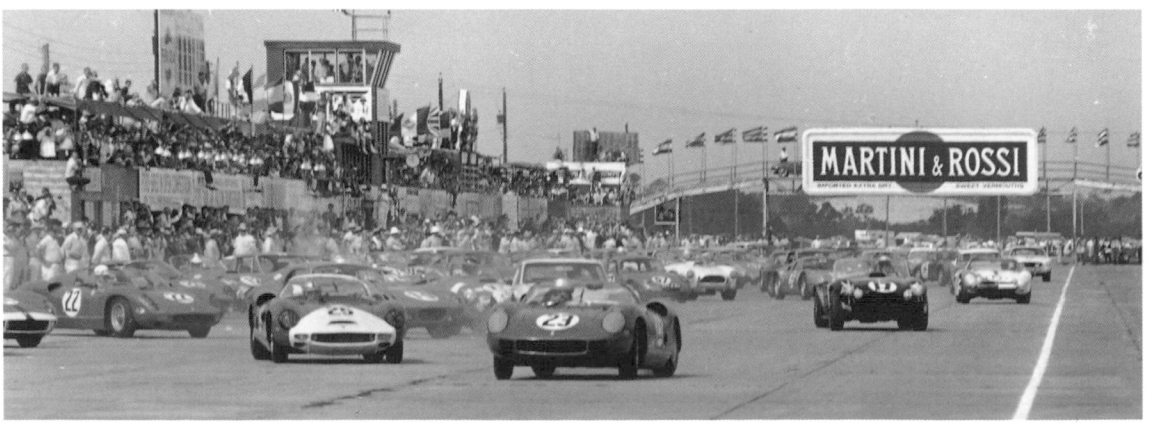

4

(1) A Sebring tradition. Drum majorettes lead the band past the pits.
(2) The John Ryan/William Bencker Porsche 904 gets pushed toward its starting spot.
(3) The Le Mans start. The 275 P Ferrari of Lodovico Scarfiotti/Nino Vaccarella got away first. Twelve hours later they were 2nd.
(4) The great French champion, René Dreyfus, served as "Blue Flag Marshall" to help keep slower cars out of the way of the faster ones.

(1) Eine Sebring-Tradition: Tambourmajoretten führen die Marschkapelle an den Boxen vorbei.
(2) Der Porsche 904 von John Ryan und William Bencker wird an die Startposition geschoben.
(3) Le-Mans-Start. Der 275 P Ferrari von Lodovico Scarfiotti und Nino Vaccarella startete als Erster und kam zwölf Stunden später als Zweiter ins Ziel.
(4) Der berühmte französische Champion René Dreyfus hielt als »Blue Flag Marshall« die langsameren Fahrzeuge den schnelleren vom Leib.

(1) Une tradition à Sebring : les majorettes précèdent l'orchestre devant les stands.
(2) La Porsche 904 de John Ryan/William Bencker est poussée vers son emplacement de départ.
(3) Départ Le Mans ; La Ferrari 275 P de Lodovico Scarfiotti/Nino Vaccarella s'est élancée la première. Douze heures plus tard, elle finira seconde.
(4) Le grand champion français René Dreyfus servait en tant que commissaire au drapeau bleu pour signaler aux voitures lentes de laisser passer les plus rapides.

1

2

3

(1) Jo Schlesser, Cobra (6th with Phil Hill/Sechster mit Phil Hill/6ème avec Phil Hill).

(2) Ken Miles, Cobra prototype. DNF/nicht im Ziel/abandon.

(3) Bob Bondurant/Lew Spencer, Cobra (5th/Fünfter/5ème).

Nino Vaccarella, Ferrari 275 P.

1

2

3

4

5

6

(1) Tom Fleming/Otto Linton/Jim Diaz, Abarth Simca (24th overall, 1st in class).
(2) Mike Parkes, Ferrari 275 P (winner with Umberto Maglioli).
(3) Ed Cantrell in his Ferrari 250 GTO (28th with Harry Heuer and Don Yenko).
(4) Roger Penske, Corvette GS (18th overall, 1st in class with Jim Hall).
(5) Lorenzo Bandini, Ferrari 330 P (3rd overall, 1st in class with John Surtees).
(6) Briggs Cunningham/Lake Underwood, Porsche 904 (9th overall, 1st in class).
(7) Jim Clark, Lotus Cortina (21st, 2nd in class with Ray Parsons).

(1) Tom Fleming/Otto Linton/Jim Diaz, Abarth Simca (24. im Gesamtklassement, Klassensieger).
(2) Mike Parkes, Ferrari 275 P (Sieger mit Umberto Maglioli).
(3) Ed Cantrell in his Ferrari 250 GTO (28. mit Harry Heuer and Don Yenko).
(4) Roger Penske, Corvette GS (18. im Gesamtklassement, Klassensieger mit Jim Hall).
(5) Lorenzo Bandini, Ferrari 330 P (Dritter im Gesamtklassement, Klassensieger mit John Surtees).
(6) Briggs Cunningham/Lake Underwood, Porsche 904 (Neunter im Gesamtklassement, Klassensieger).
(7) Jim Clark, Lotus Cortina (21., Klassenzweiter mit Ray Parsons).

(1) Tom Fleming/Otto Linton/Jim Diaz, Abarth Simca (24ème au général, 1er de catégorie).
(2) Mike Parkes, Ferrari 275 P (vainqueur avec Umberto Maglioli).
(3) Ed Cantrell in his Ferrari 250 GTO (28ème avec Harry Heuer and Don Yenko).
(4) Roger Penske, Corvette GS (18ème au général, 1er de catégorie avec Jim Hall).
(5) Lorenzo Bandini, Ferrari 330 P (3ème au général, 1er de catégorie avec John Surtees).
(6) Briggs Cunningham/Lake Underwood, Porsche 904 (9ème au général, 1er de catégorie).
(7) Jim Clark, Lotus Cortina (21ème, 2ème de catégorie avec Ray Parsons).

7

(1) Jerry Grant, Corvette Stingray (16th with Skip Hudson).
(2) Chuck Cassel/Don Sesslar, Porsche Abarth Carrera (12th overall, 2nd in class).
(3) Dan Gurney, Cobra (10th with Bob Johnson).
(4) Chuck Stoddard, AIfa Romeo 1600 TZ (13th overall, 1st in class with Jim Kaser).

(1) Jerry Grant, Corvette Stingray (16. mit Skip Hudson).
(2) Chuck Cassel/Don Sesslar, Porsche Abarth Carrera (Zwölfte im Gesamtklassement, Klassenzweite).
(3) Dan Gurney, Cobra (Zehnter mit Bob Johnson).
(4) Chuck Stoddard, AIfa Romeo 1600 TZ (13. im Gesamtklassement, Klassensieger mit Jim Kaser).

(1) Jerry Grant, Corvette Stingray (16ème avec Skip Hudson).
(2) Chuck Cassel/Don Sesslar, Porsche Abarth Carrera (12èmes au général, 2èmes de catégorie).
(3) Dan Gurney, Cobra (10ème avec Bob Johnson).
(4) Chuck Stoddard, AIfa Romeo 1600 TZ (13èmes au général, 1er de catégorie avec Jim Kaser).

1

Troubled pit stop. Pedro Rodriguez, Ferrari 330 P (with John Fulp) went out after 40 laps. Pedro switched to 250 GTO #30 and finished 7th with David Piper and Mike Gammino.

Ärger in der Box. Pedro Rodriguez, Ferrari 330 P (mit John Fulp), schied nach 40 Runden aus. Pedro wechselte auf den 250 GTO mit der Startnummer 30 und endete als Siebter mit seinen Teamkollegen David Piper und Mike Gammino.

Problèmes au ravitaillement. Pedro Rodriguez, Ferrari 330 P (avec John Fulp) abandonna après 40 tours. Pedro reprit la 250 GTO n° 30 et se classa 7ème avec David Piper et Mike Gammino.

The damaged John Ryan/William Bencker Porsche 904 managed a "classified" finish.

Der beschädigte Porsche 904 von John Ryan und William Bencker schaffte immerhin den Zieleinlauf.

La Porsche 904 de John Ryan/William Bencker, malgré ses dégâts, fut classée à l'arrivée.

A.J. Foyt/John Cannon, Corvette (23rd, 2nd in class/23., Klassenzweite/23ème, 2ème de catégorie).

Tom Hitchcock/Zourab Tchkotoua, Cobra (14th/14./14ème).

NART entry Ferrari 250 LM. Charlie Kolb left the race dramatically after 30 laps. He was unhurt, the fire was extinguished and the car repaired only to burn again in a later race. ▶

Der Ferrari 250 LM des NART. Charlie Kolb schied nach 30 Runden auf dramatische Weise aus, blieb aber unverletzt. Das Feuer wurde gelöscht und der Wagen repariert, nur um in einem späteren Rennen erneut in Flammen aufzugehen.

La Ferrari 250 LM de Charlie Kolb, engagée par le NART, quitta la course de façon dramatique après 30 tours ; le pilote était indemne, l'incendie circonscrit et la voiture fut réparée pour brûler à nouveau dans une autre course.

1

2

3

4

(1) Graham Shaw shared this Cobra with Tiny Lund of NASCAR fame and Charlie Hayes. DNF.
(2) Ralph Noseda/Jeff Stevens, Cobra. DNF.
(3) Graham Hill, Ferrari 330 P with Jo Bonnier. DNF.
(4) George Wintersteen, Cobra (35th with Ed Lowther).
(5) Carroll Shelby had the 4th place Cobra pushed to the winner's circle, much to the consternation of Alec Ulmann, race organizer. Three Ferraris were ahead of it but the Bob Holbert/Dave MacDonald Cobra had won the GT category.

(1) Graham Shaw teilte diesen Cobra mit Charlie Hayes und dem NASCAR-Star Tiny Lund. Nicht klassiert.
(2) Ralph Noseda/Jeff Stevens, Cobra. Nicht klassiert.
(3) Graham Hill mit Jo Bonnier, Ferrari 330 P. Nicht klassiert.
(4) George Wintersteen, Cobra (35. mit Ed Lowther).
(5) Sehr zur Verärgerung des Rennorganisators Alec Ulmann ließ Carroll Shelby den viertplazierten Cobra in den Kreis der Sieger schieben. Vor ihm lagen zwar drei Ferraris, aber der Cobra von Bob Holbert und Dave MacDonald hatte das GT-Rennen gewonnen.

(1) Graham Shaw partageait cette Cobra avec Tiny Lund, qui est connu par les stock-cars du NASCAR et Charlie Hayes. Abandon.
(2) Ralph Noseda/Jeff Stevens, Cobra. Abandon.
(3) Graham Hill, Ferrari 330 P avec Jo Bonnier. Abandon.
(4) George Wintersteen, Cobra (35ème avec Ed Lowther).
(5) Carroll Shelby fit pousser la Cobra classée 4ème dans l'enceinte des vainqueurs, à la grande consternation d'Alec Ulmann, l'organisateur de la course. Trois Ferrari la précédaient, mais la Cobra de Bob Holbert/Dave McDonald avait remporté la catégorie GT.

5

SEBRING 1965

The Americans were really beginning to get into their home-soil 12-Hour race and Ferrari didn't cotton to that one bit. Indeed, the factory team did not officially appear in 1965. A group of loyal Ferrari owners supposedly banded together in a grass roots movement to enter an assortment of Ferraris. Odd, then, that all the mechanics were the familiar brown-clad speakers of Italian and that drivers such as Graham Hill, Pedro Rodriguez, Willy Mairesse, Lucien Bianchi, Giancarlo Baghetti and Umberto Maglioli arrived to drive the cars which were disguised in nearly every color but Italian red.

The reason for the Ferrari factory's pique was that the rules now allowed large-bore American engines in the sports racing cars thus giving them a better chance at an overall victory. Chevrolet 5.4-liter V-8s powered the two-car Chaparral team from Texas. The Ford GT40s displaced 4.7 liters and the Chevrolet Corvette Grand Sports 6.2. Shelby Cobras (4.7 liters) were back in force, too. Ferraris, at 3 and 4 liters, were out-powered.

On practice day it was clear that Ferrari's concern was well-founded when the Chaparral, complete with automatic transmission, struck 12 seconds off the lap record. The wisdom of the pits held that the Chaparrals could not last the distance. Jim Hall, the builder/driver, thought otherwise, and, teamed with Hap Sharp, lasted the 12 hours and won the race – handily.

The victory came despite a passing cloudburst that struck in the fifth hour and flooded the course. Perhaps it was even worse than the deluge during the l959 race. Tires floated down pit lane, and blinded drivers lost their way on the expansive runways.

Only one Ferrari, a 275 LM (David Piper/Tony Maggs) made the top ten. It finished third, six laps behind the winning all-American Chaparral.

Sehr zum Mißfallen von Ferrari gewannen die Amerikaner in ihrem hauseigenen 12-Stunden-Rennen immer mehr an Boden. Tatsächlich trat das Werksteam 1965 offiziell gar nicht an. Angeblich schloß sich eine Gruppe treuer Ferrari-Besitzer zusammen und meldete in Eigeninitiative einige Ferraris für das Rennen. Seltsam war allerdings, daß alle Mechaniker die vertrauten braunen Overalls trugen und Italienisch sprachen, und daß Fahrer wie Graham Hill, Pedro Rodriguez, Willy Mairesse, Lucien Bianchi, Giancarlo Baghetti und Umberto Maglioli eintrafen, um die Fahrzeuge zu fahren, die in allen denkbaren Farben – nur nicht dem typischen Italienischrot – an den Start rollten.

Grund für die Verärgerung bei Ferrari war, daß das Rennsportwagen-Reglement inzwischen den Einbau großvolumiger amerikanischer V8-Motoren erlaubte, die eine bessere Chance für Gesamtsiege boten. Das mit zwei Wagen vertretene Chaparral-Team aus Texas fuhr mit 5,4-Liter-V8-Aggregaten. Der Ford GT40 hatte 4,7 Liter, der Chevrolet Grand Sports sogar 6,2 Liter Hubraum. Auch Shelbys Cobras (4,7 Liter) kehrten mit voller Kraft zurück. Die Ferraris waren mit nur drei und vier Litern Hubraum stark benachteiligt.

Während der Trainingsläufe zeigte sich, daß die Sorgen bei Ferrari durchaus begründet waren, da der überdies mit einem Automatikgetriebe ausgestattete Chaparral die bisherige Rundenbestzeit um ganze 12 Sekunden unterbot. In den Boxen glaubte man, daß die Chaparrals nicht über die gesamte Distanz gehen könnten. Konstrukteur und Fahrer Jim Hall hielt aber dagegen, überstand gemeinsam mit Hap Sharp die zwölf Stunden und gewann das Rennen ganz locker.

Er holte sich den Sieg trotz eines plötzlichen Wolkenbruchs, der in der fünften Stunde des Rennens den Kurs unter Wasser setzte und vielleicht sogar noch schlimmer war als die Sintflut von 1959. In den Boxenstraßen schwammen die Reifen, und die Fahrer, die kaum mehr sehen konnten, verfuhren sich auf den weitläufigen Rollfeldern.

Unter den ersten Zehn war nur ein einziger Ferrari plaziert, ein 275 LM (David Piper/Tony Maggs). Er kam als Dritter ins Ziel, sechs Runden hinter dem amerikanischen Siegerfahrzeug.

Ferrari voyait d'un mauvais œil les Américains commencer à s'imposer dans les épreuves de 12 Heures qui se déroulaient chez eux. L'équipe d'usine était même si contrariée qu'elle ne se présenta pas officiellement aux épreuves de 1965. Des propriétaires de Ferrari mordus se seraient alors rassemblés pour inscrire quelques Ferrari, de leur propre initiative. On s'étonna certes que tous les mécaniciens soient des Italiens revêtus de la tenue brune distinctive du clan et que des pilotes tels que Graham Hill, Pedro Rodriguez, Willy Mairesse, Lucien Bianchi, Giancarlo Baghetti et Umberto Maglioli viennent pour conduire les voitures camouflées sous toutes sortes de couleurs, sauf le rouge typique.

Ferrari était mécontent parce que le règlement autorisait désormais les gros moteurs suralésés américains dans les voitures de courses, ce qui augmentait leurs chances de victoire globale. Les deux voitures de l'écurie Chaparral du Texas avaient des moteurs Chevrolet V8 5,4 litres. La Ford GT40 était équipée d'un moteur de 4,7 litres et la Chevrolet Corvette Grand Sport d'un moteur de 6,2 litres. Les Shelby Cobra (4,7 litres) étaient de retour en force. Les Ferrari 3 et 4 litres n'avaient pratiquement plus de chances de s'imposer.

Le jour des essais révéla combien les craintes de Ferrari étaient fondées. La Chaparral équipée d'une transmission automatique améliora le record du tour de 12 secondes. On eut beau affirmer dans les stands que les Chaparral ne tiendraient pas les douze heures, Jim Hall, constructeur et pilote, prouva le contraire et gagna l'épreuve haut la main en compagnie de Hap Sharp.

Ils remportèrent la victoire en dépit de l'averse diluvienne qui inonda soudain la piste à la cinquième heure de course – pire peut-être que le déluge de 1959. Des pneus flottaient à la dérive dans les aires des stands et les pilotes aveuglés s'égaraient sur les vastes pistes d'envol.

La 275 LM pilotée par David Piper et Tony Maggs fut la seule Ferrari à se classer dans les dix premières. Elle termina troisième, à six tours de la championne américaine.

Jim Hall/Hap Sharp, Chaparral 2A (winners/ Sieger/vainqueurs).

Jim Hall and Carroll Shelby, American drivers turned designers and builders, pitted their respective Chaparrals and Cobras against each other.

Jim Hall und Carroll Shelby, zwei US-Fahrer, die zu Fahrzeugdesignern und -bauern geworden waren, traten mit ihren Chaparrals und Cobras gegeneinander an.

Jim Hall et Carroll Shelby, pilotes américains devenus constructeurs ont opposé leurs Chaparrals et leurs Cobras.

Jim Hall, Chaparral 2A.

The Chaparral 2As.

Cobra GT coupes.

The Chaparral 2As.

The Chaparral 2As.

(1) Shelby garage. Phil Hill, Carroll Shelby.
(2) Ford GT40 leads a parade of Cobras.
(3) Three Cobra GT Coupes and a Ford GT40 (against wall).

(1) Die Shelby-Werkstatt. Phil Hill, Carroll Shelby.
(2) Der Ford GT40 führt eine Parade von Cobras an.
(3) Drei Cobra GT Coupés und ein Ford GT40 (an der Mauer).

(1) Le garage Shelby, Phil Hill, Carroll Shelby.
(2) Ford GT40 est tête de liste d'une colonne de Cobras.
(3) Trois Cobra GT coupés et une Ford GT40 (contre le mur).

1

2

Don Yenko/John Bushell, Corvette (#6); John
Cannon/Jack Saunders, Lola T70-Ford (#22)
(neither finished).

Don Yenko/John Bushell, Corvette (Nr. 6) und
John Cannon/Jack Saunders, Lola T70-Ford
(Nr. 22) (beide nicht im Ziel).

Don Yenko/John Bushell, Corvette (No 6) ; John
Cannon/Jack Saunders, Lola-Ford T70 (n° 22)
(Aucun ne termina).

◀ Cobra GT Coupe, Jo Schlesser/Bob Bondurant
(4th, 1st in class/Gesamtvierter, Klassensieger/
4ème, 1ers de catégorie).

Gaston Andrey/Chuck Stoddard, Alfa Romeo TZ
(#55); Richard Robson/Art Baggely, Jaguar XKE
(#28) (neither finished).

Gaston Andrey/Chuck Stoddard, Alfa Romeo TZ
(Nr. 55) vor Richard Robson/Art Baggely, Jaguar
XKE (Nr. 28) (beide nicht im Ziel).

Gaston Andrey/Chuck Stoddart, Alfa-Romeo TZ
(n° 55) Richard Robson/Art Baggely, Jaguar XKE
(n° 28) (Aucun ne termina).

Porsche 904s: Ben Pon/Joe Buzzetta (#39, 6th).
Lake Underwood/Gunther Klass (#40, 5th).

Zwei Porsche 904: Ben Pon/Joe Buzzetta (Nr. 39,
Sechste). Lake Underwood/Gunther Klass
(Nr. 40, Fünfte).

Porsche 904 : Ben Pon/Joe Buzzetta (n° 39 – 6ème).
Lake Underwood/Gunther Klass (n° 40 – 5ème).

MARTINI & ROSSI
IMPORTED EXTRA DRY
SWEET VERMOUTHS
22
35
Esso
23

First the sun shone...
Zuerst schien die Sonne...
Au début, le soleil brilla...

Ferrari 330 P, Graham Hill (37th with/37. mit/
37ème avec Pedro Rodriguez).

Ferrari 330 P, Umberto Maglioli/Giancarlo Baghetti (8th/Achte/8ème).

Ferrari 330 P, Bob Grossman/Skip Hudson (34th/
34./34ème).

Ford GT40, Phil Hill/Richie Ginther. DNF/kam
nicht ins Ziel/abandon.

Ferrari 250 LM, David Piper/Tony Maggs (3rd/
Dritter/3ème).

Dan Gurney, Lotus 19B. DNF/kam nicht ins Ziel/abandon.

Then the rains came....
Dann kam der Regen…
Et la pluie survint…

Ferrari 275 P, Willy Mairesse/Lucien Bianchi (23rd/23./23ème).

Corvette GS, George Wintersteen/Peter Goetz/Milton Diehl (14th/14./14ème).

Porsche 904, Ben Pon/Joe Buzzetta (6th/Sechster/6ème).

Ferrari 275 P, Tom O'Brien/Ed Hugus/Paul Richards (12th/12./12ème).

And night fell...
Und es wurde nacht..
Et la nuit tomba...

Chaparral 2A, Jim Hall/Hap Sharp (winners/Sieger/vainqueurs).

Ford GT 40, Bruce McLaren/Ken Miles (2nd/Zweiter/2ème).

Austin-Healey 3000, Warwick Banks/Paul Hawkins (17th/17./17ème).

Chaparral 2A, Ronnie Hissom/Bruce Jennings
(22nd/22./22ème).

MOSPORT 1965

The Player's 200 was run in two heats of 100 miles each on a record setting day in June. The largest crowd ever to witness a Canadian sporting event (58,312 people) set the tone. Then Jim Hall in his Sebring-winning Chaparral broke the 100 mph barrier in setting the fastest lap. And set another record in winning the first heat – 100 miles in less than an hour.

But it was John Surtees, the 1964 world driving champion, who won the day overall with a victory in the second heat and his second place in the first. The Hall Chaparral did not last the second heat.

The race was notable for the assortment of large American V-8 engines represented. In the Chaparral, of course, but even those cars with a British skin beat with an American heart. An Oldsmobile in a McLaren-Elva, a Ford in another. A Chevrolet in a Lotus, another in a Cooper, still another in a Lola. That is the combination Surtees had – a Lola T70 with a 7-liter Traco Chevrolet.

Compound names were growing common in the under 2-liter class, as well. For instance, Joe Buzzetta won top honors for the smaller cars, driving an Elva-Porsche.

Also evident was the beginning of another trend, this less than welcome, which was to reach a greater than nuisance level in the 1970s: Rowdiness of the fans. Not yet dangerous, although one incident might have been. John Surtees, in taking his victory lap, was struck in the face by an apple thrown from the crowd.

Das Player's 200 wurde in zwei Läufen über jeweils 100 Meilen an einem rekordträchtigen Junitag ausgetragen. Insgesamt 58 000 Zuschauer, mehr als jemals zuvor bei einem kanadischen Sportereignis, gaben den Ton an. Dann überbot Jim Hall in seinem Chaparral, mit dem er bereits in Sebring gewonnen hatte, die Barriere von 160 km/h Durchschnittsgeschwindigkeit und erreichte zugleich eine neue Rundenbestzeit. Überdies gewann er den ersten Lauf über 160 Kilometer in weniger als einer Stunde – auch das ein neuer Rekord.

Gesamttagessieger wurde jedoch John Surtees, der Formel-1-Weltmeister von 1964, durch den Sieg im zweiten und einen zweiten Platz im ersten Lauf. Halls Chaparral fiel im zweiten Lauf aus.

Bemerkenswert an diesem Rennen war die Vielzahl der eingesetzten amerikanischen V8-Motoren. Im Chaparral, aber auch unter den meisten britischen Karossen schlug ein Herz aus Dearborn oder Detroit. Da steckte ein Oldsmobile-Motor in einem McLaren-Elva, ein Ford-V8 in einem anderen. Ein Lotus, ein Cooper und ein Lola fuhren mit einem Chevrolet-Motor. Diese Kombination fuhr auch Surtees – einen Lola T70 mit einem 7-Liter Traco-Chevrolet-Motor.

In der Klasse unter 2 Litern Hubraum gab es immer mehr Fahrzeuge mit Doppelnamen. Joe Buzzetta erreichte beispielsweise in der kleinen Fahrzeugklasse die Spitzenplätze mit einem Elva-Porsche.

Ansatzweise zeichnete sich auch ein anderer, weniger willkommener Trend ab, der in den 70er Jahren zu einem echten Problem werden sollte: das Rowdytum der Fans. Ein damals noch ungefährlicher Trend, mit einer möglichen Ausnahme: John Surtees, der gerade seine Ehrenrunde absolvierte, wurde von einem aus der Menge geworfenen Apfel im Gesicht getroffen.

La Player's 200 se déroula en deux épreuves de 100 miles au cours d'une journée de juin qu'on appellera la journée des records. D'abord, le chiffre record de 58 000 spectateurs : on n'avait jamais vu un public aussi nombreux à un événement sportif canadien. Ensuite, Jim Hall pulvérisa le record du tour de 160 km/h sur la Chaparral (la gagnante de Sebring) et établit un autre record en courant la première épreuve de 100 miles en moins d'une heure.

Mais c'est John Surtees, le champion du monde de 1964, qui fut le vainqueur du jour en s'octroyant la victoire dans la deuxième épreuve et une seconde place dans la première. La Chaparral de Hall ne termina pas la deuxième épreuve.

Cette course fut notamment marquée par le nombre de gros V 8 américains. Outre la Chaparral, ils vrombissaient aussi sous le capot de presque toutes les voitures anglaises. Un Oldsmobile et un Ford équipaient une McLaren-Elva, un Chevrolet était monté sur une Lotus, une Cooper et une Lola. Surtees pilotait cette dernière version : une Lola T70 avec un Traco Chevrolet 7 litres.

Les noms doubles se multipliaient également dans la catégorie des voitures de moins de deux litres. Par exemple, Joe Buzzetta s´adjugea les plus grands succès dans cette catégorie au volant d'une Elva-Porsche.

Une autre tendance – dont on aurait bien voulu se passer – était en train de poindre et allait prendre de sérieuses proportions dans les années 70 : le comportement de plus en plus agressif des fans. On ne pouvait pas encore parler de danger à cette époque bien qu'un incident aurait pu mal se terminer : alors qu'il effectuait son tour d'honneur, John Surtees fut frappé à la tête par une pomme qu'un spectateur avait lancée.

Jim Hall, Chaparral.

(1) John Surtees, Lola T70-Chevrolet (1st overall, 2nd in first heat).
(2) Harley-Davidsons proudly bearing Canadian flags, old and new, amid pup tents overlooking the course.
(3) Bob Johnson, Cobra 289 (4th) leading Walt McKay, Cooper-Ford.
(4) Jim Hall's Chaparral leading Wayne Kelly, Porsche Special (10th).

(1) John Surtees, Lola T70-Chevrolet (Erster im Gesamtklassement, Zweiter im ersten Rennen).
(2) Harley-Davidsons mit alter und neuer kanadischer Flagge inmitten kleiner Zelte, die den Blick auf die Rennstrecke freigibt.
(3) Bob Johnson, Cobra 289 (Vierter) vor Walt McKay, Cooper-Ford.
(4) Jim Halls Chaparral vor Wayne Kelly, Porsche Special (10.).

(1) John Surtees, Lola-Chevrolet T70 (1er au général, 2ème de la lère manche)
(2) Une Harley-Davidson arbore fièrement le drapeau canadien, l'ancien et le nouveau au-milieu de tentes miniatures surplombant la course.
(3) Bob Johnson, Cobra 289 (4ème) devant Walt McKay, Cooper-Ford.
(4) La Chaparral de Jim Hall devant Wayne Kelly, Porsche Special (10ème).

2

3

4

1

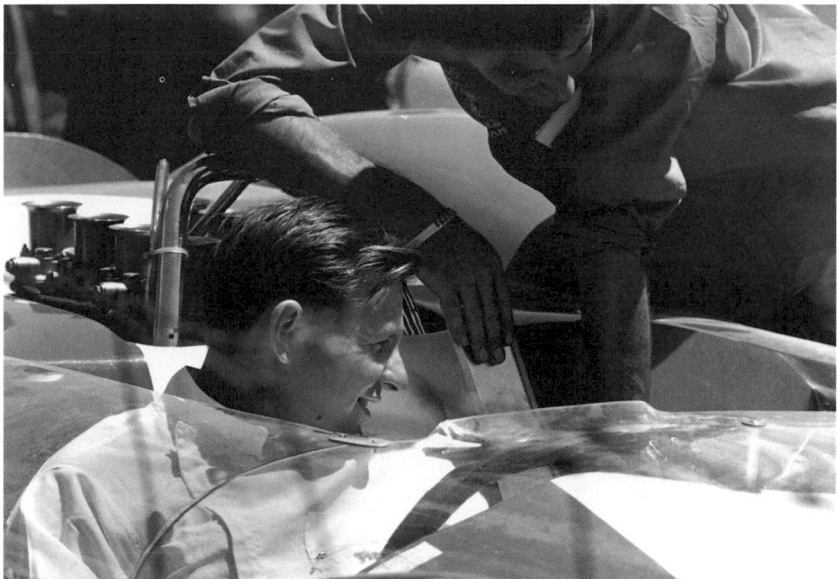

Bruce McLaren, McLaren-Olds.

Sign of the future.
Vorzeichen der Zukunft.
Présage.

Bruce McLaren, McLaren-Olds.

Lola T70-Chevrolet (John Surtees). Colin Chapman sitting on pit wall.

Lola T70-Chevrolet (John Surtees). Colin Chapman sitzt auf der Boxenmauer.

Lola T70-Chevrolet (John Surtees). Colin Chapman est assis sur la clôture.

Augie Pabst, McLaren-Elva.

Bruce McLaren, McLaren-Olds.

Start of the first heat: Jim Hall, Chaparral (#66); Walt McKay, Cooper-Ford (#93); Hugh Dibley, Lola T70-Chevrolet (#5); Bob Johnson, Cobra 289 (#33); Ludwig Heimrath, McLaren Elva-Ford (#1); Rob Slotemaker, Porsche 904 (#10); Joe Buzzetta, Elva-Porsche (#3).

Start zum ersten Rennen: Jim Hall, Chaparral (Nr. 66); Walt McKay, Cooper-Ford (Nr. 93); Hugh Dibley, Lola T70-Chevrolet (Nr. 5); Bob Johnson, Cobra 289 (Nr. 33); Ludwig Heimrath, McLaren, Elva-Ford (Nr. 1); Rob Slotemaker, Porsche 904 (Nr. 10); Joe Buzzetta, Elva-Porsche (Nr. 3).

Départ de la première manche : Jim Hall, Chaparral (n° 66) ; Walt McKay, Cooper-Ford (n° 93) ; Hugh Dibley, Lola-Chevrolet T70 (n° 5) ; Bob Johnson, Cobra 289 (n° 33) ; Ludwig Heimrath, McLaren Elva-Ford (n° 1) ; Rob Slotemaker, Porsche 904 (n° 10) ; Joe Buzzetta, Elva-Porsche (n° 3).

John Surtees, Lola T70-Chevrolet.

(1) Jim Hall, Chaparral (#66, 2nd), Joe Buzzetta, EIva-Porsche (#3, 6th).
(2) Jacques Duval, Porsche 904 (#58, 13th); Jim Hall, Chaparral; Ludwig Heimrath, McLaren-Ford (#7, 3rd).
(3) Jerry Grant, Lotus 19B (#8); Charlie Hayes, Cooper-Chevrolet (#97, 5th); Hugh Dibley, Lola T70-Chevrolet (#5).

(1) Jim Hall, Chaparral (Nr. 66, Zweiter), Joe Buzzetta, EIva-Porsche (Nr. 3, Sechster).
(2) Jacques Duval, Porsche 904 (Nr. 58, 13.); Jim Hall, Chaparral; Ludwig Heimrath, McLaren-Ford (Nr. 7, Dritter).
(3) Jerry Grant, Lotus 19B (Nr. 8); Charlie Hayes, Cooper-Chevrolet (Nr. 97, Fünfter); Hugh Dibley, Lola T70-Chevrolet (Nr. 5).

(1) Jim Hall, Chaparral (n° 66 – 2ème), Joe Buzzetta, Elva-Porsche (n° 3 – 6ème).
(2) Jacques Duval, Porsche 904 (n° 58 – 13ème) ; Jim Hall, Chaparral, Ludwig Heimrath, McLaren-Ford (n° 7 – 3ème).
(3) Jerry Grant, Lotus 19B (n° 8) ; Charlie Hayes, Cooper-Chevrolet (n° 97 – 5ème) ; Hugh Dibley, Lola-Chevrolet T70 (n° 5).

Jim Clark, Lotus 30.

(1) Porsche 904s: Rob Slotemaker (#10, 9th), Ben Pon (#9).
(2) Tom Payne, Cobra 289 (#113); Walt McKay, Cooper-Ford (#93); George Wintersteen, Cooper-Chevrolet (#12); Jim Hall, Chaparral (#66); Bob Johnson, Cobra 289 (#33).

(1) Zwei Porsche 904: Rob Slotemaker (Nr. 10, Neunter), Ben Pon (Nr. 9).
(2) Tom Payne, Cobra 289 (Nr. 113); Walt McKay, Cooper-Ford (Nr. 93); George Wintersteen, Cooper-Chevrolet (Nr. 12); Jim Hall, Chaparral (Nr. 66); Bob Johnson, Cobra 289 (Nr. 33).

(1) Des Porsche 904 : celles de Rob Slotemaker (n° 10 – 9ème) et de Ben Pon (n° 9).
(2) Tom Payne, Cobra 289 (n° 113) ; Walt McKay, Cooper-Ford (n° 93) ; George Wintersteen, Cooper-Chevrolet (n° 12) ; Jim Hall, Chaparral (n° 66) ; Bob Johnson Cobra 289 (n° 33).

Bob McLean, Lotus 23 Ford (15th/15./15ème).

1

2

Charlie Hayes, Cooper-Chevrolet (5th/Fünfter/5ème).

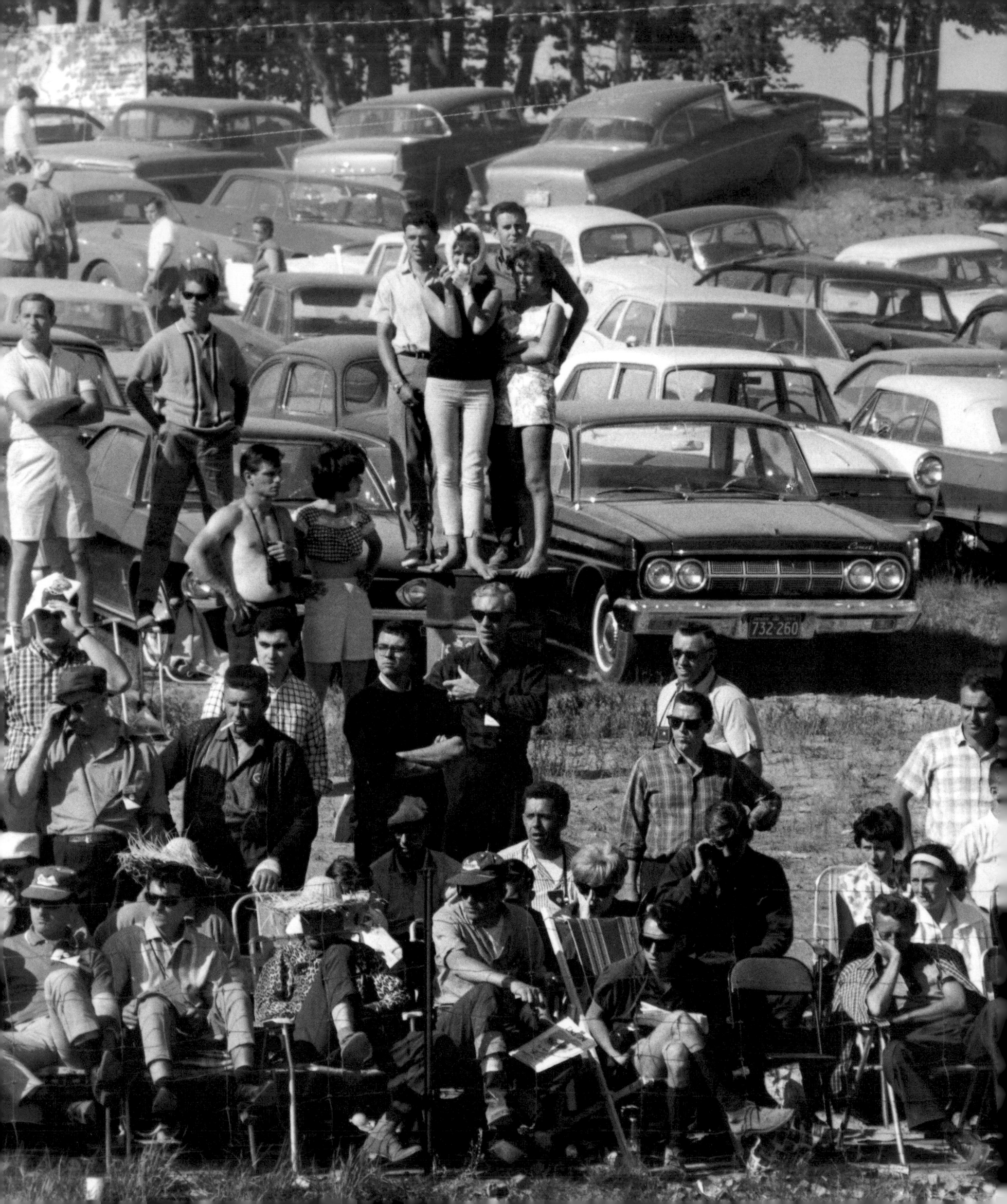

(1) A record crowd for any Canadian sporting event. They got their money's worth.
(2) Jim Hall, Chaparral, and John Surtees, Lola T70-Chevrolet, finished 1-2 in Heat 1.
(3) Surtees, Heat 2 (overall winner).

(1) Die am besten besuchte Sportveranstaltung Kanadas. Und die Zuschauer bekamen für ihr Geld einiges geboten.
(2) Jim Hall, Chaparral, und John Surtees, Lola T70-Chevrolet, Erster bzw. Zweiter im ersten Rennen.
(3) Surtees im zweiten Rennen (Gesamtsieger).

(1) Une foule record pour n'importe quel évènement sportif au Canada, ils en ont eu pour leur argent.
(2) Jim Hall, Chaparral et John Surtees, Lola Chevrolet-T70 ont terminé premier et second de la 1ère manche.
(3) Surtees, 2ème manche (vainqueur absolu).

BRIDGEHAMPTON 1968

At the Bridgehampton CanAm races in September, 1968, the future was present. Cars had begun to envelop the drivers in anonymity. The rear-mounted engines were piped like a church organ. Wings had begun to sprout on some of the cars. Sponsors' logos were proliferating on both the cars and the drivers. The business of racing was a rising tide as the sport of racing receded.

The rounder, fuller sounds and the more savage appearance of the machinery stirred the blood nonetheless, and the "old days" were too recent, yet, to generate nostalgia. A new era was discernible, one that would have its own history.

The full name of the race was "The Bridgehampton Grand Prix for the Canadian American Challenge Cup." The cars were almost all Chevrolet and Ford powered – McLarens, Lolas, and the be-winged Chaparral 2G. The time had begun when the drivers had to take a memory course to be able to reel off the full name of their "Sunoco Special McLaren M6B Chrevrolet," which was what Mark Donohue drove to victory over the sand dunes of Bridgehampton. He could have preceded it all with "the Roger Penske," because Roger had left driving behind for a rousingly successful career as a car owner.

Another portent: Only Ferrari had a single name to cover both engine and chassis. And only one was entered – a 347 P4 driven by Pedro Rodriguez. It ended stuck in the sand on the ninth lap after a brush with Sam Posey and his Autodynamics Lola T160 Chevrolet.

Closing on Donohue at the finish was Jim Hall in his Chaparral followed by Lothar Motschenbacher, Swede Savage, Richard Brown, Dan Gurney, Brian O'Neil and Sam Posey – the only finishers out of a field of 26 cars. Among the non-finishers: Bruce McLaren, Denis Hulme, Peter Revson, John Surtees, Jo Bonnier and Mario Andretti. CanAm was tough.

Bei den CanAm-Rennen von Bridgehampton im September 1968 hatte die Zukunft bereits begonnen. Die Wagen hüllten ihre Fahrer in schützende Anonymität. Die Ansaugstutzen der Mittelmotoren glichen Orgelpfeifen. Die ersten Heckspoiler tauchten auf. Fahrzeuge und Fahrer waren mit den Logos ihrer Sponsoren plakatiert. Das Geschäft mit dem Automobilsport schlug hohe Wellen, während der eigentliche Wettbewerb in den Hintergrund rückte.

Dennoch – die runderen, satteren Motorengeräusche und das aggressivere Aussehen der Boliden gingen ins Blut, und die »gute alte Zeit« war noch zu präsent, um schon nostalgische Gefühle zu wecken. Eine neue Ära kündigte sich an, und sie sollte ihre eigene Geschichte schreiben.

Vollständig hieß das Rennen »The Bridgehampton Grand Prix for the Canadian American Challenge Club«. Fast alle Wagen fuhren mit Motoren von Chevrolet und Ford – McLaren, Lola und auch der »beflügelte« Chaparral 2G. Damals begann die Zeit, in der die Fahrer Gedächtnistraining brauchten, um Typennamen wie »Sunoco Special McLaren M6B Chevrolet« herunterleiern zu können. Vor dem ohnehin langen Namen des Fahrzeugs, mit dem Mark Donohue durch die Sanddünen von Bridgehampton zum Sieg fuhr, hätte noch die Ergänzung »Roger Penske« stehen können, denn Roger hatte die Rennfahrerei zugunsten einer phantastisch erfolgreichen Karriere als Rennstallbesitzer aufgegeben.

Ein weiteres Omen: Nur bei Ferrari stand auf Motor und Chassis noch derselbe Herstellername. Und es war nur ein einziger Ferrari angemeldet – ein 347 P4 mit Pedro Rodriguez im Cockpit. In der neunten Runde endete er nach einem Scharmützel mit Sam Posey und dessen Autodynamics Lola T160 Chevrolet im Sand.

Dicht hinter Donohue erreichte Jim Hall in seinem Chaparral die Ziellinie, gefolgt von Lothar Motschenbacher, Swede Savage, Richard Brown, Dan Gurney, Brian O'Neil und Sam Posey – die einzigen Übriggebliebenen aus einem Starterfeld von 26 Fahrzeugen. Aufgeben mußten unter anderem Bruce McLaren, Denis Hulme, Peter Revson, John Surtees, Jo Bonnier und Mario Andretti. Die CanAm-Serie war ein hartes Brot.

L'avenir se dessinait d'ores et déjà à la course CanAm de Bridgehampton en septembre 1968. Les voitures commençaient à envelopper les pilotes d'un manteau d'anonymat. Les moteurs montés à l'arrière sifflaient des concerts d'orgue et des ailerons poussaient sur quelques bolides. Pilotes et voitures exhibaient les logos des sponsors. Le business du sport automobile déferlait en une vague qui emportait le sport à l'état pur.

Néanmoins, le cœur battait plus vite devant les bolides aux lignes de plus en plus hardies, aux moteurs de plus en plus perfectionnés. Les « bons vieux jours » étaient encore trop proches pour engendrer la nostalgie. On sentait qu'une ère nouvelle approchait, une ère qui allait écrire sa propre page d'histoire.

« The Bridgehampton Grand Prix for the Canadian American Challenge Cup » était le nom complet de la course. Presque toutes les voitures avaient des moteurs Chevrolet ou Ford – les McLaren, les Lola et la Chaparral 2G qui fendait les airs. Leur appellation était si longue que les pilotes allaient désormais devoir faire des exercices de mémoire pour les retenir. La voiture que Mark Donohue conduisit à la victoire à travers les dunes de sable de Bridgehampton portait le nom de « Sunoco Special McLaren Chevrolet M6B », mais on l'appelait en bref la « Roger Penske » car son heureux propriétaire était Roger qui avait quitté le volant pour une carrière éblouissante de patron d'écurie.

Un autre présage : le moteur et le châssis portaient le même nom seulement chez Ferrari. Une unique voiture était alignée – une 347 P4 pilotée par Pedro Rodriguez. Elle termina le nez dans le sable après un effleurage avec l'Autodynamics Lola Chevrolet T160 de Sam Posey.

Donohue franchit la ligne d'arrivée, serré de près par la Chaparral de Jim Hall que suivaient Lothar Motschenbacher, Swede Savage, Richard Brown, Dan Gurney, Brian O'Neill et Sam Posey – les seuls rescapés d'un plateau de 26 voitures. Parmi ceux qui abandonnèrent: Bruce McLaren, Denis Hulme, Peter Revson, John Surtees, Jo Bonnier et Mario Andretti. CanAm était bien une course redoutable.

McLaren M6B-Ford, Peter Revson qualified 3rd fastest behind Team McLaren.

McLaren M6B-Ford; Peter Revson qualifizierte sich als Drittschnellster hinter dem McLaren-Werksteam.

McLaren-Ford M6B, Peter Revson s'est qualifié 3ème, le plus rapide derrière les McLaren d'usine.

Mario Andretti, Lola T70-Ford.
DNF/Ausfall/abandon.

Lothar Motschenbacher, Leader Card McLaren M6B-Ford (3rd/Dritter/3ème).

Dan Gurney, AAR McLaren M6B-Ford
(6th/Sechster/6ème).

Denny Hulme, McLaren M8A-Chevrolet.
DNF/Ausfall/abandon.

Bruce McLaren, McLaren M8A-Chevrolet.
DNF/Ausfall/abandon.

John Surtees, Lola-Chevrolet TS160-Chevrolet.
DNF/Ausfall/abandon.

Pace lap. The lone Ferrari (#22), a NART 347 P4 driven by Pedro Rodriguez, was out on the 9th lap after an encounter with Sam Posey's Autodynamics Lola T160-Chevrolet (#2, behind #26) who went on to finish 8th.

Einführungsrunde. Der einsame Ferrari (Nr. 22), ein von Pedro Rodriguez pilotierter NART 347 P4, schied in der neunten Runde nach einer Auseinandersetzung mit Sam Posey (Nr. 2, hinter Nr. 26) aus, der als Achter ins Ziel fuhr.

Le tour de formation. La seule Ferrari (n° 22), une NART 347 P4 conduite par Pedro Rodriguez, fut éliminée au 9ème tour par une collision avec Sam Posey (n° 2, derrière le n° 26) qui continua pour se classer 8ème.

Chuck Parsons, Simoniz Lola T160-Chevrolet. DNF/Nicht klassiert/abandon.

Mario Andretti, Lola T70-Ford. DNF/Nicht klassiert/abandon.

Jo Bonnier, McLaren M6B-Chevrolet. DNF/Nicht klassiert/abandon.

Lothar Motschenbacher, Leader Card McLaren M6B-Ford (3rd/Dritter/3ème).

Jim Hall, Chaparral 2G-Chevrolet (2nd/Zweiter/2ème).

Denny Hulme, McLaren M8A-Chevrolet. DNF/Nicht klassiert/abandon.

Brett Lunger, Autodynamics Caldwell D7B-Chevrolet. DNF/Ausfall/abandon.

Mob scene around the winner, Mark Donohue.
Die Masse belagert den Sieger, Mark Donohue.
On se presse autour du vainqueur, Mark Donohue.

Sam Posey, Autodynamics Lola T160-Chevrolet
(8th/Achter/8ème).

MEMBERS OF THE CAST

DAS ENSEMBLE · MEMBRES DE LA DISTRIBUTION

Racing was theater. The players arrived, set up the props, rehearsed, improvised a grand entertainment before an appreciative audience and then struck the set and moved on. Sometimes the drama was greatest behind the scenes. Sometimes a supporting player took a star turn. Sometimes there were death scenes.

It was a tighter company in those days. The drivers who vied for the World Championship in Formula I cars also competed in the sports car races. Sometimes in rallies, as well. That's what a driver did – *drive*.

There were fewer drivers then. Even the 24-hour races rarely saw more than two to a car, not the arm-long list of participants of recent years.

The professionals played with the amateurs and always with an amateur spirit. They made money, but laughably little by the standards of the '90s. Still, they gave the impression that if they weren't paid to race they would be racing anyway.

The atmosphere was more relaxed then. Competitive – always competitive – but friendlier. Drivers were more accessible. To each other, to the press, to the fans. They had fun, they kidded each other, they cared for each other. Maybe the modern multi-millionaires do too, but they conceal it well.

Drivers came in a variety of sizes, they spoke many languages, they wore overalls and bow-ties and sometimes went shirtless in the pits. They were a unique breed. Players, all.

They put on a fine show.

Rennfahren war eine Theaterinszenierung. Die Akteure kamen, bauten die Kulissen auf, probten, improvisierten vor dankbarem Publikum ein großes Spektakel, bauten die Bühne wieder ab und zogen weiter. Manchmal spielten sich die größten Dramen hinter der Bühne ab. Manchmal wurde ein Statist zum Star. Manchmal gab es auch Sterbeszenen.

In jenen Tagen war das Ensemble eine enge Gemeinschaft. Die gleichen Fahrer, die in der Formel-1-Weltmeisterschaft gegeneinander antraten, trafen auch bei den Sportwagenrennen wieder aufeinander, zuweilen auch noch bei den Rallyes. Denn genau das tat ein Fahrer nun einmal – fahren.

Es gab damals noch nicht so viele Fahrer. Selbst bei 24-Stunden-Rennen traten selten mehr als zwei Piloten pro Fahrzeug an, die ellenlangen Teilnehmerlisten von heute waren unbekannt.

Die Profis spielten mit den Amateuren auf einer Bühne und blieben im Herzen selbst Amateure. Sie verdienten an der Rennfahrerei, allerdings lächerlich wenig, gemessen an den Standards der 90er Jahre. Dennoch, sie wirkten, als würden sie auch ohne Geld noch Rennen fahren.

Die Atmosphäre war damals spürbar entspannter. Konkurrenzbewußt – immer konkurrenzbewußt – aber freundschaftlicher. Die Fahrer waren zugänglicher – sie waren füreinander, für die Presse und für die Fans da. Sie hatten Spaß, scherzten miteinander, mochten einander. Mag sein, daß das bei den heutigen Multimillionären am Lenkrad auch noch so ist – aber dann können sie es gut verbergen.

Und die Fahrer waren ein bunt gemischter Haufen: Sie kamen in allen Größen, sprachen die verschiedensten Sprachen, trugen Overall und Fliege und standen manchmal auch mit nacktem Oberkörper in der Box. Sie waren einzigartig. Schauspieler allesamt.

Und ihre Show war hervorragend.

Le sport automobile ressemblait à du théâtre. Les acteurs arrivaient, montaient les coulisses, répétaient, présentaient un spectacle inédit devant un public ravi, puis démontaient le décor et reprenaient la route. Parfois, le suspense était plus grand dans les coulisses que sur les planches. Parfois, un acteur de second plan volait la vedette à une star. Parfois, il y avait des scènes de morts tragiques.

La troupe était une véritable communauté à cette époque. Les pilotes se retrouvaient aux Grands Prix de Formule I, mais aussi à des courses de voitures de sport et même parfois à des rallyes. Car un pilote effectuait tout simplement son travail : monter dans une voiture et courir.

Il y avait aussi moins de coureurs automobiles. Même aux courses de 24 heures, on voyait rarement plus de deux pilotes par voiture, alors qu'aujourd'hui, les listes de participants sont interminables.

Les professionnels partageaient la scène avec les amateurs et jouaient surtout pour le plaisir de jouer. Ils gagnaient certes de l'argent, mais des sommes risibles comparées aux normes des années 90. De toute façon, on sentait qu'ils courraient quand même, qu'ils soient payés ou non.

L'atmosphère était bien plus relax à l'époque. Compétitive – toujours compétitive – mais plus amicale. Les pilotes étaient plus accessibles, entre eux, à la presse et à leurs fans. Les pilotes s'amusaient ensemble, se jouaient parfois des tours, étaient toujours solidaires. Il se peut que les multi-millionnaires d'aujourd'hui ressemblent à leurs prédécesseurs, mais ils le cachent bien.

Les pilotes formaient un groupe très hétérogène. Ils parlaient toutes sortes de langues, portaient des combinaisons aussi bien que le nœud papillon et on les voyait parfois torse nu dans les stands. Ils faisaient partie d'une race unique. Ils étaient tous des comédiens.

Et ils présentaient un spectacle de grande classe.

Roger Penske. Puerto Rico, 1962.

John Edgar, Carroll Shelby. Brynfan Tyddyn, 1956.

Briggs Cunningham, Sherwood Johnston, John Gordon Bennett, Chuck Wallace. Beverly, 1956.

Luigi Chinetti. Montgomery, 1956.

From front to back/von vorne nach hinten/de l'avant à l'arrière : Briggs Cunningham, Walt Hansgen, Sherwood Johnston. Beverly, 1956.

Carroll Shelby, Masten Gregory. Beverly, 1956.

Masten Gregory. Nassau, 1955.

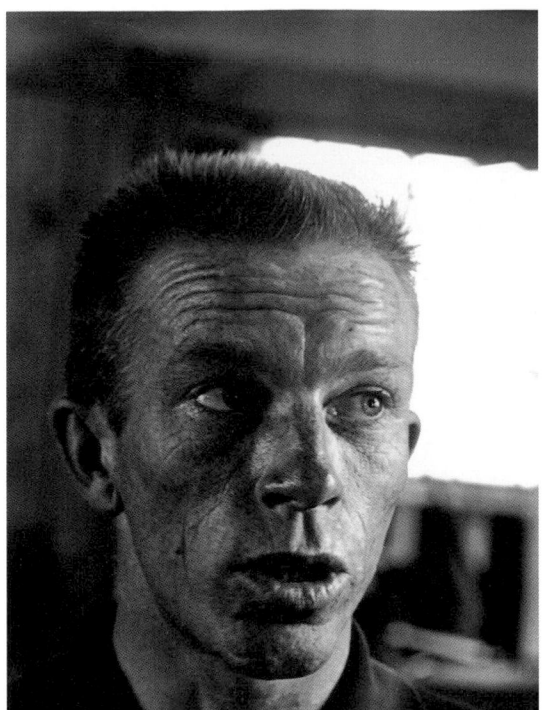

Richie Ginther. Sebring, 1965.

Denise McCluggage. Elkhart Lake, 1956.

Jim Hall. Sebring, 1965.

Augie Pabst. Mosport, 1965.

Chuck Wallace. Nassau, 1955.

Jack McAfee. Brynfan Tyddyn, 1956.

Luigi Musso. Sebring, 1958.

Jo Bonnier. Venezuela, 1957.

Peter Collins. Venezuela, 1957.

Juan Manuel Fangio. Sebring, 1956.

Eugenio Castellotti. Cuba, 1957.

Huschke von Hanstein. Cuba, 1960.

Fon de Portago. Nassau, 1956.

Mike Hawthorn. Sebring, 1957.

Mike Hawthorn. Venezuela, 1957.

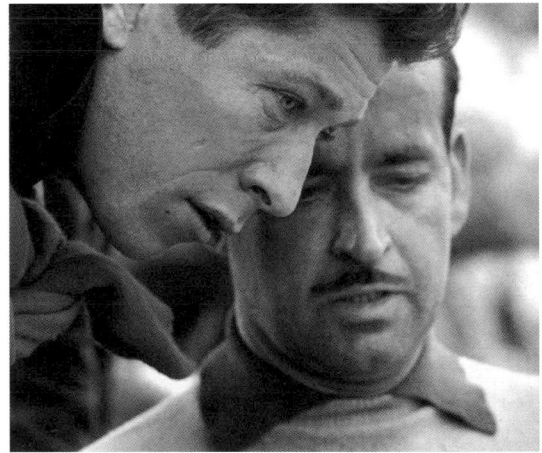

Olivier Gendebien, Maurice Trintignant.
Venezuela, 1957.

Stirling Moss. Sebring Grand Prix, 1959.

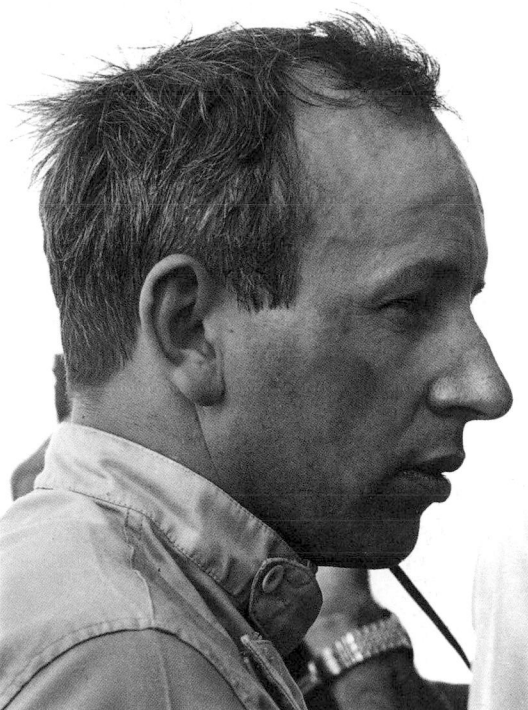

John Surtees. Sebring, 1964.

Jack Brabham. Indianapolis, 1961.

Colin Chapman. Indianapolis, 1964.

Jim Clark, Lotus-Ford. Indianapolis, 1964.

Bruce McLaren, Cooper-Climax. Sebring Grand Prix, 1959.

ACKNOWLEDGMENTS
DANKSAGUNG · REMERCIEMENTS

For their devotion to motor racing history, their determination to unravel its mysteries and their enthusiasm and generosity in sharing their knowledge we wish to thank Alexis Callier, Michael T. Lynch, Harald Mergard and Jim Sitz. Any inaccuracies that remain are our own.

Tom Burnside and Denise McCluggage

Wir danken Alexis Callier, Michael T. Lynch, Harald Mergard und Jim Sitz für ihre Liebe zur Rennsportgeschichte, für ihre Entschlossenheit, die Geheimnisse dieser Geschichte zu lüften und für die Großzügigkeit, dieses Wissen mit uns zu teilen. Alle etwa noch vorhandenen Ungenauigkeiten gehen zu unseren Lasten.

Tom Burnside und Denise McCluggage

Pour leur attachement à l'histoire de la course automobile, leur détermination à éclaircir ses mystères et leur enthousiasme et leur générosité à partager leur savoir nous désirons remercier Alexis Callier, Michael T. Lynch, Harald Mergard et Jim Sitz. Nous sommes seuls responsables des inexactitudes qui pourraient encore subsister.

Tom Burnside und Denise McCluggage

Endpapers / Vorsatzpapier / Papiers de grade:
MG B 1800 and Cobra GT. Sebring, 1965.

Pages / Seiten 2/3
Le Mans start. Sebring, 1964.

Pages / Seiten 4/5
Eagle Mountain, 1956. D-type Jaguars:
Jack Douglas, Lou Brero, Walt Hansgen.

© 1996 Könemann Verlagsgesellschaft mbH
Bonner Straße 126, D-50968 Cologne
© Photographs Tom Burnside
For information concerning the photographs please contact the photographer at:
Tom Burnside Motorsport Archive, Post Office Box 158, Pawlet, VT 05761-0158, USA
e-mail: tbside@aol.com
Text: Denise McCluggage, Santa Fe, NM, USA
Executive editor: Elinor Burnside, Pawlet, VT, USA
Art director: Peter Feierabend, Berlin
Layout and typesetting: vierviertel gestaltung, Cologne
Project coordinator: Kristina Meier, Cologne
German translation: Barbara Schellnack, Straelen
French translation: France Varry, Cologne;
Gérard Crombac, Paris
Production manager: Detlev Schaper, Cologne
Colour separation: Imago Publishing Ltd., Thame
Printing and binding: Partenaires Fabrication
Printed in France

ISBN 3-89508-246-5